Kierkegaard:
A Critical Reader

CRITICAL READERS

Blackwell's *Critical Readers* series presents a collection of linked perspectives on continental philosophers, and social and cultural theorists. Edited and introduced by acknowledged experts and written by representatives of different schools and positions, the series embodies debate, dissent and a committed heterodoxy. From Foucault to Derrida, from Heidegger to Nietzsche, *Critical Readers* address figures whose work requires elucidation by a variety of perspectives. Volumes in the series include both primary and secondary bibliographies.

Already published:

Foucault: A Critical Reader
Edited by David Hoy

Heidegger: A Critical Reader
Edited by Hubert L. Dreyfus and Harrison Hall

Deleuze: A Critical Reader
Edited by Paul Patton

Althusser: A Critical Reader
Edited by Gregory Elliott

Derrida: A Critical Reader
Edited by David Wood

Fanon: A Critical Reader
Edited by Lewis R. Gordon, T. Denean Sharpley-Whiting and Renée T. White

Nietzsche: A Critical Reader
Edited by Peter Sedgwick

Bataille: A Critical Reader
Edited by Fred Botting and Scott Wilson

Baudrillard: A Critical Reader
Edited by Douglas Kellner

Kierkegaard: A Critical Reader
Edited by Jonathan Rée and Jane Chamberlain

Forthcoming titles:

Habermas: A Critical Reader
Edited by Peter Dews

Lacan: A Critical Reader
Edited by David Macey

Wittgenstein: A Critical Reader
Edited by Hans-Johann Glock

Angela Davis: A Critical Reader
Edited by Joy Ann James

Frederick Douglass: A Critical Reader
Edited by Lawson

Kierkegaard:
A Critical Reader

Edited by

Jonathan Rée and Jane Chamberlain

BLACKWELL
Publishers

Copyright © Blackwell Publishers, 1998

Introduction, apparatus and selection copyright © Jonathan Rée and Jane Chamberlain, 1998

First published 1998

2 4 6 8 10 9 7 5 3 1

Blackwell Publishers Ltd
108 Cowley Road
Oxford OX4 1JF
UK

Blackwell Publishers Inc.
350 Main Street
Malden, Massachusetts 02148
USA

British Library Cataloguing in Publication Data

A CIP catalogue record for this book is available from the British Library.

Library of Congress Cataloging-in-Publication Data

Kierkegaard: a critical reader / edited by Jonathan Rée and Jane Chamberlain.
    p.   cm.—(Blackwell critical readers)
    Includes bibliographical references and index.
    ISBN 0–631–20198–X (hardcover: alk. paper).—ISBN 0–631–20199–8 (pbk.: alk. paper)
    1. Kierkegaard, Søren, 1813–1855. I. Rée, Jonathan, 1948–
II. Chamberlain, Jane. III. Series.
B4377.K45 1998
193—dc21   97-22299
                                                     CIP

Typeset in 10 on 12 pt Plantin
by Best-set Typesetter Ltd, Hong Kong
Printed in Great Britain by T.J. International Ltd., Padstow, Cornwall

This book is printed on acid-free paper

Contents

a be like this &
Nietzsche?
or only
Corp.

☐ more

15 · 18

Contributors

Sylviane Agacinski is a philosopher who – from *Aparté: Conceptions and Deaths of Søren Kierkegaard* (1977) to *Critique de l'égocentrisme* (1996) – has been conducting investigations into the human experience of otherness, largely inspired by Kierkegaard. She has also published on the philosophy of architecture and is at present working on the role of experience in painting, and on concepts of sexual difference. She teaches at the Ecole des Hautes Etudes en Sciences Sociales in Paris.

Wilhelm Anz fell under the spell of Kierkegaard when studying philosophy and theology at Marburg with Heidegger, Bultmann and Gadamer in the 1920s. His subsequent career was devoted to exploring the relations between Christian faith and the western philosophical tradition, especially as expressed in Kierkegaard's attitudes to Plato and Socrates. He worked as a schoolteacher before becoming Professor of Philosophy at the Kirchlichen Hochschule Bethel, and was for many years the leader of German Kierkegaard scholarship. His books include *Kierkegaard und der Deutsche Idealismus* (1956). He died in 1994 at the age of 89.

Jacques Derrida taught for many years at the Ecole Normale Supérieure in Paris, and is now at the Ecole des Hautes Etudes en Sciences Sociales. His prolific output of writings about literature, politics and the 'deconstruction' of metaphysics began in 1967 with the publication of *Grammatology, Speech and Phenomena*, and *Writing and Difference*.

Joakim Garff is Associate Research Professor at the Søren Kierkegaard Research Centre in Copenhagen, where he is part of a team producing a new edition of Kierkegaard's writings. He is co-editor of *Kierkegaardiana*, and his publications include *'Den Søvnløse'*, *Kierkegaard læst aestetisk/biografisk* (1995).

Gabriel Josipovici is Professor of English at the University of Sussex. He is the author of *The World and the Book* (1971), *The Book of God: A Response to the Bible* (1987) and *Touch* (1996), as well as ten novels, two volumes of short stories, and plays for radio and the stage.

Emmanuel Levinas was born in Lithuania, studied with Husserl and Heidegger in 1928–9, and spent the rest of his career teaching in France. The main ambition of his work was to draw attention to an 'ethical' dimension of experience that had, he argued, been covered up by the intellectualist tradition of 'western ontology' (see *Totality and Infinity*, 1961). He died in 1995 at the age of 89.

Paul Ricoeur has taught philosophy in Paris, Chicago and elsewhere, always seeking an indirect approach to truth based on understanding why conflicting interpretations of human existence are possible. His books include *The Symbolism of Evil* (1960), *Freud and Philosophy* (1965), *The Rule of Metaphor* (1975) and *Time and Narrative* (1983–5).

George Steiner is Professor of English and Comparative Literature at the University of Geneva and Fellow of Churchill College, Cambridge. His works include *The Death of Tragedy* (1961), *After Babel* (1975), *Heidegger* (1978) and *Antigones* (1984).

David Wood taught at the University of Warwick until 1994, and is now Professor of Philosophy at Vanderbilt University. He is author of *Philosophy at the Limit* (1990), *The Deconstruction of Time* (1989), and *Thinking after Heidegger* (forthcoming).

Acknowledgements

With thanks to the Department of Søren Kierkegaard Research at Copenhagen University, and to the Anglo-Danish Society whose generous grant enabled Jane Chamberlain to work there during 1996–7.

Thanks also to Stacey Ake, Margarethe Anz, Andrew Bruce, Thor Arvid Dyrerud, Robert Eaglestone, Anne-Marie Eastwood, Hans Fink, Hans-Georg Gadamer, Christiane Gehron, Karin Jakobsen, Bruce Kirmmse, Valli Melchior, Belinda Ioni Rasmussen, Stella Sandford, Ulrich-Johannes Schneider, Nick Smith, Rachael Strange, Stephan Stuchlik, Iben Thranholm, Steffi Vogel, Maria Wagner.

The editors and publishers wish to thank the following for permission to use copyright material:

'Philosopher après Kierkegaard' ('Philosophy after Kierkegaard'), first published in *Revue de Théologie et de Philosophie*, vol. 13 (1963), no. 4, pp. 303–16, reprinted in Ricoeur's *Lectures 2* (Seuil, Paris, 1992), pp. 29–45, and translated for this volume by Jonathan Rée with the author's permission. Translation copyright © Jonathan Rée 1998.

'Existence et Éthique' ('Existence and Ethics') was originally published in German in the *Schweizer Monatshefte* in 1963, and first appeared in French in Emmanuel Levinas, *Noms Propres* (Fata Morgana, Montpellier, 1976), pp. 99–109. The two comments ('A propos de *Kierkegaard Vivant*') are based on spoken interventions at a UNESCO conference on Kierkegaard held in Paris in 1964. They appeared in print in *Kierkegaard Vivant* (Gallimard, Paris, 1966), pp. 232–4 and 286–8, but in a form with which Levinas was dissatisfied. They were published in an approved version in *Noms Propres*, pp. 111–15. These translations appear with the permission of Fata Morgana. Translation copyright © Jonathan Rée 1998.

'Kierkegaard über Sterben und Tod' ('Kierkegaard on Death and Dying') was first published in *Wort und Dienst*, (Jahrbuch der Kirchlichen Hochschule Bethel) 11, 1971, pp. 9–20. This translation appears with the permission of the editors of the Yearbook and of Frau Margarethe Anz. Translation copyright © Jonathan Rée 1998.

'Argus' øjne' ('The Eyes of Argus') was first published in Danish in *Dansk Teologisk Tidsskrift* 4, 1989, and is translated here, with permission, by Jane Chamberlain and Belinda Ioni Rasmussen. Translation copyright © Jane Chamberlain and Belinda Ioni Rasmussen, 1998. References have been given to English-language editions, where available, although the translations have frequently been altered.

'The Wound of Negativity' was originally published as the Introduction to the Everyman edition of *Fear and Trembling and The Book on Adler* (David Campbell, London, 1994) and is reproduced here with permission, copyright © George Steiner, 1994, 1997.

'Nous ne sommes pas sublimes' ('We are not Sublime') was first published in this version in Sylviane Agacinski, *Critique de l'égocentrisme* (Galilée, Paris, 1996), pp. 107–32. An earlier version appeared in the special Kierkegaard edition of *Les Cahiers de Philosophie*, 8–9, autumn 1989, pp. 167–85. It has been translated for this volume by Jonathan Rée and is published with permission of Galilée and the author. Copyright © Editions Galilée 1996. Translation Copyright © Jonathan Rée 1998.

'Whom to give to' was originally Chapter 3 of Derrida's *Donner la mort*, first published in *L'éthique du don, Jacques Derrida et la pensée du don*, edited by Jean-Michel Rabaté and Michael Wetzel (Métailié-Transition, Paris, 1992). It was published in English as chapter 3 of Jacques Derrida, *The Gift of Death*, translated by David Wills (University of Chicago Press, Chicago, 1995) and is reprinted here with permission.

The publishers apologize for any errors or omissions in the above list and would be grateful to be notified of any corrections that should be incorporated in the next edition or reprint of this book.

Introduction

A rumour is gaining ground concerning Kierkegaard. A new Kierkegaard is coming forward, it seems, at the end of the twentieth century, comparable perhaps to the proto-deconstructionist 'new Nietzsche' who emerged from the shadows in the 1970s. Søren Kierkegaard – the prodigious and unpredictable Dane who wrote nearly a dozen theological and philosophical works in the early 1840s, before being shattered by a terrible but mysterious crisis between 1846 and 1848, and then going into a slow mental decline and dying in 1855 at the age of forty-two – would appear to be changing. The mask of the implacable preacher of doom is falling away, and he is presenting himself not only as a rigorous fundamental theorist, but also an effervescent wit, a captivating storyteller, and a mercurial ironist – a seductive philosophical artist, in short, to rival Plato himself.

It is a remarkable transformation. Bertrand Russell's *History of Western Philosophy*, first published in 1946, devoted a whole chapter to Hegel, and another to Nietzsche, with Byron and Schopenhauer in between. But there was not so much as a mention of Kierkegaard. No doubt part of the problem was that Kierkegaard wrote in Danish, which Russell could not understand. There were extensive translations in German or French; but – despite a few pioneering efforts in the 1930s and 1940s[1] – many of Kierkegaard's most important philosophical works were not easily accessible in English until the sixties, and the Princeton *Collected Writings* in twenty-six volumes is only now nearing completion.

When Kierkegaard first came to public attention, it was not through the works published in his lifetime, so much as selections from the amazing horde of manuscripts found in his desk after he died. The publication of these *Journals and Papers* began in 1869, and the current Danish edition – the third – fills twenty-five bindings. In much of this posthumously published material, especially the parts written after 1848, Kierkegaard comes across as a religious fundamentalist, and a hyperbolical and hysterical scourge of all the waffle, pomp and finery of Danish Christendom. But he also confesses his ordeals as a confused lover, at first tormented by his ardent courtship of the glorious young Regine Olsen, and then so upset by obtaining her consent that he broke off the engagement, and spent the rest of his life tormented by remorse about his cruelty (or sometimes by absurd suspicions about hers) till it all drove him to an early grave.

Kierkegaard was interpreted, therefore, not as a challenging thinker, but as a curious pathological case – half Don Juan, half Grand Inquisitor, a dandified moralizer and a hellfire ladies' man. Publishers enhanced this impression by producing cheap versions of isolated *Edifying* (or *Upbuilding*) *Discourses*, together with a chapter brusquely ripped from its context in Kierkegaard's *Either/Or* and marketed enticingly as *The Seducer's Diary*.

And on the whole the philosophers went along with this interpretation too.[2] In an essay of 1909, Georg Lukács focused on the relationship with Regine Olsen, concluding that 'Kierkegaard was a troubadour and a Platonist, and he was both these things romantically and sentimentally.'[3] And in the 1920s and 1930s the same romantic and sentimental Kierkegaard came to be seen as the unwitting forerunner of a philosophical 'movement' called existentialism – an unconscious harbinger of Jaspers, Heidegger, Gadamer, Sartre and de Beauvoir in their revolt against the complacencies of idealist rationalism, and especially in their revulsion from Hegel.[4]

It was pretty clear, of course, that if Kierkegaard really was a 'Christian existentialist', then he must have been in severe conceptual trouble: for how could he have thought he was returning humbly to Christ if he also imagined he was freely inventing himself out of nothing? And according to the confident historical materialism of the time, this fractured incoherency was precisely what made Kierkegaard interesting – interesting, that is, as a symptom of bourgeois malaise, not a source of continuing philosophical inspiration. According to Theodor Adorno, for example, Kierkegaard had 'absolutised' the spiritually isolated individual in his writings, just as capital had 'absolutised' the economically isolated individual in the bourgeois social order that was taking shape around him.[5] Heidegger was equally swift to put Kierkegaard in his historical place, though from a very different standpoint: 'Kierkegaard is not a thinker but a religious writer,' he wrote, and 'the only one in accord with the destining belonging to his age.'[6]

English-language readers had even less awareness of Kierkegaard's claims to be recognized as a philosopher. Their attention was focused on Alexander Dru's generous selections from the *Journals and Papers* and various devotional texts,[7] together with versions of *The Seducer's Diary* such as one by Knud Fick.[8] Two of the leading introductions to Kierkegaard in the 1950s were called *Kierkegaard the Cripple* and *Kierkegaard the Melancholy Dane*,[9] and in 1956, W. H. Auden – whose conversion to Christianity owed much to reading Kierkegaard – edited an anthology drawn from existing translations, designed to confirm Kierkegaard's reputation as a prophet of 'existentialism', but a prophet who was 'fated to be an exception and a sufferer'. Kierkegaard was an exotic Cardinal Newman, according to Auden 'neither a poet, nor a philosopher, but a preacher, an expounder and defender of Christian doctrine and Christian conduct'.[10] It is hardly surprising that such God-fearing sentimentality failed to stir Bertrand Russell.

But if you look behind his posthumous reputation to the books published in Kierkegaard's lifetime – *The Concept of Irony* in 1841; *Either/ Or* and *Fear and Trembling* in 1843; *Philosophical Fragments*, *The Concept of Anxiety* and four others in 1844; the *Concluding Unscientific Postscript* (1846); and *Sickness unto Death* (1849) – then a far different Kierkegaard emerges: one whom Bertrand Russell would have had to recognize as an intellectual brother, though not exactly an ally or a friend. This is a Kierkegaard who rejoiced not so much in Christ the redeemer as in Socrates the ironist: 'Of all men old Socrates is the greatest,' as he wrote in his journal: 'Socrates, the hero and martyr of intellectuality'.[11] This Kierkegaard is a Socratic gadfly who aimed to educate his readers by not telling them anything, by refusing to express his opinions, refusing even to have any. 'To have an opinion is both too much and too little for my uses,' he wrote, since 'to have an opinion presupposes a sense of ease and security in life, such as is implied in having a wife and children.'[12] He is a philosopher who thought that Socrates had been betrayed by professorial philosophy, just as Jesus had been betrayed by theological Christendom; he loathed the know-it-all complacency of Kant's 'Religion within the limits of reason alone', and regarded the overpoweringly systematic intelligence of Hegel as the cynosure of intellectual dishonesty. But this philosophical Kierkegaard was no romantic irrationalist. For him the trouble with philosophical rationality was not that it was too rational but that it was not rational enough: philosophical religion and philosophical ethics were betrayals of the ironic enigma that was Socrates.

If there is a single governing thought in Kierkegaard's work, it is that of the paradox. For the professorial philosophers, paradox was a cardinal sin against scientific truth – leading straight to intellectual blindness, sterility and death. For Kierkegaard, however, a capacity for paradox was the mark not of weakness but of passionate wisdom. 'One must not think slightingly of the paradoxical,' he wrote, 'for the paradox is the source of the thinker's passion, and the thinker without a paradox is like a lover without feeling: a paltry mediocrity.'[13] Paradoxes were not, as the professors thought, a fault in our conception of the world; still less were they faults that might soon be remedied thanks to new advances in philosophical technique. Paradoxes were the essential truth of the world: 'the paradox', as he wrote in his journal, 'is not a concession but a category.'[14]

Kierkegaard's conception of genuine philosophy as an activity founded in paradox was matched by a writing style that was crisp and light, and intensely focused like lyrical poetry. But it was also wise in its large-scale literary plans: grand narrative strategies that were deployed not only within each of his books but between them as well. *Either/Or* is, as its title implies, a presentation of two incompatible views of life – one 'aesthetic' (in the sense of feckless debauchery, not artistic tastefulness), and the other 'ethical' (formal, reasonable, professional and dull). And of course Kierkegaard does not tell his readers which side he thinks is right. Indeed, he does not speak in his own voice at all, for the conceit governing *Either/Or* is that it consists of two sets of papers, found one day by a literary gentleman called Victor Eremita inside his second-hand writing-desk when he smashed it up with an axe in a fit of rage and frustration. When he came to read the documents, he found that the two groups represented two opposed 'views of life', but still he was convinced that they were all written by a single unknown author – a view which he clung to even though he knew it was 'unhistorical, and . . . improbable'. Certainly any sincere and unbiased readers will encounter two authors in the body of *Either/Or*; indeed they will encounter more than two, for 'The Seducer's Diary' is presented as the work of a third person, and includes transcripts of letters by Cordelia, his victim, which makes four. And then 'The Upbuilding that lies in the Thought that in relation to God we are always in the wrong' is a sermon written by a fifth. If we add Victor Eremita to the list, then this book alone features at least six authors, or rather six characters – six characters in search of an author.

Kierkegaard's other great books are also authorless, attributed to a range of pseudonyms who themselves become characters in the developing story of his publications, representing now an ethical, now an aesthetic point of view, now a Christian one, now a dialectical one. Above all there is the great Johannes Climacus, author of *Philosophical Fragments* and *Concluding Unscientific Postscript*, as well as the eponymous hero of a novella. But then there is Johannes de Silentio, author of *Fear and Trembling*; and *Stages on Life's Way* consists of 'studies by various

difference between aesthetic & ethical.

persons' – William Afham, A Married Man (apparently identical with the author of the second part of *Either/Or*), and Frater Taciturnus (who mainly copies out the confessions of another writer, an amorous young man) – all 'collected and published' by a humble bookbinder called Hilarius. *The Concept of Anxiety* was published under the name Vigilius Haufniensis, and, to cap it all, *The Sickness Unto Death* is attributed to someone called Anti-Climacus.

But then Kierkegaard wrote another book, which seems designed to put all these paradoxes in the shade. *The Point of View for my Work as an Author* (written in 1848 but not published till 1859, four years after his death) shows Kierkegaard finally offering his public the key to the interpretation of all his works. He casts all pretence aside, or at least he says he does, and speaks plainly at last, in the style of confessional autobiography. He tries to impose a final order on his unruly brainchildren, and to demonstrate how, with God's help, all the paradoxes of the pseudonymous works cancel each other out, their dilemmas gathered up and resolved in the revelation that 'I am and always was a religious author, that the whole of my work as an author is related to Christianity, to the problem "of becoming a Christian".'[15] Thus *The Point of View* promises a convenient short cut to Kierkegaard's system, whilst removing the dangerous Socratic sting of his paradoxes.

When an author does us the courtesy of explaining the meaning of all his writings, and not-quite-accidentally leaves behind a pile of private notebooks that will be published after his death, it would be ungrateful to spurn the help they may provide us as his readers. And the dominant traditions of Kierkegaard interpretation have accepted this assistance wholeheartedly, and depended on it heavily. They have focused compassionately on the awfulness of Kierkegaard's existence as presented in the *Journals and Papers*, and bowed to the authorial opinions expressed in the *The Point of View*. But should we really allow these posthumous publications to guide our reading of everything Kierkegaard wrote, when his other works not only embody an ideal of Socratic elusiveness, but make fun of the whole idea of an all-embracing authorial opinion as well?

That is the main question that the nine essays in this anthology collectively address. Paul Ricoeur's 'Philosophy after Kierkegaard', written in 1963, is one of the earliest attempts to take the full measure of Kierkegaard's challenge to philosophy. Even where Kierkegaard's work is, as Ricoeur puts it, 'non-philosophical', it raises issues of central philosophical importance. Moreover, Ricoeur argues, the standard view of Kierkegaard as an extreme opponent of Hegel's dialectical rationalism, or a representative of a so-called 'existentialist' reaction to 'ideal-

ism', drastically underestimates the manifold ambiguities of the history
of philosophy.

Emmanuel Levinas's 'Existence and Ethics', also written in 1963,
raises the other leading issue of this collection: Kierkegaard's contribution to ethics. He does it by means of a diatribe which presupposes an
interpretation of Kierkegaard as a crude egoistic existentialist who was
insensitive on principle to the ethical claims of others; but between the
lines of Levinas's alternative – the idea that otherness has priority over
selfhood – one may perhaps glimpse a Kierkegaard who was far more
Levinasian than Levinas realized. And that is what Wilhelm Anz's study
of death and anxiety provides. He shows how Kierkegaard's idea that we
should permit ourselves to be instructed by anxiety makes the prospect
of our death into a source not of sickness, closure and sullen immanence,
but of faith, transcendence and openness. The theme is echoed by
David Wood, who weaves together threads from Sartre, Wittgenstein,
and Derrida in order to present Kierkegaard's religiousness as a way of
articulating a transcendence or mystery that is actually more ethical than
theological. Intelligent atheism, he implies, may be closer to intelligent
theism than either theists or atheists usually suppose.

Joakim Garff returns us to the other crux of Kierkegaard interpretation: the question of Kierkegaard's own pronouncements on the meaning of the pseudonymous publications. Garff demonstrates the internal
contradictions at the heart of Kierkegaard's supposedly direct communi-
cations about his work, thus suggesting that even in *The Point of View for
my Work as an Author* Kierkegaard was Socratically undermining his own
authority as he went along. George Steiner, in his essay on *Fear and
Trembling* and *The Book on Adler*, also explores the relation of life and
literature in the case of Kierkegaard, whilst Gabriel Josipovici shows how
Kierkegaard's preoccupations with narrative and identity continue to
resonate with the theory and practice of the novel.

The analysis in *Fear and Trembling* of the *akedah* – the story in Genesis
22 of Abraham binding his beloved son Isaac and preparing to sacrifice
him on the command of an unintelligible and unethical God – is
central for any philosophical interpretation of Kierkegaard's work.
Kierkegaard's suggestion that the greatness of Abraham may lie in the
fact that his deed was beyond justification is the basis for Sylviane
Agacinski's account of ethics, love and the sublime: is it God who was
incomprehensible to Abraham, or simply Abraham who is incomprehensible to us, precisely because of our intolerance of incomprehension? In
conclusion, Jacques Derrida's essay attempts to derive a conception of
absolute responsibility from the same nexus: Abraham's attitude to God,
he suggests, could provide a model for our absolute responsibility to
each other (an argument criticized in David Wood's essay). Derrida

emphasizes the incommunicability of such responsibility, but concludes by linking this essential secrecy with the open conflict between Judaism, Islam and Christianity at the very site in Jerusalem where the *akedah* is supposed to have taken place: different languages, different books, different names, but – precisely because of these differences, he suggests – the same infinite responsibility.

Kierkegaard has moved a long way in the course of the century; and perhaps it will be him and his paradoxical pseudonyms who shed the last tear, and laugh the last laugh.

NOTES

Square brackets have been used in chapter notes throught the book to indicate notes and interpolations added by the editors in order to distinguish them from authors' notes.

1 The work of Walter Lowrie and David Swenson, though unsystematic about technicalities, is often excellent (and still unsurpassed) in reproducing Kierkegaard's supple style. See in particular *Philosophical Fragments*, translated by David Swenson (Princeton University Press for the American Scandinavian Foundation, Princeton, 1936); *Stages on Life's Way*, translated by Walter Lowrie (Oxford University Press, Oxford, 1940); *Concluding Unscientific Postscript to the Philosophical Fragments*, translated by David Swenson, completed by Walter Lowrie (Princeton University Press for the American Scandinavian Foundation, Princeton, 1941); and *Either/Or*, translated by David Swenson and Walter Lowrie (2 vols, Princeton University Press, Princeton, 1944).

2 The pioneer of the critical philosophical interpretation was Harald Høffding, author of *Kierkegaard som Filosof* (Gyldendal, Copenhagen, 1892). His allusions to Kierkegaard in a brief essay, 'A philosophical confession', in *The Journal of Philosophy, Psychology and Scientific Methods*, vol. 2, February 1905, pp. 85–92, attracted the enthusiastic attention of William James. See William James, 'Is Radical Empiricism Solipsistic?' (1905) in *Essays in Radical Empiricism* (Longmans, Green, New York, 1912), pp. 234–40.

3 'The Foundering of Form against Life, Sören Kierkegaard and Regine Olsen' (1909), translated by Anna Bostock in Georg Lukács, *Soul and Form* (Merlin, London, 1974), pp. 28–41, p. 35. Lukács gives an emphatic Marxist repetition of his interpretation of Kierkegaard in *The Destruction of Reason* (1962), translated by Peter Palmer (Merlin, London, 1980), pp. 243–96.

4 For Gadamer's recollections of the 'enormous impact' of Kierkegaard's works (in Schrempf's dubious and hostile German edition), and how they 'effected an epoch in Germany in the years before and after World War I' leading, through Jaspers, to 'the movement that was later given the name

of philosophy of existence', see Hans-Georg Gadamer, *Philosophical Hermeneutics*, translated by David E. Linge (University of California Press, Berkeley, 1976), p. 125, and *Heidegger's Ways*, translated by John W. Stanley (State University of New York Press, Albany, 1994), pp. 2, 54–5.

5   Theodor W. Adorno, *Kierkegaard: Konstruktion des Ästhetischen* (Mohr, Tübingen, 1933), translated by Robert Hullot-Kentor as *Kierkegaard, Construction of the Aesthetic* (University of Minnesota Press, Minneapolis, 1989).

6   'Nietzsche's Wort "Gott ist tot"' (1943) translated by William Lovitt in *The Question Concerning Technology and Other Essays* (Harper and Row, New York, 1977), p. 94. Cf. our editorial note (n. 16) to Levinas's essay, below, p. 38.

7   For example *Purify Your Hearts!*, *The Lilies and the Birds*, and *The Gospel of Sufferings*, all translated by Mrs A. S. Aldworth and the Rev. W. S. Ferrie (Daniel, London, 1938, 1941, 1942).

8   *The Journals, 1834–55*, selected and translated by Alexander Dru (Oxford University Press, Oxford, 1938), *The Diary of a Seducer*, translated by Knud Fick (The Dragon Press, Albany, 1935).

9   See Theodor Haecker, *Kierkegaard the Cripple* (1947), translated by C. V. O. Bruyn, introduction by Alexander Dru (Harvill, London, 1948), and Harold V. Martin, *Kierkegaard the Melancholy Dane* (Epworth Press, London, 1950).

10 *Kierkegaard*, selected and edited by W. H. Auden (Cassell, London, 1955), pp. 1–2. Auden showed a better understanding of Kierkegaard in his poetry, for example 'Atlantis' (1941) with its Ionian logicians: 'Learn their logic, but notice/How its subtlety betrays/Their enormous simple grief.'

11 X 2 A 559; *Journals and Papers*, translated by Howard V. Hong and Edna H. Hong (7 vols, Indiana University Press, Bloomington, 1967–78), 2514, vol. 3, p. 80.

12 *Philosophical Fragments*, translated by Walter Lowrie, p. 6. This translation has been superseded in the *Collected Writings* by the following: 'To have an opinion is to me both too much and too little; it presupposes a security and well-being in existence akin to having a wife and children in this mortal life.' See *Philosophical Fragments, Johannes Climacus*, translated by Howard V. Hong and Edna H. Hong (Princeton University Press, Princeton, 1985), p. 7.

13 *Philosophical Fragments*, translated by Walter Lowrie, p. 46. Compare the translation in the *Collected Writings*: 'But one must not think ill of the paradox, for the paradox is the passion of thought, and the thinker without the paradox is like the lover without passion: a mediocre fellow.' See *Philosophical Fragments, Johannes Climacus*, translated by Howard V. Hong and Edna H. Hong (Princeton University Press, Princeton, 1985), p. 37.

14 VIII A 11; *Journals and Papers*, 3089, vol. 3, p. 406.

15 *The Point of View for my Work as an Author: a Report to History*, translated by Walter Lowrie (1939), 2nd edn (Harper and Row, New York, 1962), pp. 5–6.

1
Philosophy after Kierkegaard

Paul Ricoeur

In the 1920s and thirties, when Kierkegaard was first becoming known in Germany (thanks to the courageous translation by Gottsched and Schrempf – a very risky venture at the time),[1] and then in France (with the fine translations by Tisseau and Jean Wahl's celebrated *Études Kierkegaardiennes*),[2] he was called on to play a double role: on the one hand as a thinker of protest, on the other as a thinker of renewal. So what function can he have now, thirty or forty years after he made his first entrance into European philosophy and theology?

It must be admitted that the nature and significance of Kierkegaard's philosophical contribution no longer seem quite so straightforward. If he was a thinker of protest, then what was he protesting against? It is easy for us all to repeat, in unison, that Kierkegaard was opposing the system, or Hegel, or German idealism – and this would of course have been Kierkegaard's view as well. And if he was the thinker of a new awakening, then what was it all about? The fashionable answer might simply be: existentialism. But these two assumptions are precisely what I shall now try to call into question, in the hope of suggesting a different interpretation of Kierkegaard – an approach which may perhaps open up a new future for his work, now that the earlier interpretations have run their course.[3]

This chapter is the text of a lecture given in Geneva in 1963, to mark the 150th anniversary of Kierkegaard's birth. First published in *Revue de Théologie et de Philosophie*, vol. 13 (1963), no 4, pp. 303–16, reprinted in Ricoeur's *Lectures 2* (Seuil, Paris, 1992), pp. 29–45, and translated for this volume by Jonathan Rée with the author's permission. Translation copyright © Jonathan Rée 1998.

To begin with the first doubt: was Kierkegaard really the father of existentialism? With the hindsight of several decades, this attribution reveals itself as a pure illusion, a *trompe-l'oeil*, a convenient way of domesticating Kierkegaard by subsuming him under a familiar category. It is now quite easy to see that the supposed family of 'existentialist' philosophies never really existed, and this should enable us to restore some autonomy to Kierkegaard. He used to be seen as the forefather of Gabriel Marcel, Karl Jaspers, Heidegger and Sartre. But this grouping has obviously collapsed – if indeed it was ever a reality outside a few academic textbooks. The existential philosophy that they supposedly held in common does not exist. They share neither a set of leading doctrines, nor a method, nor even a group of fundamental questions: Gabriel Marcel prefers to call himself a neo-Socratic; Jaspers emphasizes his commitment to classical philosophy; Heidegger's fundamental ontology has broken down into a practice of archaizing, poetic meditation; and Sartre now regards his own existentialism as an ideology which needs to be reinterpreted in terms of Marxism. As these extreme cases indicate, it is much less illuminating now than it was in the forties to use existentialism as a key to the interpretation of Kierkegaard.

This doubt has been reinforced by our reading of *The Concept of Anxiety* and *The Sickness unto Death*, which – so we have argued – should be seen as the work of a thinker who transposed living experiences into a well-honed dialectic which was based not on experience but on abstractly imagined artificial stages of existence. These stages were then elaborated into a fractured dialectic of the finite and the infinite, the possible and the actual, the unconscious and consciousness, etc. And this fractured dialectic, we suspect, had rather more in common with Kierkegaard's own best enemy – Hegel – than with his supposed intellectual heirs.[4]

But this suggestion immediately collides with an apparently stronger certainty. Everyone knows that Kierkegaard was an anti-Hegelian. He said so himself. In fact he hardly ever said anything else. And everyone also knows that he was the creator of a new intellectual epoch, following on from German idealism: the era of post-philosophy. Thus it is taken for granted that philosophy came to an end with Hegel, that philosophical discourse reached its completion in and through him, and that what came after Hegel must be something very different – something no longer discursive at all. This interpretation of modern thought has been encouraged by the convergence of Marx, Nietzsche and Kierkegaard in their attacks on idealism. The realization of philosophy as revolutionary practice, European nihilism and the transvaluation of values, and the defiant individual standing alone before God: these three great tendencies of modern thought are said to represent the end of philosophy conceived as a total discourse, and the beginning of post-philosophy.

But is it any more illuminating to associate Kierkegaard with Marx and Nietzsche than to incorporate him into something called existentialism? Is the concept of the end of philosophy any clearer than that of existentialism? There are two main doubts on this score. First: who is to be regarded as the last philosopher? Is it Hegel? Can we be sure? And second: is the trilogy of post-philosophers really independent of German idealism, rather than an integral part of it?

So who really was the last philosopher? It is easy to see Kant, Fichte, Schelling and Hegel as constituting a single sequence which reached its culmination in Hegel's *Encyclopedia*. But this view is itself part of a Hegelian interpretation of German idealism. It entails forgetting that Schelling buried Hegel (and prophetically, too); it means neglecting the unexplored riches of Fichte and the later Schelling; and above all, it involves a misunderstanding of Hegel himself. We might, after all, be victims of a Marxian and Kierkegaardian misinterpretation of Hegel. At any rate a fresh interpretation of Kierkegaard must certainly entail a reconsideration of Fichte, Schelling, and Hegel himself.

But I want to press home my doubts about the concept of a completion of western philosophy, by suggesting that the so-called post-philosophies themselves belong to the philosophical epoch of German idealism. Heidegger has argued quite plausibly that Nietzsche fulfilled one of the deepest yearnings of western thought: if it has always been driven by a kind of aggrandizement of subjectivity, and the realization of the *subjectum* as subject, then Nietzsche must be the final completion of the western philosophical adventure. On the other hand, if we accept the Marxian view that philosophy has hitherto 'interpreted the world without changing it', then Kierkegaard and Nietzsche must still be classified as discursive philosophers.[5] For Nietzsche, however, Marx would still be enslaved to the idols of the crowd, to the mythology of science ('our last religion') – the last breath of Christianity and Platonism. And for the reader of Kierkegaard too, Marx remains a Hegelian, though for rather different reasons: to the extent that the dialectic of history is still a logic of reality, Marx represents the triumph of generality and the fulfilment of the Hegelian postulate that the real is the rational and the rational the real.[6]

My motive for playing off Schelling against Hegel in this way, and Hegel against himself, and Nietzsche, Kierkegaard and Marx against each other, is simply to free the interpretation of Kierkegaard from the whole idea of a fulfilment or end of western philosophy. If we can avoid making a sharp separation between his fate and that of German idealism, and if we can give up regarding him as a source of existentialism, then we shall be in a position to consider the question: how can one conduct philosophy after Kierkegaard?

My answer will have three levels. First I wish to separate off the genuinely *irrational* aspects of Kierkegaard. Then I shall consider his contribution to a *critique of existential possibilities*. Finally, I shall try to relate this critique to *the ideal of philosophical discourse as a system*.

'The Exception'

There is one aspect of Kierkegaard's work that can never be taken over and carried forward, either by philosophers or by theologians, and that is his incommunicable existence. But there are other elements that can be built upon, because they belong to philosophical argumentation, to reflection and speculation: these are the elements represented by the pseudonyms. And while it is impossible to philosophize in succession to Kierkegaard the existing individual, it may be possible to philosophize in succession to his pseudonyms, at least to the extent that they belong to the same philosophical sphere as German idealism.

Let us consider the first aspect of this paradox. On the one hand, Kierkegaard holds himself aloof from both philosophy and theology. We are then confronted by the question of *genius*, considered as a non-philosophical source of philosophy. The extent of this genius is of course very large: it includes not only the real (unknown) Kierkegaard, but also the mythical Kierkegaard, a creation of his own writings. Everyone would agree that the story of his real existence constitutes something quite unique in the history of thought: the dandy from Copenhagen, with his bizarre engagement to Regine, the devastating critic of Bishop Mynster, the unfortunate victim of the *Corsair*, the sick man dying in the public hospital – none of these characters can be repeated, or even correctly understood. But of course the same applies to any other existence as well.

But the case of Kierkegaard is exceptional all the same: no one else has ever transposed autobiography into personal myth as he did. By means of his identifications with Abraham, Job, Ahasuerus and several other fantastical characters, he elaborated a kind of fictive personality which conceals and dissimulates his real existence. And this poetic character – like a character in fiction, or the hero of a Shakespearean tragedy – can never be situated within the framework or landscape of ordinary communication.

Of course, what is here offered to our philosophical understanding, and withheld as well, is a character, a hero, created by his own writings;

an author, the creature of his works, an existing individual who has de-realized himself and thus avoided capture by any known discipline. He does not even fit in with his own 'stages on life's way'. He was not enough of a seducer, a Don Juan, to be an aesthete. Nor did he succeed with the life of ethics: he was unmarried and childless, and he did not earn his living by practising a profession, so he was excluded from the ethical existence described by Judge Wilhelm in *Either/Or*. Surely his family were right: 'how could you not be melancholy, squandering all your fortune like that!'

But if Kierkegaard failed to live either an aesthetic or an ethical life, what then of religion, in his sense? Surely the Christianity he described is so extreme that no one could possibly practise it. The subjective thinker before God, the pure contemporary of Christ, suffering crucifix-ion with Him, without church, without tradition, and without ritual, can only exist outside of history. 'I am the poet of the religious', he says, and I think we should take him at his word.[7] But what does it actually mean? We cannot possibly tell. Kierkegaard is there somewhere, in the gaps between his stages, in the interstices and the transitions, as a kind of synopsis of the aesthetic and religious stages, but omitting the ethical stage. Thus he escaped the choice that he himself propounded in *Either/Or*. Kierkegaard does not fit his own categories. To understand him one would need to be able to grasp him unprecedented combination of irony, melancholy, purity of heart and corrosive rhetoric, add a dash of buffoonery, and then perhaps top it off with religious aestheticism and martyrdom . . .

So Kierkegaard is certainly 'an exception'. But apart from simply reiterating that fact, we need to deepen our understanding of it too: we need to read Kierkegaard, and let him be what he is, where he is – that is to say, outside both philosophy and theology. We must allow him to be what he is; it is no use trying to correct him, refute him, or complete him. Some readers may wish he had shown more sense of forgiveness and less sense of guilt, or more sense of collective guilt and of the Church. Others will say: if only he had had a bit more sense of community, of dialogue. Still others will add: and perhaps a greater sense of history too, and more respect for the crowd, more affection for the people. Finally there are those who will say: if only he had been simpler, clearer, more coherent. No doubt all of us – philosophers, political theorists or theologians – have complained about Kierkegaard in this way. But we also realize that it is a ridiculous conceit: would you presume to correct Othello, or Cordelia? Or the Bourgeois Gentilhomme? Nietzsche used to say: 'you cannot refute a sound!' What is irrefutable, in Kierkegaard, is the existing individual – both the real existing individual, the author of his works, and the mythical existing individual, who is their creature. You cannot refute Kierkegaard: you must simply read him, consider, and then get on with your work – but 'with your eyes fixed on the exception'.

But what exactly can it mean, to work as a philosopher with your eyes fixed on the exception? In the first place, I think, it must mean paying renewed attention to the close relationship between philosophical thinking, or philosophical work of all kinds, and non-philosophy. The exception that is Kierkegaard, the rhetorical–religious genius, the dandy–martyr: these do not constitute a unique situation. Philosophy must always be concerned with non-philosophy, because it has no object of its own. It is a reflection on experience, on the whole of experience, and on experience as a whole. Philosophy is a reflection on scientific, ethical, aesthetic and religious experience, so its *sources* are clearly external to it. But philosophy's starting point is a different matter. Philosophy is responsible for its own starting point, its method, its completion; it seeks it out, and goes towards it. (Our lamented friend Pierre Thévenaz was firm and persuasive on this point: the starting point of philosophy always lies ahead of it.)[8] But if it is obliged to seek out its starting point on its own, it must still receive its sources from outside. It controls its starting point but not its sources, that is to say its basic supplies, its underpinnings. That is how I would interpret the saying of Karl Jaspers: 'we are not the exception, but we must philosophise with our eyes fixed on the exception.'[9]

And Kierkegaard, with his aesthetic–religious–rhetorical genius, is one such source, in the same way as Stirner, Kafka and Nietzsche. Of course Nietzsche must also be treated as possessing philosophical genius, though this is as inadequate a characterization of him as it would be of Kierkegaard. (I refer here to the Nietzsche of Sils-Maria, the Nietzsche who gave up his chair at the University of Basle, the hermit of Engadine, Nietzsche the aphorist, the Nietzsche invented by Zarathustra, the Nietzsche who conversed with Dionysus and with the Crucified, the Nietzsche who drifted into madness – the Nietzsche who resembles Kierkegaard the martyr, or Kierkegaard the insolent insulter of the Bishop.) Thus philosophy must engage with Kierkegaard as with any other genius of non-philosophy. But philosophy still has its own distinct tasks – the search for origins and principles, for order and coherence, for the meaning of truth and reality – and these tasks must always remain theoretical and reflective.

So much for the first response. But of course, to recognize the aesthetic–religious genius of Kierkegaard in this way might lead to him being excluded from philosophy. And everyone can sense that Kierkegaard is not – or not only – a non-philosopher. What makes

Kierkegaard awkward is that he belongs both inside philosophy and outside it at one and the same time.

The Critique of Existential Possibilities

Kierkegaard thrust himself into both philosophy and Christian dogmatics, and this somewhat upsets and destabilizes our relationship to him. So we must now turn to his actual argumentation, as opposed to his unique genius – whether real or fictional, biographical or mythical, that of the *Journals* or that of the poetic transposition of his living experience. The riddle of the pseudonyms has already introduced us to this other side of the question of Kierkegaard; for even if Kierkegaard always held himself aloof from philosophy, still Constantin Constantius, Johannes de Silentio, Vigilius Haufniensis – the supposed aliases of Kierkegaard – are clearly philosophical authors. But the problem of the pseudonyms is the same as that of indirect communication; and indirect communication, in its turn, involves a particular form of argumentation.

Hence we cannot simply classify Kierkegaard as the exception, and exclude him from philosophy on account of his genius for exceptionality. His terrifying power of argumentation will simply return him to us. So we find ourselves confronting the same question we previously left unanswered. Kierkegaard, as we said, not only produced arguments; he also worked out concepts: the *concepts* of anxiety, despair, sin or position, for example. And he constructed these concepts on the territory of the Hegelian dialectic, building an anti-dialectic out of those unresolved contradictions he called paradoxes.

But paradoxes still have a logical structure – the structure appropriate to the methods of proof required by the problematic of the existing individual, the individual before God. Here it is necessary to turn to Kierkegaard's most extraordinary work, the *Concluding Unscientific Post-script*. The *Postscript* deploys an entire network of categories: eternity and the moment, the existing individual, choice, singularity, subjectivity, the 'before God', and the absurd. And this is not non-philosophy: it is hyper-philosophy, even to the point of caricature and ridicule. It is in connection with these categories of the existing individual that the crucial problem arises – that of the logic of Kierkegaard discourse.

But this problem cannot be tackled without a thorough reappraisal of the relations between Kierkegaard and German idealism. A new approach to Kierkegaard must also be a new approach to German idealism. But no such reinterpretation will be possible until we have unravelled the apparent logic of the sequence 'from Kant to Hegel' (as Kroner called it in his great book).[11] Let me now offer a few pointers towards such a reinterpretation.

In a sense, Kierkegaard can be regarded as part of the general movement in German philosophy after 1840 generally known as the 'return to Kant'. The phrase 'the paradox calls for faith, not understanding'[12] is clearly an echo of Kant's celebrated adage about the necessity 'to deny *knowledge*, in order to make room for *faith*'.[13] But the similarities go further than that, for the philosophical function of 'paradox' in Kierkegaard is closely parallel to that of 'limits' in Kant. One might even go so far as to say that Kierkegaard's fragmented dialectic resembles the Kantian dialectic, understood as a critique of illusion. In each case, there is an essential truth that can be stated only fragmentarily. Thus there is something in Kierkegaard that cannot be understood except against a Kantian background, and something in Kant that only makes sense in terms of a Kierkegaardian struggle with paradox.

Of course this way of comparing Kierkegaard and Kant is not entirely adequate. It is only within a philosophical perspective which presumes that the essential choice lies between Kant and Hegel that such a connection needs to be made. And in addition, Kierkegaard was not really a critical thinker in the Kantian sense: he had no interest in conditions of possibility, at least not as an epistemological problem. But it might perhaps be argued that Kierkegaard's categories of existence constitute a different kind of critique, a *critique of existence*, and that they address the question of the possibility of *speaking* about existence. The existence of the singular individual is not a mystical experience that must be passed over in silence. Kierkegaard was far from being an intuitionist: he was a reflective thinker.

In order to identify a deeper connection between Kierkegaard and Kant, it will be necessary to work our way past another distinction, concerning the structure of reflection itself. Kantian reflection follows a particular model, based on a separation between the *a priori* and the *a posteriori* at the heart of experience. This Kantian formalism may well be both meaningful and functional within the field of physical experience. That is not at issue here; but it is possible that the source of all the difficulties of Kant's practical philosophy lies in his attempt to transpose this formalism from natural science to ethics. Kant's practical philosophy was constructed on the model of his theoretical philosophy, and reduced the critical problem of action to the formalization of the categorical imperative. Thus the Kierkegaardian categories of existence could be regarded as a response to problems of practical reason that Kant had rendered insoluble. The categories of existence are to ethics what the categories of objectivity are to natural science. They are the *conditions of possibility of experience* – not the possibility of physical experience, however, but the possibility of the fundamental experience of *the fulfilment of our desire and striving for existence*.

But the idea of freeing practical reason from the chains of formalism takes us from Kant to Fichte. As I have already remarked, Fichte and Schelling are the most misunderstood thinkers of their period, and the most constantly plagiarized. Everything that is strong and valuable in modern philosophy, everything that did not reach us through Hegel or Kant, must be due to Fichte or Schelling; and I am convinced that closer attention to them would transform our understanding of Kierkegaard. Let me offer two examples of the kind of reinterpretation that might be possible. First, as everyone knows, Fichte distinguished between *Tathandlung* and *Tatsache*, or *act* and *fact*, and this distinction provided the philosophical foundation for any ethic, or theory of action, that aspired to get beyond a simple doctrine of duty. The task of a philosophy of existence was then to work out the conditions of possibility and actuality of this act of existence. And despite all the differences between Kierkegaard and Fichte, it was this Fichtean problematic that defined the ground upon which Kierkegaardian experience could be *put into words*. But of course the point bears not on Kierkegaardian experience as such, but only on Kierkegaard's philosophical means of expression, which were derived from Fichte.

Our second remark concerns Schelling as well as Fichte. We are perhaps too much inclined to regard idealism, especially German idealism, as a pure play of abstractions. The great problem of 'idealism', however, is the problem of reality: fundamentally, idealism is the doctrine that the distinction between the ideal and the real is itself entirely ideal. In the later Schelling, human finitude – to the extent that it has a structure of its own – becomes irreducible to the limitation of one object by another, and the connection between finitude, freedom, and evil acquires a philosophical meaning of its own. The problem is no longer one of pure emotion, passion or poetry: it is a philosophical problem, the problem of finite reality.

Such then are the three philosophical structures – taken over from Kant, Fichte and Schelling – which give Kierkegaardian discourse its philosophical dimension. First there is the Kantian idea of a critique of practical reason as distinct from a critique of physical experience; then the Fichtean distinction between act and fact, and the definition of a practical philosophy in terms of the conditions of possibility and actualization of the act of existence; and finally there is the Schellingian problematic of finite reality, and specifically the connection between finitude, freedom and evil.

It seems to me, therefore, that in order to think philosophically after Kierkegaard we must not only go back behind Kierkegaard, toward this threefold problematic. We also need to release this problematic from its Hegelian yoke, and show that it could not achieve its meaning – or at any rate one of its meanings – except in the living experience of Kierkegaard.

System and Critique after Kierkegaard

We can now turn to a last comparison, in which we will find a reflection of the existential and dramatic conflict which sets Kierkegaard in total opposition to Hegel. This final comparison will bring us back to our starting point. We began with the simple and naïve conflict between Kierkegaard and Hegel – the existence of which is of course beyond dispute. The task is not to soften it, but to learn how to *think* it as a significant disagreement, a disagreement with a *meaning*. The conflict was of course part of Kierkegaard's own self-understanding, and in that sense it is clearly impossible to understand Kierkegaard apart from Hegel. And it is more than just a fact of his biography, a fortuitous encounter; it is a constitutive structure of Kierkegaardian thought that it is unthinkable apart from Hegel. A correct understanding of this paradoxical situation is a necessary condition for any fresh interpretation of Kierkegaard.

Let us begin with what the Hegelians would say about Kierkegaard. For them, Kierkegaardian discourse is merely a subsidiary part of Hegelian discourse. Indeed it can be given an exact location within the system: it is the discourse of the 'unhappy consciousness', and its logical place is at the beginning, not the end, of the *Phenomenology of Spirit*.[14] And Kierkegaard himself demonstrated that he was part of the system: he showed it in his own discourse. Once he had lost the key to the true dialectic – namely the self-movement of contents, and the self-supersession of these contents through contradiction and mediation – it was inevitable that he would try to replace the true dialectic with an artificial play of paradoxes, his fractured dialectic, which was really a mere rhetoric of pathos, wrapped up in laborious didacticism. Considered in this light, Kierkegaard appears as no more than a parasite of the system, by turns denying it and reinventing it in a derisory form.

Kierkegaardians will have to accept that the Hegelian response has some merit. The role of philosophical renegade or buffoon was indeed an element of Kierkegaard's vocation. Only someone with the courage to act out such a role could adopt the name of 'existential thinker', and write a *Concluding Unscientific Postscript to the Philosophical Fragments*. The title itself proclaims that derision forms part of the structure of

Kierkegaardian discourse, and that is why it cannot be separated from the philosophical discourse of Hegelianism.

But this connection between Kierkegaard and Hegel – this dependence through derision – is evidence of a still closer relationship: a connection which can only be detected by means of a fresh interpretation of Hegel himself. The Hegelian accusation – that Kierkegaard is either excluded from the system by his own discourse, insofar as it lacks sense, or included within it as a partial discourse (for example, that of the 'unhappy consciousness') – presupposes that the system exists. But we need to recognize that for Hegel himself the possibility of the system was not only a presupposition but a question as well. The truth of the conflict between Hegel and Kierkegaard cannot be understood apart from Hegel's own questioning of the system.

It follows that Kierkegaard and Hegel are put in question together, and put in question by each other. Let us just consider three critical points arising from this mutual destabilization.

1   The *Phenomenology of Spirit* enables us to question the meaning of Kierkegaard's entire enterprise. But on the other hand, what is the real position of the *Phenomenology of Spirit* within the system as a whole? It is clearly inadequate to say that it is a propaedeutic to Hegel's doctrine of logic: there must surely be some hidden discord between a schematic history of spirit and a logic of the absolute? Surely the prodigious wealth of this history – a kind of gigantic novel of humanity – could never be contained and recapitulated by the system?

This reciprocal questioning, at the level of the 'unhappy consciousness' itself, is strengthened by a curious similarity between Kierkegaard and the Hegel of the *Phenomenology*: are they not both ranged on the same side, against all kinds of superficial rationalism – against the Enlightenment, the *Aufklärung*? But then the struggle between Hegel and Kierkegaard suddenly appears in a different light. Kierkegaard is neither included nor excluded by a system which is a question for itself. The conflict between the Hegelian and the Kierkegaardian dialectic raises a question for each of them. Would not a fractured dialectic be unthinkable without a philosophy of mediation? But on the other hand, could a philosophy of mediation ever be final? In this way, the conflict between Hegelian and Kierkegaardian dialectics becomes a dialectical figure in itself, a figure that needs to be understood in its own terms, as constituting a new structure of philosophical discourse.

If this general interpretation of the relation between Hegel and Kierkegaard – as a conflict which itself needs to become a moment of philosophical discourse – is accepted, then it may become possible to discover a deeper understanding, both in Hegel and in Kierkegaard, of two other fundamental issues: the critique of ethics, and the meaning of religious faith.

2   I must immediately emphasize a point which is easily missed or misunderstood: the paradoxical fact that both Hegel and Kierkegaard constructed a critique of the ethical stage of existence. But if, for Hegel, Kantianism as a whole represented the 'ethical view of the world', for Kierkegaard it was Hegelianism that represented the 'ethical stage of existence'. Both the similarity and the disagreement are highly significant, and they both lead to the question: what is the meaning of the ethical stage?

Hegel would say that the ethical stage is about a conflict between the ideal and the real, that it denigrates the real in the name of the ideal, and ultimately that it postulates a transcendence cut off from rational reality: without this transcendence consciousness could not sit in judgement, or weigh and condemn. For Hegel, therefore, any philosophy that depends on a dualism of heaven and earth, God and world, or transcendence and immanence, is trapped within an ethical view of the world and must be overcome; in this sense, the 'before God' of Kierkegaard also arises from the ethical view of the world, and it too must be overcome. But having made this criticism, Hegelians will also admit that, to the extent that Kierkegaard managed to get beyond his own ethical view of the world, it was because he brought in another idea – that of the contemporaneity of Christ and the Christian believer. But this is a poetic relation which short-circuits rational discourse, and it would be unthinkable except as the interiorization of the 'before God' by means of which the philosophy of transcendence becomes subsumed in a philosophy of love. But if this can indeed be said, then it needs to be thought as well; and how could that be done without the help of the categories which bear witness to the triumph of the religion of the Spirit over the religion of the Father, through the mediation of the death of the Son? And that, of course, is the central theme of the Hegelian philosophy of religion. Such is a Hegelian interpretation of Kierkegaard, and it ought to be accepted by Kierkegaardians in the same way they have to accept their inclusion within the *Phenomenology of Spirit* under the heading of 'the unhappy consciousness'.

But this second critique, this second attempt to include Kierkegaard within the system, is no more conclusive than the first. For we will not be able to make sense of Hegel until we have understood the Kierkegaardian critique of the ethical stage: that Hegel could not get beyond the ethical stage because he reduced the individual to the general, the subjective thinker to impersonal objective thought. The principal contention of any Hegelian philosophy – 'the rational is the real, the real rational' – is the contention of any ethics that reduces the individual to the general. But this proposition also expresses either a hypocritical omission of Hegel as an existing individual, or his delirious ascension to the rank of Spirit.

Surely this conflict between Hegel and Kierkegaard ought itself to become a part of philosophical discourse. On the one hand, the distance between humanity and the totally other is unthinkable except in terms of an inclusive relation which would dispense with any idea of pure transcendence. Anyone who speaks of transcendence is thinking of a totality which embraces the relation between the Other and the self. In this sense, the idea of transcendence is bound to be self-defeating, and Hegel will always be able to triumph over any attempt to think the absolute separation between humanity and the absolutely other. In this sense too, any ethical view negates itself as soon as it tries to make itself explicit. On the other hand, this point of view without a viewpoint, from which one is supposed to be able to see the deep identity between the real and the rational, existence and meaning, individual and discourse, is never vouchsafed to us. It is always necessary to return, with Kierkegaard, to this admission: that I am not absolute discourse; that to exist is to be ignorant, in a strong sense of the word; and that singularity is constantly regenerated at the margin of discourse. A different discourse is needed, therefore – one which will attend to singularity and give it expression.

3   The struggle enters a third phase with the problem of religious faith. For Hegel, religion was just a preliminary to philosophy in the sense of Absolute Knowledge. For Kierkegaard, in contrast, there was nothing beyond faith, because it is God's gracious response to unfathomable evil. This conflict appears to be total, but do we really have to make a choice? Ought we not rather to treat these two opposed philosophies of religion as parts of a single whole? We should perhaps move beyond the level of the 'unhappy consciousness' to the seventh chapter of the *Phenomenology*, which contains Hegel's real philosophy of religion – a doctrine that remained almost unchanged up to the *Lectures on the Philosophy of Religion* of 1820–1. This chapter poses a problem which throws light on Kierkegaard, and which Kierkegaard illuminates in his turn: that of religious language and of *representation* in general. In one sense, it is impossible to transcend religion – that is to say, true religion or revealed religion, as Hegel calls it – because it is both the agony of representation and the representation of agony, on the threshold of Absolute Knowledge. However, we are not actually in possession of Absolute Knowledge. All we can really say is that there must be such a thing, and that this is why representation must be both transcended and sustained. But

in that case, religion can never be abolished by anything external to it: it must simply continue living its own agony, and comprehending its own meaning as its own suppression. Religion exists nevertheless; and within a religious community and its rituals of worship, religion has to learn to think this suppression – the destruction of idols, figures and representations, the death of God – as its own truth.

We have thus reached the point where the opposition between the Hegelian system and the passionate subjective thinker can attain its full meaning. The relation between Hegel and Kierkegaard has itself become a paradox, and the explanation lies in the philosophical function of the idea of system. Perhaps we have discovered or rediscovered that the system is both the ultimate aspiration of philosophy and its unachievable goal. Religion is the place within philosophical discourse where it is possible to contemplate both the necessity of transcending images, representations and symbols, and the impossibility of giving them up. This is the 'locus' of the struggle between Hegel and Kierkegaard. But from now on the struggle itself can become a part of philosophical discourse.

I shall now try to bring together the partial responses that I have given to the question: how to philosophize after Kierkegaard?

Firstly, philosophy always has a relation to *non-philosophy*. In this way, the irrational aspect of Kierkegaard is a resource for philosophy like any other work of genius. If the vital link between philosophy and non-philosophy were to be severed, philosophy would be in danger of degenerating into a mere word game, ultimately becoming a pure linguistic nihilism.

Secondly, there is more to Kierkegaard than the romantic genius, the individual, the passionate thinker. He opened up a new mode of philosophizing, which I have described as the *critique of existential possibilities*. This discourse on existence is no longer the poetic expression of an emotion; it is a form of conceptual thinking, with its own principles of rigour and its own type of coherence, and it requires a logic of its own. To use Heideggerian language, one could say that the problem is to move from the *existenziell* to the *existenzial*, from personal decision to anthropological structures.[15] The development of such a discourse requires a new interpretation of both Kierkegaard and German idealism. In this sense, Kierkegaard answers the Kantian demand for a practical philosophy that will be quite distinct from the critique of physical experience; but at the same time his existential analysis has its philosophical grounding, first in Fichte's distinction between act and fact (between the act of existence and the existing fact), and second in Schelling's philosophy of reality, which was the first to tie together questions of finitude, freedom and evil.

Thirdly, we concluded by returning to the initial problem of the conflict between individual and system. It appeared to us that it would be a mistake to regard them as alternatives between which we are condemned to make our choice. A new philosophical situation arises from this conflict, inviting us both to reinterpret Hegel's *Phenomenology* and *Philosophy of Religion*, and to locate Kierkegaard's paradoxes within the field of a Hegelian philosophy of 'representation' and Absolute Knowledge.

It is to be hoped that these partial answers will prevent us from giving way to the disastrous disjunction between rationalism and existentialism. Scientific knowledge is not everything. Beyond science, there is always thinking. The question of human existence does not imply the death of language and logic; on the contrary, it calls for yet more lucidity and rigour. The question: What is it to exist? is inseparable from another question: What is it to think? Philosophy lives in the unity of these two questions; and when they are separated, it dies.

NOTES

1 [Ricoeur refers to the translations by Christoph Schrempf and Hermann Gottsched in the 12-volume *Gesammelte Werke*, edited by Schrempf (Diederichs, Jena, 1922–5).]

2 [Paul-Henri Tisseau's translations include *La Répétition* (Alcan, Paris, 1933), *Crainte et Tremblement* (Aubier, Paris, 1935), *Le Concept d'Angoisse* (Alcan, Paris, 1938); Jean Wahl's *Études Kierkegaardiennes* (Paris, Aubier, 1938) is a wide-ranging philosophical study, supplemented with translated selections from Kierkegaard's *Journals and Papers*.]

3 [Ricoeur remarks that this interpretation 'has been prepared for in our preceding meditation', i.e. in a companion piece entitled 'Kierkegaard et le mal' – a lecture on *The Concept of Anxiety* and *The Sickness Unto Death*, published in *Revue de Théologie et de Philosophie*, vol. 13 (1963), no. 4, pp. 303–16, reprinted in *Lectures 2*, pp. 15–28, and translated by David Pellauer as 'Kierkegaard and Evil', in *Kierkegaard's Truth: The Disclosure of the Self*, edited by Joseph H. Smith (Yale University Press, New Haven, 1981), pp. 313–25.]

4 [See above, n. 3.]

5 [Ricoeur alludes to the eleventh of Marx's 'Theses on Feuerbach' (1845): 'The philosophers have only *interpreted* the world, in various ways; the point is to *change* it.' See Karl Marx, *Early Writings*, translated by Rodney Livingstone and Gregor Benton (Penguin, Harmondsworth, 1975), p. 423.]

6 [See G. W. F. Hegel, *The Encyclopedia of the Philosophical Sciences*, Part One, §6, translated by William Wallace as *The Logic of Hegel* (Oxford University Press, Oxford, 1892), p. 10.]

7 [Kierkegaard's idea of himself as a poet was ambivalent. In 1840, he wrote his in his Journal (III A 62): 'the poetic is the divine woof of the purely human existence . . . it is the cord through which the divine holds fast to existence. The poetic life in the personality is the unconscious sacrifice . . . because it is first in the religious that the sacrifice becomes conscious and the misrelationship is removed.' And in 1851: 'I am a poet. But long before I became a poet I was intended for the life of religious individuality. And the event whereby I became a poet was an ethical break or a teleological suspension of the ethical. And both these things make me want to be something more than "the poet"' (X 3 A 789). A little later, repeatedly: 'I am only a poet – alas, only a poet. . . . I love this earthly life all too much' (X 4 A 33). See *Journals and Papers*, translated by Howard V. Hong and Edna H. Hong (7 vols, Indiana University Press, Bloomington, 1967–78), 1027, 6718, 6727; vol. 1 pp. 449–50, vol. 6, pp. 371, 377–9. The phrase 'poet of the religious' is also in *The Sickness Unto Death*, translated by Howard V. Hong and Edna H. Hong (Princeton University Press, Princeton, 1980), p. 78. Cf. note 29 to Agacinski, p. 149, below.]

8 [Pierre Thévenaz, Swiss philosopher and theologian, to whom Ricoeur paid tribute in 'Un philosophe protestant: Pierre Thévenaz' (1956), reprinted in *Lectures 3* (Seuil, Paris, 1994), pp. 245–59.]

9 [See Karl Jaspers, *Vernunft und Existenz: Fünf Vorlesungen* (J. B. Wolters, Groningen, 1935), translated by William Earle as *Reason and Existenz* (Routledge and Kegan Paul, London, 1956), p. 129, translation modified.]

10 [On the concept of position (or positing), as opposed to negation, see *The Sickness Unto Death*, translated by Howard V. Hong and Edna H. Hong (Princeton University Press, Princeton, 1980) Part 2, Ch. 3, pp. 96–100: 'Sin is not a negation but a position.']

11 [Richard Kroner, *Von Kant bis Hegel* (2 vols. Mohr, Tübingen, 1921, 1924).]

12 [This theme is discussed extensively in *Philosophical Fragments*, esp. chs 3 and 4. 'When the understanding and the paradox happily encounter each other in the moment, when the understanding steps aside and the paradox gives itself, . . . the third something, the something in which this occurs . . . is that happy passion to which we shall now give a name, although for us it is not a matter of the name. We shall call it *faith*.' See *Philosophical Fragments, Johannes Climacus*, translated by Howard V. Hong and Edna H. Hong (Princeton University Press, Princeton, 1985) p. 59. See also 'Subjective Truth, Inwardness' in *Concluding Unscientific Postscript*, translated by Howard V. Hong and Edna H. Hong (2 vols. Princeton University Press, Princeton, 1992), vol. 1, esp. pp. 213–28; see esp. p. 224: 'With the understanding in direct opposition, the inwardness of faith must grasp the paradox.']

13 [See Immanuel Kant, *Critigue of Pure Reason*, Preface to second edition, B xxx; translated by Norman Kemp Smith (Macmillan, London, 1929), p. 29.]

14 [The 'unhappy consciousness' is the culmination of the discussion of self-consciousness in Ch. 4 of G. W. F. Hegel, *The Phenomenology of Spirit*

(1807), translated by A. V. Miller (Oxford University Press, Oxford, 1977), pp. 119–38.]

15 [Ricoeur alludes to Heidegger's distinction between the everyday 'existentiell' interpretation of existence, and the 'existential' interpretation, in which the structure of existence is made 'theoretically transparent', See *Being and Time*, §4, translated by John Macquarrie and Edward Robinson (Blackwell, Oxford, 1962), p. 33.]

2
Existence and Ethics

Emmanuel Levinas

1 Truth in Victory

The strong conception of existence which was Kierkegaard's contribution to European thought insists on two basic points. The first is that human subjectivity, together with its dimension of interiority, needs to be maintained as an absolute, as something separate but located on this side of objective Being rather than beyond it. But secondly, and paradoxically, the irreducibility of the subject must be protected – on the basis of pre-philosophical experience – from the threat of idealism, even if it was idealism that first accorded a philosophical status to subjectivity.

For idealism either sought to reduce humanity to an impervious disembodied point whose interiority was constituted by timeless logical activity; or, following Hegel, it attempted to absorb the human subject into the very Being which it was simultaneously engaged in revealing. The basic claim of idealism was that the explication of Being by thought would allow the subject to transcend itself and hand over its ultimate

'Existence et Éthique' was originally published in German in the *Schweizer Monatshefte* in 1963, and first appeared in French in Emmanuel Levinas, *Noms Propres* (Fata Morgana, Montpellier, 1976), pp. 99–109. The two comments ('A propos de *Kierkegaard Vivant*') are based on spoken interventions at a UNESCO conference on Kierkegaard held in Paris in 1964. They appeared in print in *Kierkegaard Vivant* (Gallimard, Paris, 1966), pp. 232–4 and 286–8, but in a form with which Levinas was dissatisfied. They were published in an approved version in *Noms Propres*, pp. 111–15. These translations appear with the permission of Fata Morgana. Translation copyright © Jonathan Rée 1998.

mysteries to Reason. It was like imagining an artist carried off into a world of his own creation, becoming incorporated into the painting as it emerged under his brush.

Kierkegaard attacked these claims by arguing that the subjectivity which idealism wanted to grasp was not originally a movement of thought at all. Subjectivity was not a capacity for 'thematization', which somehow totalized different experiences, revealing them all to be commensurable and therefore generalizable, and generating the Idea and the System out of their differences and mutual contradictions. Subjectivity could not be subsumed into a power which makes the thinker into the measure of all beings, and reduces beings to expressions of the thinker or the act of thinking. Being, according to Kierkegaard, was not the correlative of thought.

But what could then become of the subjectivity of the subject? Kierkegaard was not able to appeal to the particularity of sensation and pleasure as opposed to the productive generosity of the concept. The kind of sensory dispersal which he referred to as the 'aesthetic stage' led to the depths of despair, where subjectivity is dissipated and destroyed. The alternative was the 'ethical' stage, in which the inner life finds expression and fulfilment in the world of law and society, putting its trust in principles and institutions and human communication. However this kind of totalizing and generalizing would itself turn out to be incapable of containing the thinker. Exteriority could never match up to human inwardness: the subject had a secret, forever inexpressible, and it was this secret that defined its subjectivity. The secret was not like a piece of information passed over in silence, but was essentially inexpressible and associated above all with the burning pain of sin. There was no victory for rational and universal truth; nor was there any means of expression that could either cover up the secret or extinguish it.

This incommunicable burning, this 'thorn in the flesh', testified to subjectivity as a *tension over itself* [*tension sur soi*]. This conception can be traced back beyond the philosophical notion of subjectivity to a Christian form of experience, and even to the pagan sources of Christianity. Subjectivity in this sense is an existence in tension over itself [*tendue sur elle-même*], which opens onto exteriority in an attitude of impatient expectation, but is incapable of finding fulfilment in the kind of exteriority – whether of persons or of things – that could be comprehended by an impervious mode of thinking which was itself without tension. And beyond this thirst for salvation, there lies a still more archaic tension of the human soul – 'naturally Christian', perhaps – the tension of the soul consumed by desire.

The traditional subjectivity that derives from this ancient experience, and which is common to both speculative and existential philosophy, is a means by which a being can produce itself; but it does not achieve its self-identification through a simple logical tautology about being, a repeated 'A is A' which is merely *said*, and which has no real bearing on it as it soars meteorically over nothingness [*sa météorie*]. The tautology is somehow able to launch subjectivity into flight, and activate its emergence out of nothingness. The identification of subjectivity is thus prior to language, and depends simply on the way a being clings to its being. The identification of A as A is the same as A's anxiety for A. The subjectivity of the subject is an identification of the Same in its concern for the Same. It is egoism, and its subjectivity is a Self [*un Moi*].

The idealistic Hegelian conception of subjectivity started out from the same egocentric orientation of the subject. The dialectic was called upon to demonstrate that this egoism was bound to be converted into a consciousness of Being and Truth, thereby revealing a structure of thought that had always been slumbering within the subjectivity of the subject. At some point its tension over itself would relax and be replaced by self-consciousness, and the Self would at last be able to understand itself, within a totality, as subject to a general law based on the ultimate victory of truth – on a truth leading towards rational discourse. In other words subjectivity was converted into philosophy.

The great value of the Kierkegaardian notion of existence, with its deeply protestant protest against systems in general, is that it saw an impossibility within the very *capacity to speak* that was the achievement of totalizing thought. It descried within this discourse a faraway impossibility of discourse – the shadow of the evening hidden in the light of the midday sun. Behind the philosophy of totality which assuages the tension (possibly a sublime thirst for salvation) of subjective egoism it foresaw the end of philosophy, and how it would lead to a political totalitarianism in which we would cease to be the source of our own language and become mere reflections of an impersonal *logos*, or roles enacted by anonymous figures.

On the other hand, though, we must surely wonder whether this return to a subjectivity which holds itself aloof from thought, that is to say from truth in perpetual victory – this suspicion of any thought that might allay our unease, on the ground that it might possibly be a delusion or a *distraction* – could not itself give rise to further acts of violence? In the end, we must ask whether a subjectivity which is irreducible to objective being might not be rendered intelligible through some principle other than its egoism, and whether Kierkegaard was really right to describe the ethical stage in terms of generality and the equivalence of the outer and the inner. Surely it is possible that existence is inaccessible not only to speculative totalitarianism, but to Kierkegaardian non-philosophy as well?

2 Truth Under Persecution

Kierkegaard made a contrast between knowable victorious truth, in which existence could have the illusion (but only the illusion) of 'explicating itself', and an authentic belief which would reflect the incommensurability of subjectivity. Belief was not an imperfect understanding of a truth which was essentially complete and victorious, and which had always held sway over all our thinking. If belief were merely uncertain knowledge of a truth, then it would simply be a defective form of knowledge. The subjectivity of belief would be no more than a slight opacity, passing through the sun-drenched field of exteriority before eventually vanishing.

Belief is the expression of an existence that can never be comprehended by any 'outside', a condition of neediness and poverty, a poverty which is radically and irremediably poor – poor with the absolute hunger which, in the final analysis, is the meaning of sin. *Belief always exists in relationship with a suffering truth.* And a truth which *suffers* and is persecuted is by no means the same as a truth that has simply been mistreated or misunderstood. For Kierkegaard, the two are so different that the suffering truth proves to be a way of delineating the manifestation of divinity: the simultaneity of All and Nothing, the Relation with a Person who is both present and absent, with a humbled God who has suffered and died, and brought despair to those he has led to salvation. Here is a certainty that coexists with absolute doubt – so much so, that one may even wonder whether Revelation itself does not contradict the essence of the crucified truth, and whether the suffering of God and the misrecognition of truth might not reach their sublime fulfilment in a total lack of recognition, an *incognito*.

Belief stands in the midst of this conflict between presence and absence – a conflict which remains for ever irreconcilable, an open wound, unstaunchable bleeding. But this failure to synthesize is not an intellectual deficiency. It is exactly appropriate to the new mode of truth: the suffering and humbling of truth are not an accident, an external contingency. They are part of its essence as truth; in a way they are part of its very divinity. Faith is henceforth the exit from the self, the exit to subjectivity, the isolation of the individual relationship with the being to which, for Kierkegaard, no other kind of relationship is possible: that is to say, with God. The *salto mortale* or leap of faith which is necessary if existence is to move from absence to presence must be perpetually remade. Possession can never be secured. If synthesis were ever to succeed, then the individual relationship would have been destroyed. It would have been *expressed*. Subjectivity would have lost its searing tension over itself, its deep egoism, and it would have been incorporated into exteriority and generality. Subjectivity would be converted into philosophy, or the Life of the Future. In belief, existence is always trying to secure recognition for itself, just like consciousness in Hegel. It struggles for this recognition by seeking forgiveness and salvation. But this recognition comes to it through a truth which is always spurned and unrecognized, always in need of *renewed recognition*: the subjectivism of subjectivity never comes to an end.

But the idea of truth as suffering utterly changes the nature of the search for truth. It converts relations to exteriority into inward dramas. Any relationship between truth and outwardness comes to be marked by indiscretion and scandal. When the discourse of truth addresses the external world it is filled with anger and invective. It is merciless. The suffering truth does not open us out to others, but to God in isolation.

This kind of existence, whose inwardness exceeds exteriority and cannot be contained by it, thus participates in the violence of the modern world, with its cult of Passion and Fury. It brings irresponsibility in its wake and a ferment of disintegration. Cursing and accursed philosophers rise up like accursed poets. But we may also wonder whether the exaltation of pure faith as the counterpart of crucified truth (the 'phenomenology' of which has never been better described than by Kierkegaard) is not a final consequence of that tension over itself that I earlier described as egoism: egoism not as a vile defect in the subject, but as its ontology. It is expressed for example in Spinoza's *Ethics*: 'Everything, insofar as it is in itself, endeavours to persist in its own being';[1] and again in Heidegger's formulation of the existence which exists in such a way that its existence is always an issue for it.[2]

The impact of Kierkegaard's philosophy on contemporary thought has been so profound that even the reservations and rebuttals that it has provoked can be seen as further evidence of its influence. The seductiveness of the later Heidegger is partly due to the rigorously ontological style of the Heideggerian thinking of Being. Its trenchant opposition to Kierkegaardian subjectivism would surely not have been so severe if it had not previously pursued the adventure of existence to the very end, and if *Being and Time* had not taken over certain notions from Kierkegaard and elevated them from mere subjective expressions to the status of philosophical categories.[3] Moreover the current fascination with Hegelian thought is due not only to its fundamental connection with the pressing political questions that currently preoccupy both the advocates and the enemies of Marxism (that is to say the whole of thinking humanity at the middle of the twentieth century). Neo-Hegelianism also benefits from its opposition to the exaggerated subjectivism of existence.

After a century, there is a widespread desire to move beyond the pathos of Kierkegaardian protestation. The distractedness of the systematic spirit to which Kierkegaard objected (echoing Pascal's notion of diversion),[4] is gradually being replaced by mere impertinence.

But one may wonder whether the authenticity which Kierkegaard succeeded in promoting does not bring with it a certain forgetting or repression of Kierkegaardian subjectivity in its tension over itself, and whether a certain self-renunciation ought not to accompany that concern for salvation which systematic philosophizing tends to make too cheap.

In the dialogue between Anima and Animus, between individuality and sensibility within universal Spirit, it would appear that the voice of the Spirit – even in its Hegelian form – may help to curb the self-satisfaction of the Soul in its interiority.

The Heideggerian appeal to the self-concealing Being of beings, whose truth and mystery call forth our human subjectivity, is capable – just like the Hegelian appeal to impersonal structures of Spirit which lie beyond contingency and imagination – of taking on a hard masculine tone. And anyone emerging from the existentialist experience will be able to respond to this tone – not only in the way one responds to a change of climate, but also with the affection we have towards everything that is already familiar. And Kierkegaardian thought has contributed to this through its intransigent vehemence and its taste for scandal. Hence the new tone in philosophy, the tone promoted by Nietzsche when he began to 'philosophize with a hammer'.

This hard and aggressive style of thinking, which had always been associated with the most unscrupulous and cynical forms of action, could now be taken seriously as a kind of justification for violence and terror. This is not just a matter of literary form. Kierkegaardian violence begins when existence, having moved beyond the aesthetic stage, is forced to abandon the ethical stage (or rather, what it took to be the ethical stage) in order to embark on the religious stage, the domain of belief. But belief no longer sought external justification. Even internally, it combined communication and isolation, and hence violence and passion. That is the origin of the relegation of ethical phenomena to secondary status and the contempt for the ethical foundation of being which has led, through Nietzsche, to the amoralism of recent philosophies.

3 Stewardship [*La Diaconie*][5]

The entire debate between Kierkegaard and speculative philosophy presupposes a subjectivity in tension over itself, and existence as concern for one's own existence, as a torment over oneself. For Kierkegaard the ethical was essentially general. The individuality of the Self would be dissipated in any rule that was valid for everyone. Generality could neither contain nor express the secret of a Self that was infinitely impoverished and anxious for itself.[6]

But does our relation with Others [*Autrui*][7] really entail our incorporation and dispersal into generality? *That is the question we must raise, against both Kierkegaard and Hegel.* If it is impossible for a relation with exteriority to constitute a totality whose elements can be compared and generalized, this is not because the Self manages to cling to its secret despite the system, but because the exteriority in which the human face is revealed disrupts and destroys totality.[8] The idea of a systemic collapse precipitated by Others is not an apocalyptic figure of speech. It expresses the fact that the mode of thinking which reduces otherness to sameness is simply incapable of encompassing Others. But this incapacity is not purely negative, for it also puts the Self into question. And this in turn is sufficient to indicate the Self's responsibility for the Other [*l'Autre*]. Subjectivity *exists* within this responsibility, and only an irreducible subjectivity can take on a responsibility. That is the meaning of the ethical.

Being a Self means not being able to hide from responsibility. This excess of being, this existential exaggeration which is called 'being a self', this irruption of *selfhood* or *ipseity* into being, is equivalent to an explosion of responsibility. By calling the self into question, the face of Others creates a new tension in the Self – but not a tension over itself. The Self is not annihilated when it is called into question; on the contrary, it acquires a unique solidarity with Others. But this solidarity has nothing in common with the way a piece of matter can be incorporated into a larger lump, or the relation between a particular organ and the organism of which it is a part. Mechanical or organic solidarity would simply dissolve the Self back into a totality.

The Self is in mutual solidarity with the non-self, as if it held the entire destiny of the Other in its hands. The singularity of the Self resides in the fact that no one else can answer on its behalf. Being called into question by the Other does not lead the Self to an act of reflection through which it will rise up and transcend itself in glorious serenity; but neither does it lead to the incorporation of the Self into a universal and systematic suprapersonal discourse. When the Self is put in question by the Other it is thereby chosen, promoted to a special position on which everything else depends.

To be chosen involves the most radical commitment conceivable: total altruism. The responsibility through which the Self is emptied of all imperialism and egoism – including the egoism of salvation – does not transform it into a mere moment within the universal order. It confirms it in its selfhood, its ipseity, in its central position within being; it confirms it as a support of the universe.

The Self is infinitely responsible when it stands before Others. The Other is poor and destitute, and nothing that touches this Stranger can be indifferent to the Self. It reaches the peak of its existence as a self precisely when it relates to everything as Others. The power which sustains the sovereignty of the Self reaches out to Others not in order to triumph over them, but in order to given them support. But at the same time, to bear the burden of the Other is to raise the Other above one's Self and confirm it in its substantiality. The Self is accountable for its burden to those it supports. Those I am answerable for are also those I am answerable to. The *for whom* and the *to whom* coincide with each other. This double movement of responsibility is what indicates the dimension of height [*hauteur*]. It forbids me to fulfil my responsibility as an act of pity, since I owe an account *to* precisely those I am accountable *for*. And it also forbids me to fulfil my responsibility as an act of unconditional obedience within a hierarchical order, since I am also responsible for whoever has power over me.

Kierkegaard was drawn to the biblical story of the sacrifice of Isaac. He saw in it an encounter between a subjectivity raising itself to the level of the religious, and a God elevated above the ethical order. But the story can also be taken in a very different sense. The high point of the whole drama could be the moment when Abraham lent an ear to the voice summoning him back to the ethical order. And there is another story that Kierkegaard never mentioned: the occasion when Abraham entered into conversation with God concerning Sodom and Gomorrah, begging him, in the name of the righteous who might be living within them, to spare those accursed cities. Abraham was fully conscious of his own nullity and mortality, and began by saying: 'I have taken upon me to speak unto the Lord, which am but dust and ashes,' whilst the consuming fire of God's anger burned before his eyes.[9] But death has no dominion, since the meaning of life is derived from infinite responsibility, from the profound stewardship which constitutes the subjectivity of the subject: – a responsibility which precludes any return to oneself, because it is wholly directed towards the Other.

Two Comments on Kierkegaard

I

[This comment is Levinas's response to a remark of Jean Hyppolite, who confessed that his 'passionate admiration' for Kierkegaard was accompanied by a 'sullen irritation', because he sometimes got the impression that Kierkegaard took himself to be God.][10]

There are two main things that irritate me about Kierkegaard.

The first is this. Kierkegaard very powerfully rehabilitated the topics of subjectivity, uniqueness and individuality. He objected to the absorption of subjectivity into Hegelian universality, but he replaced it with a subjectivity that was shamelessly exhibitionistic. I believe that the seductive attraction of the later Heidegger, no less than the current popularity of neo-Hegelianism and Marxism, and perhaps structuralism too, are due, amongst other things, to a reaction against this kind of naked subjectivity, a subjectivity which is so anxious about being dissolved into the universal that it rejects form altogether.

And second: what shocks me about Kierkegaard is his violence. An impulsive and violent style, reckless of scandal and destruction, was added to the philosophical repertory by Kierkegaard, even before Nietzsche. Philosophers could now philosophize with a hammer. The new style aspired to permanent provocation, and the total rejection of everything, and I think we can see it as anticipating certain other verbal violences that once passed themselves off as pure and considered. I refer not only to National Socialism itself, but also to the various ideas that it promoted. Kierkegaard's harshness started with his 'transcendence of the ethical'.[11] The whole of his polemic against speculative philosophy presupposes a subjectivity in tension over itself, and existence as concern for one's own existence, as a torment over oneself. For Kierkegaard, the ethical was essentially general. The individuality of the self would be dissipated, according to him, in any rule that was valid for everyone. Generality could neither contain nor express the secret of the self.[12]

But it is not at all clear that Kierkegaard located the ethical accurately. As the consciousness of a responsibility towards others [*autrui*], the ethical does not disperse us into generality [. . .].[13] On the contrary, it individualizes us, treating everyone as a unique individual, a Self. Kierkegaard seems to have been unable to recognize this, because he wanted to transcend the ethical stage, which he identified with generality. In the 'Eulogy on Abraham' he described Abraham's encounter with God in terms of a subjectivity raising itself above the ethical to the level of the religious. But the opposite interpretation is also possible: the highest point of the whole drama may be the moment when Abraham paused and listened to the voice that would lead him back to the ethical order by commanding him not to commit a human sacrifice. That he should have been prepared to obey the first voice is of course astonishing enough; but the crucial point is that he could distance himself from his obedience sufficiently to be able to hear the second voice as well. Why is it that Kierkegaard never spoke of the conversation in which Abraham pleaded with God for Sodom and Gomorrah, begging Him, in the name of the righteous who might be living within them, to spare those accursed cities?[14] For it is this action of Abraham's that contains the precondition for a victory of life over death. Death has no dominion over a finite life whose meaning is derived from an infinite responsibility for others, from a stewardship [*diaconie*] that is constitutive of the subjectivity of the subject, which in its turn is nothing but tension towards the other. It is only here in the ethical that an appeal can be made to the singularity of the subject, and that life can be endowed with meaning, in spite of death.

II

[This comment takes up a remark by Gabriel Marcel, who had described Kierkegaard as a 'tragic thinker', afflicted with 'a sort of suspicion concerning . . . peace and harmony,' and convinced of the necessity of 'distress'.][15]

But Kierkegaard was thereby [through his reference to 'distress'] introducing something absolutely novel into European philosophy: the possibility of arriving at truth through the ever-renewed distress of doubt, where doubt is not a mere occasion for reconfirming one's certainty, but an element of certainty itself. In my opinion the philosophical novelty of Kierkegaard lies in his notion of belief. For him, belief was not just an imperfect knowledge of a truth which was perfect and victorious in itself. Belief was not a deficient form of knowledge, or a minor form of truth, or a truth lacking in certainty. Kierkegaard was not concerned with the distinction between faith and knowledge, uncertainty and certainty; what interested him was the difference between a victorious truth and a persecuted one. A persecuted truth is not a truth that happens to have been mistreated and misunderstood. Persecution, and the humility that comes with it, are themselves the modalities of truth. And that thought is something altogether novel. The imposing greatness of transcendent truth, and its very transcendence, depend on this humility: transcendent truth manifests itself elusively, turning away from us as if it dared not speak its name. It cannot be one phenomenon amongst others, merging with them as if that were where it belonged: for it comes from beyond. Perhaps a Revelation which proclaims its own origin would be incompatible with the essence of transcendent truth, of a truth which can have no authentic manifestation unless it is persecuted. Perhaps the only possible mode of true revelation is the *incognito*, and perhaps a truth which has been spoken must therefore appear as one of which nothing has been said.

The idea that the transcendence of the transcendent depends on its extreme humility enables us to glimpse a kind of truth which does not take the form of un-concealment. The humility of a persecuted truth is so profound that it will not even venture to present itself in the Heideggerian 'clearing'. Or perhaps it presents itself ambiguously: it is there as if it were not there. That, for me, is Kierkegaard's great contribution to philosophy. The idea of a persecuted truth may at last permit us to put an end to the entire game of unconcealment, where immanence always has to triumph over transcendence. Once being has been unconcealed – even partially or mysteriously – it ceases to be transcendent and becomes immanent. Hence there is no genuine exteriority in such an unconcealment.

And then, with Kierkegaard, it becomes possible for something to manifest itself in such a way as to leave us wondering whether the manifestation really took place. Someone starts to speak: but no – nothing has been said. Truth is played out in two phases: the essential truth is given expression, but at the same time nothing has been said. This is the new philosophical situation: a result which is not a result, and permanent distress. First a revelation, then nothing.

But Kierkegaard's new modality of truth was not a purely philosophical invention. It was genuinely the expression of an epoch [. . .][16] – an epoch which can no longer believe in the historical authenticity of the Scriptures, but which can still hear a voice that speaks through them from beyond. Perhaps the Scriptures are of no importance. After the historical criticism of the Bible, it is possible to explain them in terms of all sorts of historical accidents. And yet there was a message. And that is why the Kierkegaardian style of truth contains a new modality of the True.

NOTES

1   ['Unaquaeque res, quantum in se est, in suo esse perseverare conatur.' See Spinoza, *Ethics*, part III, proposition VI, in *Works of Spinoza*, translated by R. H. M. Elwes (Bell, London, 1883), vol. 2, p. 136.]

2   [Levinas alludes to the description of Dasein in the Introduction to Heidegger's *Sein und Zeit* (1927), §4 (Niemeyer, Tübingen, 1984), p. 12: '. . . daß es diesem Seienden in seinem Sein *um* dieses Sein selbst geht'. See *Being and Time*, translated by John Macquarrie and Edward Robinson (Blackwell, Oxford, 1978), p. 32: 'Dasein is an entity which . . . is ontically distinguished by the fact that, in its very Being, that Being is an *issue* for it.']

3   This was recognized by Jean Wahl in relation to the concept of anxiety in the most thorough, perceptive, and philosophically acute of all accounts of Kierkegaard: see Jean Wahl, *Études Kierkegaardiennes* (Aubier, Paris, 1938), p. 211, n. 2. [Wahl's comment is as follows: 'There is clearly a considerable difference between Kierkegaard and Heidegger in their use of the concept of anxiety. Kierkegaard was concerned with a psychological anxiety, a kind of nothing within the spirit, whereas for Heidegger anxiety was connected with a cosmic fact, an absolute nothingness against which existence had to define itself. Therein lies Heidegger's originality, even in his theory of anxiety, which would at first appear to have been entirely inspired by Kierkegaard.']

4   [See *Pascal's Pensées*, edited and translated by H. F. Stewart (Routledge and Kegan Paul, London, 1950), IV, 1, p. 59: 'The one thing which consoles us for our miseries is diversion, and yet that is the greatest of our miseries. For it is this that mainly checks consideration of ourselves and ruins us unconsciously.']

5   [The term 'Diaconie' is also used in Levinas's article 'La trace de l'autre' (1963), reprinted in *En découvrant l'existence avec Husserl et Heidegger*, second edition (Vrin, Paris, 1974), p. 197, and Levinas relates it to Isaiah 53.]

6   [This paragraph reworks a passage in the first of Levinas's 'Comments on Kierkegaard'.

7   [In what follows, *autrui* is translated by 'others' and *autre* by 'other' and initial capitals are used in conformity with the original.]

8   Reference should be made at this point to the magnificent work of Max Picard, and tribute paid to the profundity with which he has spoken of the metaphysical opening in the 'human face'. [Levinas refers to the Swiss art historian Max Picard, 1888–1965, author of *Das Menschengesicht* (Delphin-Verlag, Munich, 1929). In an essay on Picard in *Noms Propres*, Levinas praised him for the manner of his 'rejection of the modern world' and endorsed his remark that 'the human face is the proof of the existence of God'.]

9   [Genesis 18: 23–33. Despite what Levinas says, Kierkegaard mentioned this incident in the 'Eulogy on Abraham' in *Fear and Trembling*. See *Fear and Trembling, Repetition*, translated by Howard V. Hong and Edna H. Hong (Princeton University Press, Princeton, 1983), p. 21.]

10   [See *Kierkegaard Vivant*, p. 218.]

11   [The 'teleological Suspension of the Ethical' ('*teleologisk Suspension af det Ethiske*') is discussed in 'Problema I' in *Fear and Trembling*, p. 54.]

12   [This sentence and the two that precede it are repeated almost unaltered in Levinas's 'Existence and Ethics'. See above p. 31–2.]

13   [Levinas adds that 'Mlle Hersch spoke just now of the infinite demand that calls us to a responsibility that no one can shoulder on our behalf.' He was referring to a remark by Jeanne Hersch, who had invoked a concept of the exception which was 'so exceptional that there are no more points of comparison'. See *Kierkegaard Vivant*, p. 227.]

14   [Cf. n. 9 above.]

15   [See *Kierkegaard Vivant*, p. 285.]
16   [Levinas adds: 'What Beaufret said yesterday about Kierkegaard as the
      thinker of our time is absolutely true, though perhaps not for Heideggerian
      reasons alone.' He was alluding to a comment by Jean Beaufret, who,
      invoking Heidegger, had claimed that Kierkegaard was the authentic
      thinker not only of his own time but of ours as well. See *Kierkegaard Vivant*,
      pp. 255–9. Beaufret was referring to Martin Heidegger, 'Nietzsches Wort
      "Gott ist tot"' (1943), translated by William Lovitt in *The Question Concern-
      ing Technology and Other Essays* (Harper and Row, New York, 1977), p. 94,
      in particular the following remark: 'The comparison between Nietzsche and
      Kierkegaard that has become customary, but is no less questionable for that
      reason, fails to recognise . . . that Nietzsche as a metaphysical thinker pre-
      serves a closeness to Aristotle. Kierkegaard remains essentially remote from
      Aristotle, although he mentions him more often. For Kierkegaard is not a
      thinker but a religious writer, and indeed not just one among others, but the
      only one in accord with the destining belonging to his age. Therein lies his
      greatness, if to speak in this way is not already a misunderstanding.']

3
Kierkegaard on Death and Dying

Wilhelm Anz

Towards the end of his life, Kierkegaard located the 'Point of View for his Work as an Author' in the attempt to 'compel' his readers to 'take notice' of the question 'how to become a Christian?'[1] To compel someone to take notice, however, is not the same as giving advice. To Kierkegaard, it involved raising our awareness of 'the Christly' out of universal incomprehension, and clearing the way for a comprehending appropriation. But in the 'present age', the conditions for such an appropriation were lacking. As Kierkegaard put it, 'the preachers we ordinarily find preaching Christianity in Christendom . . . surrounded as they are by too much illusion and rendered secure by it . . . have not the courage to make men take notice.'[2]

There were two kinds of illusions to be overcome. The first was the Danish State Church with its unquestioning identification with the existing social order: neither Christianity nor the Church could derive legitimacy from representing generality or universality (the existing order). The second was the idea that history is the earthly incarnation of the divine and that modern culture is the legitimate heir of history since Christ. 'It is a matter of getting rid of 1800 years as if they had never been,' says Kierkegaard.[3] This seems extreme, but all it means is that the ground for Christian belief cannot lie in its past (a past which is in any case highly ambiguous), but only in an origin that is always present

'Kierkegaard über Sterben und Tod' was first published in *Wort und Dienst* (Jahrbuch der Kirchlichen Hochschule Bethel), 11, 1971, pp. 9–20. This translation appears with the permission of the editors of the Yearbook and of Frau Margarethe Anz. Translation copyright © Jonathan Rée 1998.

within it. And we need to find the path that will lead us back to that ground. The illusions which have concealed it from us must be exposed, and we must open out and clarify our spontaneous and original experiences in a 'reflection of inwardness'. Only in this way can we hope to find a place within human existence which can accommodate the kind of truth to which Christian belief bears witness. That is why Kierkegaard sought to become a 'Socratic thinker inside Christianity'.[4]

Socrates had used dialectic, or the test of dialogue and discussion, to bring out the conflict between truth and mere opinion. On the path of logical or conceptual clarification he had unearthed those buried truths which are the unexpressed origin of the dialectic. As a Christian thinker, Kierkegaard sought to discover this contradiction in life itself and his quest led to an area of human existence which resisted conceptual definition – an area which is open only to the 'silent understanding of anxiety'. In states of 'anxiety' your own life has to be understood as an 'inter-esse', as a 'being between possibility and impossibility', as essentially a 'temporality' which can never be closed off and isolated from what it encounters. But this kind of comprehension is achieved only in a condition of final 'earnestness', touched by the certainty of one's own death. Thus learning to die was both the ultimate duty and the 'beginning of wisdom'.

The context in which Kierkegaard sought to grasp the whole field of human existence is vast and not immediately comprehensible. It requires a language that is prior to concepts, which naturally makes it difficult to explicate. Kierkegaard liked to crystallize his experiences epigrammatically; he worked with these compressed formulations, but did not seek to explain or justify them. Of course this is what gives them their power and allure. But it also means that we need to make an especially careful effort in order to disentangle them. We must adopt a Kierkegaardian starting-point and try to work our way back to what his epigrams are really trying to say.

Kierkegaard's suggestion that everything depends on the repetition of the Socratic distinction between understanding and understanding is one such starting point.[5] A repetition is always meant to be a repetition of sameness; but when it is carried out it is never more than a repetition of similarity. Thus Kierkegaard contrasts the 'understanding of anxiety' with another kind of understanding – one which comprises not only the perception of what is positively graspable, but also the will to philosophical or scientific knowledge itself.[6] The power of this second kind of understanding is that it identifies what is salient in our perceptions and turns it into something objective, testing it against its own principles so as to set it in the context of an integrated field of objectively correct knowledge. To borrow the language of idealistic philosophy, this is the kind of knowledge that belongs to *Verstand*. It is objectively correct, methodologically controlled, and therefore certain, and all its judgements are either true or false.

But Kierkegaard wanted to focus our attention on another kind of understanding, with a different kind of object, customarily associated with the realm that he called 'the ethical'. However the ethical consists primarily of human relationships in their generality, insofar as they are inwardly binding on our behaviour. Thus we can say: I understand that a given aspect of my life, a given relationship – my profession, or a friendship, or marriage, for example – entails certain claims upon me, and that these are duties I must not evade; and I realize that I must enter into this relationship wholeheartedly, and fashion my life in unqualified *conformity* to it. Only then can the relationship be *true*. Kierkegaard described this mode of truth, or rather of being true, as *revelation* or *disclosure* [*Aabenbarelse*]. Accordingly, its mode of deficiency and untruth is not so much error, as *closure* or *inclosing reserve* [*det Indesluttede*], or – as Kierkegaard also put it – a *lack of earnestness*.[7] Disclosure cannot come about unless it is sought with unqualified earnestness.

Thus we achieve truth to the extent that we conform to the claim of duty; and conversely the relationship comes into its own as a relationship only to the extent that we achieve truth by conforming to it. Each relationship is true, that is to say disclosed, only in and through other relationships. Truth as disclosure is thus constituted by a relationship to which I belong, and by the *manner* in which I belong to it or – to use a characteristically Kierkegaardian expression – *the way I understand myself within it*, that is to say, the way I take up my role in it. To understand a claim is always to understand a relationship as a relationship, and thus always to understand oneself in relation to something. But this always means executing a movement, an inner action which responds to an invitation which is implicit in the act of understanding.

We will always misunderstand a relationship if we try to stand outside it and dissolve it in some way into objective knowledge. The 'ethical' is the 'understanding' of a claim upon us, or – to make its inner character clearer – it is a form of self-relation in which what makes a claim on us starts out as '*intellectual ignorance*'. And Kierkegaard was trying to guide us towards this *ignorance*. It is an ignorance which leads into a dimension of which reason and scientific understanding know nothing, and Kierkegaard found it exemplified above all in Socrates. But a Socratic admission of ignorance carries within itself a secret knowledge, the knowledge that in our lives we belong to a realm which we cannot step out of, even if it is mostly concealed from us. For Kierkegaard this is the experience of the proximity of death, which carries concealed within it the untranscendable dependence of finite humanity upon God.

'Socrates was great in that he distinguished between what he understood and what he did not understand' – between what is available to knowledge, and that in the face of which he would always be ignorant.[8] That is the basis, according to Kierkegaard, on which Socrates thought through *all* relationships so as to destroy any false confidence we might have in them. Only a way of thinking that had learned its limitations in this way would be able to show us the path to the 'ethical', and also make room for a relationship with God.

Thus Kierkegaard was able to describe Socratic ignorance as the 'incognito of the ethical'. The admission of this ignorance conforms to the experience of the limit, the limit where all 'positive' knowledge finally founders. And for Kierkegaard this is the realm of faith. Hence he could say of Socrates:

> Let us never forget that Socrates' ignorance was a kind of fear and worship of God, that his ignorance was the Greek version of the Jewish saying: The fear of the Lord is the beginning of wisdom. . . . Let us never forget . . . that he was on guard duty as a *judge* on the frontier between God and man.[9]

Thus Socrates was, according to Kierkegaard, pointing to a *fundamental relationship* which is superior to knowledge and shuns it, a relationship which reveals itself only in our understanding of its claim upon us, and which reaches down to the ultimate ground of our freedom. It is only through fear or timidity that our relationship to God allows us to understand what lies within it, and the bearing it can have on our humanity; for the fear of God is the beginning of all wisdom – if 'wisdom' is the right word for our relation to that which concerns us most.

The Socratic thinker within Christianity will try to make us take notice of this fundamental relationship; but it is a matter which, of its nature, can only be *indirectly communicated*. Thus we finally arrive at our theme. By way of anticipation, we can say that learning to die is the *appropriate* comportment in relation to death, and that it carries within it a relationship to the God who grants us our capacity for death.

As a Socratic thinker, Kierkegaard started off from that which drives our spontaneous and original experience of temporality and death into concealment, and then tried to show how what is concealed is precisely the active and untranscendable ground of its concealment. The kind of objective knowledge which reduces death to a mere 'episode', or a mood of despair, or 'the sickness unto death', shuts itself off from death as that which might show us our life as either 'true' or 'closed'.

There is a form of spiritual freedom grounded upon a distance from death – a freedom which is achieved by reducing death to a mere natural process. Kierkegaard liked to quote Epicurus' famous saying: 'Death is not to be feared: when it is, I am not, and when I am, it is not.'[10] If dying is seen in this way, then it becomes a mere episode and it has no power over the innermost freedom of spirit: it 'touches' or endangers this freedom far less deeply than a prolonged illness or grinding poverty. If we refuse to see death as an authority, an *Instanz*, and it holds no terror for us, then we can of course 'keep death at a distance' and, as Kierkegaard put it, 'ideality can ideally vanquish death by thinking it' – and that is its triumph over the world.[11] But if we take this 'category' seriously we will come to understand that death can never be overcome by 'ideality', and we will learn to 'fear' it – for to turn our backs on this fear will lead to the sickness unto death, or despair. This sounds rather extreme, and could be misunderstood, as if Kierkegaard were trying to persuade our free spirit into terror. But as a Socratic thinker he was not seeking to persuade – only to indicate what is the case. That is the standard by which his thought has to be judged.

But autonomous scientific ways of thinking seek to place death entirely in the sphere of objectivity. Rigorous objective knowledge thus cuts itself off from the kind of experience which lay at the basis of Socratic ignorance. The question is how far such knowledge can really isolate itself from experience, in the context of human life as a whole.

If we are to attune ourselves in the use of our freedom in relation to death, and thus avoid contradicting ourselves, then we must control our moods (fear, terror, anxiety, melancholy). We must always remain conscious of our fate as finite beings. But it is debatable how far we can ever do so. Descartes for example was convinced that we *are* pure consciousnesses, and that, as subjects of knowledge, we can rise above all the conditions of our empirical human existence. However, Kant realized that the gap between life and knowledge is not a fact, but rather a methodological assumption which consciousness sets up for itself as an aspiration. But this did not imply that we are really masters of ourselves, and it does not say anything about the impulses to which we are subject as thinking human beings.

Kierkegaard was content to remain a thinker immersed in the natural experience we have of ourselves as human beings. He was aware that our susceptibility to moods (he sometimes spoke of contingency, and sometimes of moods as the reflection of contingency in our feelings) undermines the self-certainty of consciousness, and was thus able to show us our condition directly – but only, of course, in the mode of concealment.[12]

The titles of two of Kierkegaard's works make a direct reference to this situation: *The Concept of Anxiety* and *The Sickness Unto Death*. The second of these is explicitly addressed to the question of mood and the concealment of our authentic relationship to death. The sickness unto death is *despair*. Kierkegaard calls it the sickness *unto* death because it implies that human life is in motion towards inner death: towards boredom, melancholy, and an empty and contentless abandonment to itself; towards a 'non-being' where every relationship has lost its truth – either by inner deterioration or by breaking up or inverting itself. We are constantly retreating from whatever life indicates that we ought to be; we are always falling into a false relation to a call that lies in our understanding, and therefore into a misunderstanding of ourselves – a misunderstanding which we try to conceal from ourselves, but which cannot in truth be concealed. Thus we are divided against ourselves.

—Kierkegaard brought great insight to his descriptions and elaborations of the trivial and everyday forms of such *dividedness*: for example, curiosity, gossip or idle talk, and envy. What all these attitudes have in common is the way they allow us to 'slacken' the relationships in which we find ourselves, breaking up their continuity and extricating ourselves from them. And yet we still remain unfree: the relationship still persists, but as 'untrue'. That is what is meant by closure: we reject the claim to 'disclosure' that lies within every relationship, because it would require of us the kind of steady seriousness in which our conduct is held to account before our conscience. But closure is despair – even if, in our despair, we are not conscious that we are in despair.

Thus despair is a *state of being*, but one which is reflected in a mood – though as these examples show, it is reflected there only with a certain clouded obscurity. This is no less true of the more extreme case, where despair is the sickness unto death, or inward death, freedom trapped in its own closure.

For Kierkegaard the extreme example of despair was the figure of Macbeth, who exhibited all its elements with the greatest possible clarity.[13] First there was *dividedness*: Macbeth was desperate to be king, but then he came into contradiction with himself, because it was through crime and unlawfulness that he became the upholder of the law. Second, there was the *breaking of continuity*: being thrown into the isolation of closure – what Kierkegaard called the category of the 'sudden'. Thirdly there was *boredom or inward death*, where nothing related to truth any more.[14] Time has been emptied out, and to live through time, when there is no longer anything true, is to be in despair.

We should note that this category of despair includes utter triviality as well as manifest terror. Both modes of being – falling into closure and falling out of disclosure – lie within its sphere: and hence, for

Kierkegaard, it includes the whole range of human existence: the breaking of continuity, dividedness, and the emptiness of existence. Despair is
present, in different degrees, in all of them.

Another form of despair occurs when we make any given relationship
so central to our lives that we have to close ourselves off from the
possibility of its loss, because otherwise we would find ourselves surrounded by emptiness. We rehearse the possibility of its loss in the most
various forms, but we cannot *seriously* entertain it, because we cover up
our own finitude. We seek out those goods which will grant us full
humanity (the society of others, health, wealth, skills, reputation and so
forth) and we try to cling on to them. We desire, we strive to possess, and
we live in constant fear of loss. The intensity of this fear can vary greatly.
It can range from a slight sentiment of transience in the midst of
happiness, to the experience of exposure to time, contingency, and
terror. There is no guarantee that this fear will not itself deprive us of
those things we believe we cannot survive without, simply because we
have identified with them.

Augustine says that at this point we fear to fear (*metuimus metuere*),
but cannot do otherwise.[15] This is what is meant by anxiety: a limit case
of fear – abstract fear, fear with no object, fear trapped within itself. Grief
is always replaying the same old game of loss, and we are always losing
our lives anew.[16] This despair is the outward manifestation of the sickness unto death: we are left alone with our empty wishes and desires, and
we are at the mercy of boredom, of the pure passage of time.

Kierkegaard provided an acute description of the scale of attunement
by which despair suffuses human existence as the sickness unto death:
from the *melancholy* which insists that the purpose of human life is
fulfilment in happiness, and which can neither live nor die if this fulfilment is denied it, through the *despair* which is denied its highest happiness, namely death, to the *resentment* which turns against excellence in
life and wishes to see it destroyed. *Mood* is able to gain its power over us,
because we have lived in terms of *representations* of our lives, and lost
ourselves amongst the ideals of the comparative imagination. We have
become identical with them, but we cannot cling to this identity – and
that is why our lives are reduced to death and nothingness. Despair
concerning temporality expresses itself only in the form of moods. (Its
manifestations belong exclusively the 'aesthetic stage', the level of
reflected life-feeling.[17])

Kierkegaard here gives expression to the despair which knows itself to
be a sickness, and which is bound to follow it through to the point of
inner death, perhaps even to suicide as an attestation that there can be no
way out: the melancholy and boredom where nothing has meaning any
more, not even one's own death. (Once again I refer to the figure of

Macbeth.)(According to Kierkegaard, the only way to get out of this
situation is by clarifying our relationship to ourselves in a reflection of
inwardness – so that we can come to realize that our despair bears a
contradiction within itself – and by being ready to see the contradiction
resolved. Despair is like a double movement, and Kierkegaard explains
its contradictory tension in the following formula: we despairingly want
to be ourselves (in our identification with the wishes and representations
in terms of which we think we live our lives), because we despairingly
want not to be ourselves. What is concealed in despair is precisely what
has led us into despair: that we do not wish to be the *finite self* that we are
'from the ground up'; or in other words our 'despair of the eternal' – of
the eternal which finds expression in despair.[18] The 'eternal' is the basic
relationship through which 'knowing' is converted into Socratic ignorance, in an experience of fear and trembling. Unless we learn to understand ourselves in relation to the eternal (Kierkegaard speaks of
'self-grounding')[19] we will never be able to break through our identification with that from which we expect life; nor will we achieve that
openness – that open proximity to everything – in which our relationship
to our own death is included. What this means can only be revealed if the
pretences with which despair assails and perplexes us are dissolved by
what we understand in anxiety.

But what is *anxiety* and what does it mean? Augustine demonstrated how
anxiety develops out of fear; it is a limit case of fear, he says – fear which
has lost its object, fear trapped within itself. Kierkegaard defined it more
profoundly, by showing that it has an ontologically fundamental meaning. In anxiety, one's own life presents itself as *essentially temporal*, as
lying between possibility and possibility. We live – or perhaps rather exist
– as a *capacity-for-being* or, as Kierkegaard also puts it, as possibility.
What we are is always a possibility which is at the same time grasped and
not grasped and needing to be grasped again. This is clear in relation to
the futural, but it applies to the past as well: the past is a former
possibility and as such it too is accessible to our freedom; otherwise there
would be no such thing as regretfulness or the seriousness of repetition.
The pasts which are accessible to our freedom return to us as futures.

Possibility has to be grasped and acquired. The demand of possibility
is experienced in anxiety and it transforms our present certainty into a
relationship of possibility, destabilizing it. Possibility always exists for
possibility. This quality of possibility itself provokes anxiety. In this way,
anxiety is always anxiety over 'nothingness'.[20] This 'not' – the not yet
grasped, or not yet graspable, but yet impending – takes the certain
present away from us or, as Kierkegaard puts it, it negates all positivity
and sets us down into a kind of time which is not the measure of

movement, just as understanding is not direct acquaintance. The time which is disclosed in anxiety is the *inter-esse*, the 'between' that comes between possibility and possibility, and which is manifest in the *moment* (*øieblik, Augenblick*); it is the time which is identical with temporality and which gives rise to possibility – the time which situates us in a life of possibility, of freedom. This life of possibility – as I have already re-marked – consumes our 'objective' and 'realistic' certainties, which come to us from 'positivity'. Of course our lives contain facts and data ('I am', or 'I have'), but these facts are never pure and simple realities. This is true also of the fact of death.

~~The factical~~ is always a possible 'how': we always stand before our-selves, as something impending, and we are always summoned in our freedom. To repeat: possibility always exists for possibility. And our freedom becomes available to us through the anxious experience of temporality: although freedom is always a choice, it is always given as well. That is why Kierkegaard could also say: 'anxiety is always anxiety about one's self' – about being condemned to choose and being unable to diminish this necessity, or to reduce our relationship to death. Insofar as freedom faces up to this necessity, anxiety informs it of what it was that despair was always in flight from: the necessity to choose oneself as a 'temporal' self.[21]

Thus anxiety reveals the deceptiveness of our identification with our 'securities' by transforming everything, even the fact of death, into a possible 'how', into something that will have to be lived through in some way or other. It leads us into openness, into an open proximity to everything, and gives freedom the space in which to make a 'choice' between openness and closure. If we allow ourselves to be educated by anxiety, then we will come to understand that dying is not a process that happens to us from outside; rather it is our own ownmost being, which as a not-yet-grasped possibility 'concerns' us in anxiety. It is a possibility which has to be appropriated and made one's own, and which, if we allow ourselves to be seriously concerned with it (that is, if we can endure what we understand through anxiety), identifies us with our-selves and removes all our self-deceptions. Anxiety transforms dying as the end of our life into an inward matter of 'fearing' our death, granting it its uncertain certainty, and finally trusting in God as the ground which summons us to our capacity-for-dying.

But this would all be meaningless if it were not for the fact that in the silent language of 'self-confirming' anxiety – that is to say the anxiety which maintains itself in its truth – finite humanity experiences itself as belonging to a ground to which it owes its temporal being as a self: the possibility for possibility which is experienced in states of anxiety, and the capacity for being of freedom.

This is the only way in which we can *abide* in proximity to death, so that we can concur with ourselves as the finite self that we are from the 'ground' up, and be 'true'. By abiding in it we bring into the open our relationship to death and thus to God in his inescapable claim upon us: an openness which is also an unreserved proximity to everything. As Kierkegaard put it in a funeral oration, 'Death does not come because someone calls it (for the weaker one to order the stronger one in that way would be only a jest), but as soon as someone opens the door to uncertainty, the teacher is there.'[22]

The uncertainty of which Kierkegaard speaks here is not simply a matter of giving up the 'security' of positivity; it is an uncertainty which refuses to conceal from itself the inner limits of its freedom, the limits of which anxiety is aware. If we cling to that, then anxiety allows us to glimpse the possibility of a freedom which is self-aware and which does not cut itself off from the 'eternal' – a freedom which has experienced anxiety and learned the lesson of it own impotence, so that it can penetrate its closure with its own power, and ground itself in God as its own origin) 'God is in the ground only when everything that is in the way is cleared out.'[23]

Once we have come to understand that one is a self grounded in 'the eternal', and that nothing exists outside our abiding proximity to death, then the relationships in which we live need no longer be turned into the sickness unto death. Thus the capacity for dying becomes the highest wisdom, a wisdom imparted by anxiety. Anxiety is our teacher, and as Kierkegaard wrote, 'anxiety is freedom's possibility, and only such anxiety is through faith absolutely educative, because it consumes all finite ends and exposes all their deceptions.'[24]

Thus we finally reach the vantage point from which Kierkegaard was able to speak directly of dying and of death. At first sight, his further comments on the theme of death may appear paltry and empty. Kierkegaard simply says what all of us already know, and could easily have said for ourselves without his help. He says that death is the end, that it is where a lifetime breaks off, that it individualizes our lives, and that its eventual arrival is certain even though the time of its appearance is not. He says that the fact of death brings no enlightenment to the dying, because it refuses to be subsumed under any general concept, whereas of course from the standpoint of conceptual discourse it can be defined and described exhaustively. For obviously the understanding can provide us with a different account of death – bringing individual cases under general statistical relationships, calculating times and probabilities and assigning exact causes, in the context of medical diagnosis or life assurance for example, and on its own terms such an account may be entirely correct. But that is a different matter, and not our present concern, for we are here trying to follow the path of Socratic understanding. On this path we have learned that the 'emptiness' or lack of content to which intellectual ignorance leads us opens up a space for the experience of 'time', temporality and death, and that this emptiness corresponds precisely to the 'nothingness' of anxiety.

Seen from within the inner certainty of its impending imminence, however, death is much more than the obvious fact of the ending of a life. Death is not merely the actuality of death. As existing individuals, we live our death before we die it.[25] The manner in which we 'live' or experience our death is precisely the anxious looking forward which individualizes us in our lives and thereby places us in a necessary relationship to ourselves. This individualization does not isolate us as existing individuals. On the contrary, it makes us all *equal* to each other in an absolutely unlimited manner, requiring from the other as much as from oneself a struggle towards a 'true' relationship with death. The only real fear is that this sense of struggle will be lost, and with it our connection with God and the place of faith: that would be the sickness unto death. Our anxious proximity to our own death opens out what might be called a creaturely or dependent power of sympathy and so once again an extreme of openness, but now an openness in relation to the other.

> Only when the sympathetic person in his compassion relates himself to the sufferer in such a way that he in the strictest sense understands that it is his own case that is in question, only when he knows how to identify himself with the sufferer in such a way that when he fights for an explanation he is fighting for himself, renouncing all thoughtlessness, softness and cowardice – only then does the sympathy acquire significance.[26]

The experience of the uncertain certainty of death arouses our consciousness of the passage of time; it makes time into 'precious time'. If we do not close ourselves off from it, we will learn to understand the 'frontier dispute between life and death', and the 'moment' in which 'time' is given to us, and with it the possibility of freedom.

Thus it is the impossibility of removing death from the silent presence with which it announces itself in states of anxiety, and the impossibility of translating it into general concepts, that opens up for us an understanding in which we can understand ourselves in a 'relationship' which is simply superior to us, that is to say an understanding which does not give up on the proximity which calls to us in the final freedom, in faith.

In the preface to Kierkegaard's theologically crucial book *Philosophical Fragments*, Johannes Climacus asks: 'What is my own opinion?' and he answers: 'To have an opinion is to me both too much and too little.' He then continues: 'All I have is my life, which I promptly stake every time a difficulty appears. Then it is easy to dance, for the thought of death is a good dancing partner.'[27]

Knowledge is possible only in the realm of free opinion. But understanding, in the sense of the self-understanding in truth to which I am called, is of its nature incompatible with the sovereign freedom of holding an opinion. That is why having an opinion is too much for it. In the face of death, there can be no opinions, but only a readiness to be called into the movement of states of anxiety, which are 'freedom's possibility'.[28]

But this is a movement which will always remain concealed from objective knowledge. That is why having an opinion is too little for the uses of a Socratic thinker within Christianity. Only those who understand the 'in-between' (or 'interest') which is finite freedom, and who can think and speak from inside it, are in a position to compel us to take notice of 'the Christly' itself and to give voice to it anew – as Kierkegaard undertook to do, for example, in the *Philosophical Fragments*.

Those who have followed Kierkegaard's path are in a position to affirm that the experience of death and dying is the element through which Kierkegaard's thoughts come to language and show themselves for what they are. Purely sustained in anxiety, and unfolded out of a proximity to Socratic ignorance and Jewish learning, it leads to the stage where eschatological belief belongs: that of the moment. The moment – the *Augenblick or Øieblik* – is where the finite self, aware of the inner limits of its freedom, learns to believe and have faith. Kierkegaard allowed this place of faith to show itself, and that is why his thinking has become a touchstone for theology. And it always raises the question, whether theology has stayed in its place.

NOTES

1 ['One man may have the good fortune to do much for another, he may have the good fortune to lead him whither he wishes . . . he may have the good fortune to help him to become a Christian. But this result is not in my power; it depends on so many things. . . . But one thing I can do: I can compel him to take notice.' See *The Point of View for my Work as an Author*, translated by Walter Lowrie, 2nd edn (Harper and Row, New York, 1962), pp. 34–5.]

2 [*The Point of View for my Work as an Author*, p. 36].

3 [IX A 72; *Journals and Papers*, translated by Howard V. Hong and Edna H. Hong (7 vols, Indiana University Press, Bloomington, 1967–78), 6168, vol. 6, p. 13.]

4 [In 1848, Kierkegaard wrote in his journal of 'Socratically starving the life out of all the illusions in which Christendom has run aground' (IX A 214);

in 1850 he noted that 'in the midst of Christendom one is hardly ever aware of the Socratic' (X 2 A 380); and in 1854 he wrote: 'to proclaim Christianity really requires a person who combines personal character and dialectical power. (Socrates for example would be suitable)' (XI 1 A 477). See *Journals and Papers*, 6228, 2514, 3535, vol. 6, p. 39, vol. 1, p. 64, vol. 3, p. 617.]

5 [In a footnote to *Fear and Trembling* Kierkgaard wrote: '*Every movement of infinity is carried out through passion, and no reflection can produce a movement. This is the continual leap in existence that explains the movement, whereas mediation is a chimera, which in Hegel is supposed to explain everything and which is also the only thing he never has tried to explain.* Just to make the celebrated Socratic distinction between what one understands and what one does not understand requires passion.' See *Fear and Trembling, Repetition*, translated by Howard V. Hong and Edna H. Hong (Princeton University Press, Princeton, 1983), p. 42n. See also *The Sickness Unto Death*, translated by Howard V. Hong and Edna H. Hong (Princeton University Press, Princeton, 1980), p. 90: 'Does this mean, then, that to understand and to understand are two different things?']

6 [On the limitations of the 'scholarliness and scienticity that ultimately does not build up', see Preface to *The Sickness Unto Death*, p. 5.]

7 ['Whoever has not understood the eternal correctly . . . lacks inwardness and earnestness.' See *The Concept of Anxiety*, edited and translated by Reidar Thomte and Albert B. Anderson (Princeton University Press, Princeton, 1980), p. 151. On *disclosure* and *inclosing reserve* see *The Concept of Anxiety*, pp. 123–7.]

8 [This remark, attributed to J. G. Hammann, is quoted in Kierkegaard's epigraph to *The Concept of Anxiety*, p. 3.]

9 [*The Sickness Unto Death*, p. 99. (The biblical reference is to Psalms, 111, 10.)]

10 [See for example *Philosophical Fragments*, in *Philosophical Fragments, Johannes Climacus*, translated by Howard V. Hong and Edna H. Hong (Princeton University Press, Princeton, 1985), p. 95n; and *Johannes Climacus*, in *Philosophical Fragments, Johannes Climacus*, p. 147.]

11 [See *Concluding Unscientific Postscript*, translated by Howard V. Hong and Edna H. Hong (Princeton University Press, Princeton, 1992), vol. 1, p. 168.]

12 Kierkegaard illustrates the point by referring to the ruthless lucidity with which Macbeth described how his life was transformed by murdering the King – a clarity only available to those in despair. And yet Macbeth's speech is not open but shut in on itself – not only because he is now obliged to deceive his old comrades (he must conceal his despair like a gnawing secret) but also because he speaks about himself and his situation as if fate were working itself out through him. It is therefore impossible for him to repent. ('Had I but died an hour before this chance/ I had lived a blessed time; for, from this instant,/ There's nothing serious in mortality,/ All is but toys; renown and grace is dead,/ The wine of life is drawn, and the mere lees/ Is left this vault to brag of.' See *Macbeth* II, 3, 99–103.) [See also *The Concept of Anxiety*, pp. 146.]

13   See above, n. 12. [See also *The Sickness Unto Death*, p. 110.]

14   See *Macbeth*, V, 5, 17–28, where Macbeth reflects on the death of Lady Macbeth: 'She should have died hereafter', and then on his own life: 'Out, out brief candle!/ Life's but a walking shadow, a poor player/ That struts and frets his hour upon the stage,/ And then is heard no more; it is a tale/ Told by an idiot, full of sound and fury,/ Signifying nothing.'

15   *De diversis quaestionibus ad Simplicianum*, qu. 33.

16   See 'Silhouettes' (or 'Shadowgraphs') in *Either/Or*, translated by Howard V. Hong and Edna H. Hong (2 vols, Princeton University Press, Princeton, 1987), vol. 1, pp. 165–215.

17   [See 'Diapsalmata' in *Either/Or*. 'There are, as is known, insects that die in the moment of fertilisation. So it is with all joy: life's highest, most splendid moment of enjoyment is accompanied by death' (vol. 1, p. 20). 'What is going to happen? What will the future bring? I do not know, I have no presentiment. When a spider flings itself from a fixed point down into its consequences, it continually sees before it an empty space in which it can find no foothold, however much it stretches. So it is with me; before me is continually an empty space, and I am propelled by a consequence that lies behind me. This life is turned around and dreadful, not to be endured' (ibid., p. 24). 'So I am not the one who is lord of my life; I am one of the threads to be spun into the calico of life! Well, then, even though I cannot spin, I can still cut the thread' (p. 31).]

18   [*The Sickness Unto Death*, pp. 60–1.]

19   ['The formula that describes the state of the self when despair is completely rooted out is this: in relating itself to itself and in willing to be itself, the self is grounded transparently in the power that established it.' See *The Sickness Unto Death*, p. 14 (translation modified).]

20   [*The Concept of Anxiety*, pp. 77, 91–2, 111.]

21   [On the relation between anxiety and despair, see *The Sickness Unto Death*, pp. 22ff.]

22   [*Three Discourses on Imagined Occasions*, translated by Howard V. Hong and Edna H. Hong (Princeton University Press, Princeton, 1993), p. 102.]

23   [*Concluding Unscientific Postscript*, vol. 1, pp. 560–1n.]

24   [*The Concept of Anxiety*, p. 155 (translation amended).]

25   [As Kierkegaard observes in 'Preliminary Expectoration' in *Fear and Trembling*, 'if one believes that cold, barren necessity must necessarily be present, then one is declaring thereby that no one can experience death before one actually dies, which to me seems to be crass materialism.' See *Fear and Trembling, Repetition*, p. 102.]

26   [*The Concept of Anxiety*, p. 120.]

27   [*Philosophical Fragments*, p. 8.]

28   [*The Concept of Anxiety*, p. 155.]

4
Thinking God in the Wake of Kierkegaard

David Wood

If ever we needed proof of Sartre's genius we could do worse than read his extraordinary essay on Kierkegaard, 'The Singular Universal'.[1] In this essay, Sartre finds in the *character* of Kierkegaard's Christian faith the key to his significance even to those committed to the life-long task of 'becoming-an-atheist'. It would be a commonplace to re-mark that such a reading revealed 'more about Sartre' than about Kierkegaard. But it would also trivialize the stakes of a philosophical engagement.

About thirty years later, Derrida takes up the question of Kierkegaard's God in ways that bear close comparison:

> It is perhaps necessary – if we are to follow the traditional Judeo-Christiano-Islamic injunction, but *also at the risk of turning it against that tradition*, to think of God and of the name of God without such idolatrous stereotyping or representation. Then we might say: God is the name of the possibility I have of keeping a secret that is visible from the interior but not from the exterior. Once such a structure of conscience [or consciousness] exists . . . once there is secrecy and secret witnessing within me, then what I call God exists.

Derrida develops this thought further:

> God . . . is that structure of invisible interiority that is called, in Kierkegaard's sense, subjectivity. [This gives us] . . . a history of God and of the name of God as the history of secrecy, a history that is at the same time secret and without any secrets. Such a history is also an economy.[2]

Derrida is not merely affirming that the very word 'God' is problematic, he is demonstrating the logic or economy within which
everything we want to say about 'God' can best be located. He is
sharpening the question that Sartre rubs our noses in: is the specifically
religious character of Kierkegaard's *philosophical* reflections not best
revitalized as a recognition of the *passion* of thought? How else could it
inspire a militant atheist? I shall pursue this question by an indirect
route, commenting on the concerns of various thinkers who have
found in Kierkegaard a kindred spirit. After some remarks about
Wittgenstein, I will return to comment more fully on treatments
by Sartre and by Derrida, and then show that this same possibility of an
economic reading of Kierkegaard's religious language – a thinking of
an excess that explodes all ethical complacency – is anticipated by
Kierkegaard himself.

'The meaning of life . . . we can call God.'
(Wittgenstein)

Some time ago it was fashionable to refer to God-talk. The idea was that
it might be no deficiency for religious (and theological) language to lack
any reference to the real world, because its intelligibility rested merely on
there being appropriate and shared ways of talking. Perhaps God-talk
could best be thought of as a language-game in Wittgenstein's sense, one
which *bears witness* to the limits of language from 'within'. To speak of
a language-game is not to give up all structure to one's discourse.
Although there are many kinds of games, they all involve the possibility
of distinguishing between acting appropriately and inappropriately.
And it is no accident that Wittgenstein wrote sympathetically about
Kierkegaard. Having said that he 'can readily think what Heidegger
means by Being and Anxiety', he remarks on how tempting it is to
suppose that one can express one's astonishment that anything exists, as
had both Heidegger and Leibniz. 'Everything which we feel like saying
[here] can, a priori, only be nonsense. Nevertheless, we do run up
against the limits of language. This running-up against Kierkegaard also
recognized and even designated in a quite similar way (as running up
against Paradox). This running-up against the limits of language is
Ethics.'[3] Now we might suppose that we could continue to speak here,
because it would be what Ramsey ironically called 'important nonsense'.[4] But Wittgenstein insists that 'it is truly important that one put an
end to all the idle talk about Ethics', which would suggest that we should
stop talking about it altogether. And then he goes on 'Yet the tendency
represented by the running-up against *points to something*,' and quotes

St. Augustine's advice: 'Talk some nonsense, it makes no difference.'[5]
Where does this leave us?

There is a soft sense of a language-game which marks the local
legitimacy of any linguistic practice tied in to some stable social practice,
a legitimation acknowledging that norms are born from regular patterns
of linguistic behaviour. But Wittgenstein never quite lost the logical or
grammatical concerns of his early writing, which surface here in his
reference to 'the limits of language'. If '*the limits of my language* mean the
limits of my world', and 'God does not reveal himself *in* the world',[6] then
Wittgenstein's point sounds somewhat Kantian – our impulse to apply
reason (language) beyond the bounds of possible experience (the world)   *Alberdij*
is hard to curb but doomed to fail. Wittgenstein is, however, willing to
make remarks of another grammatical order. Consider an expanded set
of such claims:

1. 'The meaning [*Sinn*] of life, i.e. the meaning of the world, we can
    call God.'[7]   *apperson*
2. 'We *are* in a certain sense dependent, and what we are dependent on
    we can call God. In this sense God would simply be fate, or, what is
    the same thing: The world – which is independent of our will.'[8] – *God as Oedipal*
3. 'God does not reveal himself *in* the world.'[9] *yet a 'truth'*   *father.*
4. 'The feeling [*Das Gefühl*] of the world as a limited whole is the
    mystical.'[10]

In the first two cases, Wittgenstein does not simply identify or define
God by some other form of words. Instead he says 'we *can call* God', or
'we are *in a certain sense* dependent', or '*what is the same thing*', and finally
he speaks of 'the *feeling* of the world' (my emphases). In each case he
acknowledges a certain equivalence or translatability. The last example –
'the feeling of . . . as . . .' – is an extraordinary fusion of the cognitive and
the affective in which there is an uncanny echo of Heidegger, for whom
it was neither epistemology nor a constructive act of synthesis that could
give us a sense of the world 'as a whole', but *mood*. In writing that '*mood
has already disclosed, in every case, Being-in-the-world as a whole, and
makes it possible first of all to direct oneself towards something*', and that '*the
world already disclosed lets inner-worldly things be encountered*',[11]
Heidegger articulated as a requirement what Wittgenstein acknowledges
phenomenologically – that we have to make a rather special shift of
perspective from our position 'within' the world, in order to grasp the
world *as such*. That shift is brought about by mood (Heidegger) or
feeling (Wittgenstein).

While Heidegger does not here speak of God, he and Wittgenstein are
clearly on the same wavelength. Why does Wittgenstein move from 'the

meaning of life' to 'the meaning of the world' in the first remark? He is
transforming the question we ordinarily ask into one in which the structure of our *relation to the world* becomes explicit. God appears not *in* the
world, but in or as a way of thinking (or feeling) *about* the world. We may
think of Wittgenstein's proposal as either topological or grammatical.
Topologically, we would have to accept the possibility of taking
some distance from 'the world-as-a-whole', defining another sort
of space in which to locate it. Grammatically, we would have to allow
that the difference between 'in' and 'about' is such as to allow the
appearance of a different order of being.[12] What Wittgenstein (and we)
are clearly wrestling with here is the order of grounding. Might naming
(God) or spacing ('aboutness') or different orders of being simply
be attempts to fold back into the world (and into our language) the
consequences of intellectual moves that would otherwise lead us to
silence? If so, the justification would perhaps be that without this folding
back we would be unable to differentiate different dimensions of the
'beyond'. But equally, we might wonder whether there are not different
modes of being within the world, of which thinking about it would be but
one. The fate of 'God', given such reflections, will depend on the way we
construct our topology of the world and what we believe it makes sense
to say in or about it. And it is clear that some of what is in play here
derives from what could be regarded as logical properties of the terrain.
For example, the world itself is not obviously 'in' the world. If we cannot
talk about anything except what is in the world, the expression 'in
the world' would surely be unintelligible. This suggests the more radical
thesis that insofar as we can raise any of these kinds of questions,
we cannot merely be *in* the world, whether as facts or as things. The
'transcendence' of God would then be our way of recognizing the
transcendence implicit in our ability to talk *about* the world. Such a
formula would continue a tradition of inscribing 'God' in a complex
structure of self–self and self–world relationality, which would do justice
to what we know to be the case – that God is *not* a thing, not 'part' of the
world.

    Wittgenstein appears, then, to be making another attempt at thinking
God without God, as one might say. First, he finds a way of understanding God in terms of our relation to the 'world' – as a modulation of our
relation of 'dependence'. This derives from our discovery that the world
is not simply a reflection of our will. Things happen that we never will.
Our very existence is not, at least initially, a matter of our will. Somehow,
the will provides us with a route to the unification of the 'world' at the
very point where the world's independence of our will comes into focus.
Wittgenstein seems to offer 'fate' as an intermediary expression for this
unity, from which an identification with God then arises. His successive

references to our being 'in a certain sense' dependent, to God being 'in this sense . . . simply', and 'what is the same thing' records, and perhaps also masks, the process of synthetic unification and substitution by which we can give the word 'God' both a logic and a kind of phenomenological grounding. Wittgenstein seems to be saying: to the extent that we can conceptualize the world as exceeding our will, we have found a way of understanding how the word 'God' can be intelligibly deployed. This does not, of course, guarantee that all the additional things we might want to say about God would be intelligible or justified. Indeed, the exposure of such an origin, might lead to a theological minimalism. The same combination of a phenomenological with what I will call a 'structural' sense can be found in Wittgenstein's reference to the experience of 'absolute safety', which crystallizes both a separation between myself and the world, and a second-order attunement of the two. 'Absolute safety' is dependence plus faith or trust. The word 'absolute' alludes both to the scope of the experience (nothing can harm me) and the power and quality of the experience — that through it we may come to understand how it might make sense to use terms like 'God'. The sense of absolute safety is not a proof of God's existence. We might be tempted to say, rather, that it 'opens a world' (to use a Heideggerian expression) in which talking about 'God' would make sense. But given that Wittgenstein wants to place God, and the mystical, in the 'space' of our discourse 'about' 'the world', it might be better to say that it opens up 'a new way of being *in* the world'; one in which 'Being in' could include 'reflecting on', 'marvelling at', and so on. What this suggests is that God-talk is an acknowledgement and witness of the grammatical complexity of being-in-a-world, even if its form *may* be systematically misleading.

'Kierkegaard is . . . my adventure.' (Sartre)[13]

I want now to explore whether these suggestions illuminate not just Sartre's treatment of Kierkegaard, but Derrida's too, and indeed Kierkegaard's treatment of himself. I will try first to show that Sartre brought us closer to realizing the connection between Kierkegaard's religious discourse and the paradox focused in Sartre's title: 'The Singular Universal'. I will argue that Kierkegaard finds in Christianity a way of giving coherence to crucial aspects of our being in the world which he could acknowledge in no other form. In Christ, for example, Kierkegaard found a source of distance from what he construed as philosophical detachment. To be a sacrifice is to give one's individual life a significance transcending that empirical individuality. (Christ died to save our souls.) Death, for a living being, is an absolute. It is not just an event in the world but the limit of the possibility of certain kinds of events (such as *my* experiences). To talk about a limit is to talk about the sort of thing that constitutes a world. Without limits manifesting themselves *in* the world there could be no absolutes. To give up one's life for something is to take up a relation to 'the absolute'. To take up a relation to the absolute, to appropriate one's finitude, is to transform oneself – it is to bring transcendence into being. This is how dialectical thought allows us to develop forms of transcendence within immanence, life folded back upon itself.

Sartre shows exactly how Kierkegaard does this, and his success in accounting for Kierkegaard's stance in existential but non-religious terms raises the question of whether the insights expressed by religious discourse might be better understood in a different way. Wittgenstein says that God does not appear *in* the world, and I have responded by suggesting that the very idea of God (here) rests on a narrow sense of what appearing *in* the world might consist in. If we acknowledge ways-of-being-in-the-world in which the transcendent is folded back into the immanent, the infinite played out in the finite, and the absolute found in the contingent, then we may enrich our ways of thinking about *this* world. What Sartre uncovers as the key to Kierkegaard's thought could be put in a number of ways: appropriation, 'living as', repetition, bearing witness. Each of these concepts names a way of converting the straw of contingency into absolute gold. The general idea is not difficult. If I 'begin' thinking of my existence as contingent, I may oppose this to the necessity of an absolute being. And yet the discovery of my contingency, and indeed the contingency of all beings like me, is the discovery of an essential condition which *bearing witness to* allows me to rise above. How does this happen? There seem to be four different thoughts interwoven here. The first is that the character of a truth can be changed by our awareness of it: to be beautiful, and not to know it, is very different from making an exhibition of one's beauty. Second, limitations can take on a distinctive value if one becomes aware of them – for instance the fact that humans are not omniscient might seem like a deficiency, until we realize that if we knew everything life would be totally uninteresting: there would be no surprises, no news, no conversations, in some sense no tomorrow. Thirdly, to act on the distinctive and defining nature of our limitations is a way of transforming our awareness into a creative process. Lastly, by publicly bearing witness to such a feature or condition, we make something new occur. The acknowledged willingness to sacrifice one's life creates a value which was not there before. Life is no longer just life, but, . . . And here a word like 'spirit' would commonly appear.

In what sense does something new occur, or a value get *created?* Is this not a kind of idealism? The fact is that reflection, repetition, embodiment, 'living as', or witnessing are all ways of transforming the economy of significance within which the *considerations brought to bear* on action relate to our finitude, mortality and limits.

Let us now be more specific about Sartre's account of how Kierkegaard makes the moves I have outlined. The first general economy or logic in Sartre's account is that of 'Loser Wins'. His argument is that Kierkegaard's defeat by history (we can place him within Hegel's system, we can 'understand' him to have been psychosexually 'troubled', we can 'teach' him in Existentialism classes) is dialectically temporary. For the being that was 'defeated' (absorbed, forgotten, objectified, misunderstood) escapes history by anticipating and living that defeat subjectively, as *despair*.

> No knowledge could ever transmit directly (because no historical advance could recuperate it): failure lived in despair. Those who died of anguish, of hunger, of exhaustion, those defeated in the past by force of arms, are so many gaps in our knowledge in so far as they existed: subjectivity constitutes *nothing* for objective knowledge since it is a non-knowledge, and yet failure demonstrates that it has an absolute existence. In this way Søren Kierkegaard, conquered by death and recuperated by historical knowledge, triumphs at the very moment he fails, by demonstrating that History cannot recover him. As a dead man, he remains the insurpassable scandal of subjectivity; though he may be known through and through, he eludes History by the very fact that it is History that constitutes his defeat and that he lived it in anticipation. In short, he eludes History because he is historical.[14]

Underlying Sartre's argument is the idea that the negative, non-being, is not ultimately susceptible to calculation or objectification. The negative *can* be merely formal (the antelope *not* on the sofa, the Pope *not* in my seminar) but in concrete cases it functions as a form of resistance preserving significance against positivity. Sartre contrasts our knowledge *about* Kierkegaard with the singular existence of which we suppose we might have knowledge. Sartre suggests that it is Kierkegaard's way of appropriating Christianity that enables him to transcend historical determination. Should we try to prove the immortality of the soul? This is a misunderstanding. 'Immortality, even proven, could never be an object of knowledge: it is a particular absolute relationship between immanence and transcendence that can only be constituted in and through lived experience.'[15] In various ways, Sartre argues that for Kierkegaard 'the opposition of non-knowledge and knowledge is that of two ontological structures', two 'orders of discourse' we might say, or two 'language-games'. Kierkegaard's linking of truth and subjectivity marks not just the locus of truth, but a certain status for subjectivity. Sartre shows how subjectivity is the achievement we called a folding back, which Kierkegaard himself calls repetition; the move is away from any knowledge that a subject might possess towards a transformative achievement *of* a subject.

There is an inherent difficulty in the language Sartre uses here. Let me give some more examples: this non-knowledge, he says, is 'a decision of authenticity: the rejection of flight and the will to return to oneself'; '*knowledge* cannot register this obscure and inflexible *movement* by which scattered determinations are elevated to the status of being and are gathered together into a tension which confers on them . . . a synthetic meaning'; 'subjectivity is temporalization itself; it is *what happens to me*, what cannot be but in happening. It is myself in so far as I can only be born to adventure. . . .'[16] The difficulty lies in trying to determine the radically new significance – what Sartre thinks in terms of 'ontological structure' – brought about in and through a *transformative reflexive becoming*, in recognizing the existential/ontological/categorial significance of distinctions that must be understood modally rather than substantively.[17] Sartre shows that Kierkegaard's thinking is a struggle to express something that is structurally and existentially recessive, a folding back through which the absolute or the transcendent appears within history, within time, within contingency. Sartre says this explicitly in different places:

> In his life, Kierkegaard lived this paradox in passion: he desperately wanted to designate himself as a transhistorical *absolute*. In humour and in irony, he revealed himself and concealed himself at the same time.[18]

> The moment of subjective truth is a temporalized but transhistorical *absolute*.[19]

> Subjectivity constitutes *nothing* for objective knowledge . . . and yet failure demonstrates that it has an *absolute* existence.[20]

In each case, the italicizing of 'absolute' is mine. The word designates a freedom from objectifying, historicizing subordination, even if that freedom is won *through* this subordination. This 'freedom' is not so much a 'fact' in the world as a claim about the autonomy of a certain kind of achievement. But this autonomy deserves comment, for the subject is not autonomous in the sense of being a substance complete in itself. Rather, if subjectivity is an 'openness to the other', such openness is always one openness rather than another (and, as Heidegger would say, 'in each case mine'). And as an openness, it cannot itself be determinate, but rather an openness to ongoing, incalculable determinations.

To talk of an absolute here is to mark a logical/ontological distinction. If Sartre is right, we must mark and remark the presence of the absolute in history, and we can do so in a way consistent with our status as historical beings (beings essentially involved in history), because such an absolute can be realized only *through* such an involvement. Again, the absolute as Sartre unrolls it is modal, found in a way of Being, and whatever advantages any more representational version might have, it runs the risk of being disastrously misunderstood. Sartre shows that the mundane distinction between life and death needs to be redeployed within what we call life, and indeed within what we call death. For the living can be dead, and the dead can live as never before. These reflections would give a new twist to Plato's understanding of philosophy as a preparation for death, a twist presaged by Sartre's gloss on Kierkegaard's interpretation of immortality in terms of inwardness. To understand what Kierkegaard was up to is not merely to do justice to Kierkegaard. It is to do justice to what Kierkegaard tried to do justice to – the way in which 'the universal enters History as a singular, in so far as the singular institutes itself in it as a universal'.[21] The individual can take up a relation to himself through which he maximizes the significance (universality) of his historical particularity.

Sartre is perhaps a predictable ally in the project of providing a dialectical reconstruction of Kierkegaard's Christian commitments. Unlike Kierkegaard and Heidegger (and even Hegel) he does not find in Being-towards-death a source of transcendence. Rather it is the broader categories of negation and non-Being that do the work for him. By maintaining a logic of transcendence at the same time as articulating our historical contingency, he shows that transcendence and situatedness are interdependent, like swimming and water. The situatedness of freedom is not a mere limitation. But Sartre's analysis implies that Kierkegaard's response to Christianity *bears witness* to this connection, even if Kierkegaard's grasp of this dialectic is more formal than substantial.

We know that Kierkegaard emphasized the importance of indirect communication[22] and carefully distinguished objective and subjective thinking. Sartre radicalizes the implication of this when he says 'the *theoretical* aspect of Kierkegaard's work is pure illusion'. He continues:

> When we *encounter* his words, they immediately invite us to another use of language, that is to say of our own words. . . . Kierkegaard's terms refer to what are now called, in accordance with his precepts, the 'categories' of existence. But these categories are neither principles not concepts nor the elements of concepts: they appear as lived relationships to a totality, attainable by starting with the words and following their trajectory back from speech to speaker. This means that not a single one of these verbal

alliances is *intelligible*, but that they constitute, by their very negation of any effort to know them, a reference back to the foundations of such an effort.[23]

There is an echo here, perhaps, of Wittgenstein's remark that our desire to speak when we can only speak nonsense nonetheless 'points to something', as well as of his description of God as the 'meaning of life, i.e. the meaning of the world', and his claim that 'the feeling of the world as a bounded whole is the mystical'. In its displacement of objectifying discourse – religious or otherwise – into 'lived relations to the totality', this resembles what I previously called, after Heidegger, ways of being-in-the-world. But how are we to understand the lessons Sartre learns from Kierkegaard's Christianity? Sartre writes,

> Within each of us he offers and refuses himself, as he did in his own lifetime; he is my adventure and remains, for others, Kierkegaard, the other – a figure on the horizon testifying to the Christian that faith is a future development forever imperilled, testifying to myself that the process of *becoming-an-atheist* is a long and difficult enterprise.[24]

We could understand this as drawing an analogy between becoming a Christian and becoming an atheist, but a stronger claim would be that if the only difference between them is at the 'objective' level, then they are *existentially equivalent*. Is Sartre distorting Kierkegaard's thinking, or keeping faith with its deepest impulses?

'God as wholly other.' (Derrida)

The issue of the status of religious language in Kierkegaard's philosophical discourse has also been pursued by Derrida. The early Derrida understood the idea of God as no more than a symptom of a desire for a fixed stabilizing point outside language – a 'transcendental signified'. And Kierkegaard's appeals to interiority and subjectivity would seem vulnerable to the same criticism. But things were never quite that simple, and if one looks at the panoply of Kierkegaard's discursive displacements – indirect communication, pseudonyms, and so on – it is not difficult to imagine that Kierkegaard, far from being a suitable case for deconstruction, was himself engaged in a deconstructive enterprise.

Derrida's most recent engagement with these issues is in *The Gift of Death*. In the early sections of this text, he discusses an essay by Jan Patočka which plots the connection between religion and responsibility in terms of the appearance of a subject freed from the essential secrecy of ancient orgiastic cults, and capable of freely relating to itself by relating to an infinite other. Here another kind of secrecy arises,

> or more precisely a mystery, the *mysterium tremendum*: the terrifying mystery, the dread, fear and trembling of the Christian in the experience of the sacrificial gift. This trembling seizes one at the moment of becoming a person, and the person can become what it is only in being paralyzed, in its very singularity, by the gaze of God. Then it sees itself seen by the gaze of another, 'a supreme, absolute and inaccessible being who holds us in his hand not by exterior but by interior force'.[25]

Derrida draws from Patočka's work the possibility of a history of secrecy, from Plato through Christianity – a history which calls for a complex economy and topology, because what is repressed is also conserved:

> The logic of this conservative rupture resembles the *economy of a sacrifice* that keeps what it gives up. Sometimes it reminds one of the economy of sublation (*relève*) or *Aufhebung*, and at other times, less contradictory than it seems, of a logic of repression that still retains what is denied, surpassed, buried. Repression doesn't destroy, it displaces something from one place to another within the system. It is also a topological operation.[26]

This history of secrecy is also a history of responsibility, a genealogy of a subject and of a relation to an Other, a genealogy of what Kierkegaard calls subjectivity. And the reference to the *mysterium tremendum* allows Derrida to go on to discuss the *trembling* in Kierkegaard's *Fear and Trembling* as a reflection of a structure of exposure to the gaze of an Other whom one cannot see. But first he inscribes trembling in a history of trauma and repetition that silently reminds us of Kierkegaard's all-too-human biography. Why trauma? Because it too has the structure of radical secrecy, where the secret is hidden even from the subject to whom it 'belongs'. Derrida suggests that what makes us tremble is what 'exceeds my seeing and knowing', and 'concerns the innermost parts of me'. And yet it is something we recognize, 'a strange repetition that ties an irrefutable past (a shock that has been felt . . .) to a future that cannot be anticipated'.[27] This implies that what is at stake is the vulnerability of my identity, my very being. Perhaps our sense of ourselves as unified subjects has been achieved in the face of clear evidence to the contrary – what Wittgenstein called our 'dependency'.

We may suppose that much of what makes us who we are is to be found in the sorts of reasons we give for the things we do. But what of God? Derrida seems to be reporting factually on God when he writes 'God doesn't give his reasons, he acts as he intends, he doesn't have to give his reasons or share anything with us: neither his motivations, if he has any, nor his deliberations, nor his decisions.' But he then says: 'Otherwise he wouldn't be God, we wouldn't be dealing with the Other as God, or with God as *wholly other*. If the other were to share his reasons with us by explaining them to us, if he were to speak to us all the time, without any secrets, he wouldn't be the other.'[28] We find here the beginnings of a functional (or structural) understanding of the expression 'God', which Derrida goes on to intensify even as, at times, it is explicitly problematized. And he draws our attention to the parallel difficulties with straightforward reference embodied in Kierkegaard's use of pseudonyms:

> This pseudonym keeps silent, it expresses the silence that is kept. Like all pseudonyms, it seems destined to keep secret the real name *as* patronym, that is, the name of the father of the work, in fact the name of the father of the father of the work. This pseudonym . . . reminds us that a medita-tion linking the question of secrecy to that of responsibility immediately raises the question of the name and of the signature.[29]

Here Derrida is linking the question of responsibility with that of the subject, and suggesting that revisions in our sense of the significance and scope of responsibility will be played out at the level of the subject's inscription in language. Kierkegaard understands Abraham's 'silence' as displacing the framework of intelligibility and justification away from a public, universal standard towards one drawn from his relation to God, to the wholly other. But one implication of Kierkegaard's problematizing of his own name is that 'God' too might come to be seen as a mere name. We might then wonder whether all this indirectness and secrecy points not to some substantive truth, but to an essential feature of the economy of responsibility.

What is the meaning of the *experience* of sacrifice? If Derrida is right, the significance of sacrifice, and of Abraham's readiness to sacrifice Isaac, is that it marks an absolute limit to the ethics and logic of calculation, in which obligations can be weighed and balanced against one another. Sacrifice is an intrusion, an interruption of public intelligi-bility and acceptability, a repudiation of the ethical court of last appeal. As Derrida presents matters, sacrifice points to a vital component in 'the aporia of responsibility'. As he puts it, 'responsibility . . . demands on the one hand an accounting, a general answering-for-oneself with respect to the general and before the generality, hence the idea of substitution, and, on the other hand, uniqueness, absolute singularity, hence non-substitution, non-repetition, silence, and secrecy.'[30]

Responsibility, then, has a power that will break through any calculated settlement of my responsibilities, and silence is a mark of the incommensurability of this responsibility with any specific conceptualization or finite economizing of its content. And Derrida concludes that this *absolute* responsibility, as we might call it, 'puts us into relation . . . with the absolute other, with the absolute singularity of the other, whose name here is God.'[31]

> The other as absolute other, namely, God, must remain transcendent, hidden, secret, jealous of the love, requests, and commands that he gives, and that he asks to be kept secret. Secrecy is essential to the exercise of this absolute responsibility as sacrificial responsibility.[32]

In these two formulations, Derrida invokes God in the shape of a *name*: 'whose name here is God', 'namely, God'. Shortly afterwards, he writes 'the absolute other: God, if you wish'. This does not imply that 'God' is *only* a name, but it suggests that we cannot understand 'God' (or names) unless we approach the matter indirectly.[33] Thus he prepares the way for an interpretation of 'God' as the marker of a different ethical economy. Derrida's distance from his earlier understanding of 'God' as a transcendental signified now becomes clear. For as he starts to expound the broader significance of Kierkegaard's account of Abraham and Isaac, it emerges that religious concepts can be seen as preserving us – we have yet to determine at what cost – against an inane reductionism in which our ordinary obligations always have the last word. Derrida claims that the extreme horror of the Abraham story actually displays the structure of the most *everyday phenomena*: 'Isn't this the most common thing?'

> As soon as I enter into a relation with the other, with the gaze, look, request, love, command, or call of the other, I know that I can respond only by sacrificing ethics, that is, by sacrificing whatever obliges me also to respond, in the same way, in the same instant, to all the others.[34]

His argument is that if every other is wholly other, then there is nothing to allow me to respond selectively: 'I cannot respond to the call, the request, the obligation, or even the love of another without sacrificing the other, the other others. *Every other (one) is every (bit) other* [*tout autre est tout autre*], every one else is completely or wholly other.'[35] And this teaches us something vital but disturbing: 'The simple concepts of alterity and of singularity constitute the concept of duty as much as that of responsibility. As a result, the concepts of responsibility, of decision, or of duty, are condemned *a priori* to paradox, scandal, and aporia.'[36]

Finally, in confessional mode, Derrida gives voice to the *experience* from which his analysis seems to flow:

By preferring my work, simply by giving it my time and attention, by preferring my activity as a citizen or as a professorial and professional philosopher, writing and speaking here in a public language, French in my case, I am perhaps fulfilling my duty. But I am sacrificing and betraying at every moment all my other obligations: my obligations to the other others whom I know or don't know, the billions of my fellows (not to mention the animals that are even more other others than my fellows), my fellows who are dying of starvation or sickness . . . every one being sacrificed to every one else in this land of Moriah that is our habitat every second of the day.[37]

Abraham's sacrifice of Isaac is, in other words, our everyday experience writ large. But this is surely too hasty. The central move seems to be a generalization of my responsibility to the singular other, the other as absolute other ['namely God'] to every other. The argument must be that the only significant criterion for inclusion is the otherness of the other, which *increases*, if anything, as knowledge, involvement and acquaintance recede. Charity may begin at home, but justice, duty and obligation begin as I close the gate behind me on the way out. The plausibility of this argument rests on the appeal of its conclusion – which opens our eyes to the social and political horrors that surround us – and on the force of the categorial distinctions (singular versus general, absolute versus negotiable) on which it rests. But the way in which these distinctions are deployed bears closer scrutiny.

Derrida claims that I can only respond to the call of the other by 'sacrificing' the ethical, but I can see three distinct objections to this claim. (1) If I am walking down the street and interrupt my daily round to help someone bleeding in a ditch I am not 'sacrificing' any other. No doubt it is a contingent fact that I am walking down *this* street, but such contingency is an essential condition of any life. Generalizability here does not add an impossible mountain of other analogous obligations. (2) It is our responsibility always to allow the interruption of our particular ethical space, but we do not need to expand it infinitely. When we say things like 'God is the name of the absolute other as other',[38] the '*as* other' here does not mean 'treated as belonging to some other category, that of the other', but rather 'as interrupting any positive ethical space one might set up'. To say that God is the absolute other is to designate God as the iterable event of interruption. But as soon as Derrida talks about 'my obligations to the other others whom I know or don't know, the billions of my fellows' he is starting to calculate excess, to add the others together, even though they cannot be accumulated, and cannot be used to compound indebtedness. (3) The difficulty resembles that in Descartes *Meditations*, when he moves from the (true) suggestion that we might doubt any belief to the (false) conclusion that we could doubt every belief. Because the grounds for doubt always include some beliefs, we may be able to doubt anything, but not everything. Similarly, if any particular definition of our duties is provisional, open to revision in the light of an appeal we had not anticipated, this implies the need for a permanent vigilance in avoiding complacency, rather than an infinite expansion of our duties. Absolute openness takes the form of a readiness or capacity, not a total inclusion.

There is another aspect to Derrida's argument which requires a similar response. He writes: 'How would you ever justify the fact that you sacrifice all the cats in the world to the cat that you feed at home every morning for years . . . ?'[39] And his point, here and elsewhere, is that we cannot *justify* our singular attachments. Nevertheless we can explain how we come to have them – not least through chance, situation, and so on. Derrida seems to assume, furthermore, that there is no ethical difference between acts of commission and acts of omission. But this must be false. There are no *a priori* grounds for refusing to consider the ethical significance of a particular omission, but this cannot be converted into a positive claim about our absolute responsibility for everything. And perhaps Kierkegaard's discussions of silence, indirectness, and secrecy find their place here.

We have seen that Derrida encourages us to think of God as a name, or as bound up with naming. But what has happened to 'God' in the generalization we have just criticized? The justification for Derrida's reading of Kierkegaard's treatment of the Abraham story is contained in this sentence: 'If God is completely other, the figure or name of the wholly other, then every other (one) is every (bit) other.'[40] As Derrida acknowledges, 'this formula disturbs Kierkegaard's discourse on one level while at the same time reinforcing its most extreme ramifications.'[41] More explicitly, 'it implies that God, as the wholly other, is to be found everywhere there is something of the wholly other.'[42]

The point might be put like this: 'Don't ask for God, ask for the wholly other'. Derrida recognizes the distinction between preserving a particular reference (e.g. God) for 'the infinite other', and allowing it to be distributed over 'each man and woman'. And he shows that while both Levinas and Kierkegaard seek to preserve this distinction, neither is able 'to determine the limit between these two orders'. Levinas would like there to be an analogy between the face of God and the face of the other, but analogy both distinguishes and elides, and we are left without a decision.

The issue of the status of God is raised again, finally, in Derrida's discussion of the secret. Abraham keeps silent, and keeps his plans secret from Isaac. He communes with God, but can tell no one else what he is doing, or why. And Derrida shows silence at work in the logic of the gift which is the Christian message (turning the other cheek – repaying unkindness with love). There must be a secret: 'and thy Father which seeeth in secret . . . shall reward thee'.[43] But the left hand must not know what the right hand is doing, or else such a gift will become a mere strategy for achieving further goals, such as salvation. At the same time, Derrida is trying to grasp what Kierkegaard calls subjectivity, and its need for secrecy and indirect communication. What he proposes is a dramatic translation of the language of God:

> We should stop thinking about God as someone, over there, way up there, transcendent . . . capable, more than any satellite orbiting in space, of seeing into the most secret of the most interior places. It is perhaps necessary, if we are to follow the traditional Judeo-Christian-Islamic in-junction, but also at the risk of turning it against that tradition, to think of God and of the name of God without such idolatrous stereotyping or representation.[44]

How, then, are we to think of God, if not in this way?

> Then we might say: God is the name of the possibility I have of keeping a secret that is visible from the interior but not from the exterior. Once such a structure of conscience [or consciousness] exists, of being-with-oneself, of speaking, that is, of producing invisible sense, once I have within me, *thanks to the invisible word as such*, a witness that others cannot see, and who is therefore *at the same time other than me and more intimate with me than myself*, once I can have a secret relationship with myself and not tell everything, once there is secrecy and secret witnessing within me, then what I call God exists, (there is) what I call God in me, (it happens that) I call myself God – a phrase that is difficult to distinguish from 'God calls me,' for it is on that condition that I can call myself or that I am called in secret. God is in me, he is the absolute 'me' or 'self,' he is that structure of invisible interiority that is called, in Kierkegaard's sense, subjectivity.[45]

But how are we to link these remarks about secrecy and invisibility with our earlier criticisms of Derrida's account of absolute responsibility. If absolute responsibility is, as I have suggested, a kind of willingness to have one's ethical habits challenged, then it is invisible in the strongest possible sense. For it is not itself another responsibility, but rather a way of dealing with the limits of one's responsibility. Its invisibility is of the same order as that of what Heidegger calls the withdrawal of Being.

'God is this – that all things are possible. . . .' (Kierkegaard)[46]

So far we have argued (with Wittgenstein) that religious language is not referential, but expresses the limits of our possibilities of being-in-the-world, (with Sartre) that Kierkegaard's position may be existentially equivalent to an enlightened atheism, and (with Derrida) that what we call God may be inseparable from an openness to the other which is part of the structure of subjectivity. But what of Kierkegaard himself?

Of course, Kierkegaard's authorship was itself a sustained putting in question of just this 'Kierkegaard himself'. But this account of the self at the beginning of *The Sickness Unto Death*, for example, effectively argues that the self must be constituted in a relation to God. Anti-Climacus says: 'If a human self had itself established itself, then there could be only one form [of despair]: not to will to be oneself, to will to do away with oneself, but there could not be the form: in despair to will to be oneself.'[47] This implies that it is God who supplies an answer to the question of what it is to be oneself. We cannot be self-constituted, and we are selves only to the extent that we relate ourselves to 'the Power that established us'. And, yes, Kierkegaard – or Anti-Climacus – does not say 'God', but 'Power'. And that is because the argument is formal – if valid, it establishes the necessity of a relation to something other than ourselves, through which we truly become ourselves. Whether this other could be other than God – perhaps 'other people', or 'that which I cannot comprehend' – is left open.

But is the argument valid? It is a kind of transcendental argument, which begins with the way things seem (that there are different forms of despair), and then proceeds to account for these different forms. But it could be argued that my willing to be myself (in despair) does not show that I have a constitutive relation to another being, a Power, but only that *I believe I have*, or perhaps better (because mere belief could itself so easily fall to despair), that the structure of my selfhood seems to reflect such a heteronomous relation (perhaps what Wittgenstein called *dependence*). If the argument is to prove my dependence on a distinct being, then it at least needs to be supplied with some further premises. But if the argument is sufficient to demonstrate a certain dependent structure of subjectivity, then it would be valid, and this would bring Kierkegaard's view on the status of God into line with that we have gleaned from Derrida.

The interpretation of responsibility as an openness to the transformation of the boundaries of one's assumed responsibilities, which, if connected to God, would make God a modal or dispositional property of the self, is confirmed by Kierkegaard's formulation of the difference between objectivity and subjectivity. In his *Concluding Unscientific Postscript* he wrote that '*Objectively the emphasis is on **what** is said; subjectively the emphasis is on **how** it is said.*'[48] And by 'how it is said', he means not style, but 'the relation of the existing person, in his very existence, to what is said. . . . At its maximum, this 'how' is the passion of the infinite . . . [which] is precisely subjectivity.'[49] For this reason, the objective question of the existence of God is a misunderstanding. Why?

> Subjectively, [what is reflected on is] that the individual relates himself to a something *in such a way* that his relation is in truth a God-relation. . . . The objective way . . . is not achieved in all eternity, because God is a subject and hence only for subjectivity in inwardness.[50]

Here Kierkegaard makes it clear, first that God is a mode of a relationship, and secondly, that God is a subject, not a thing. This puts in perspective the nominalistic remarks in the *Philosophical Fragments*, where Kierkegaard, like Wittgenstein and Derrida, traces the emergence of the word 'God'.

> But what is this unknown against which the understanding in its paradoxical passion collides and which even disturbs man and his self-knowledge? It is the unknown. But it is not a human being, insofar as he knows man, or anything else that he knows. Therefore, let us call this unknown *the god*. It is only a name we give to it.[51]

And consider Kierkegaard's treatment of the question of immortality, which is not susceptible to objective proof, but has to do with the passion of the infinite. Socrates might sound like a doubter when he asks '*if* there is an immortality', but 'He stakes his whole life on this "if"; he dares to die, and with the passion of the infinite he has so ordered his whole life that it might be acceptable – *if* there is an immortality.'[52] In other words, Socrates, who embodied the passion of the infinite in his life, gave immortality the highest significance it could have. Again, this would testify to a modal displacement of the religious. Similarly, Kierkegaard's comment that 'since everything is possible for God, then God is this – that all things are possible',[53] could be interpreted as a way of organizing one's Being in the world. God is being glossed as hope.

If we consider, too, that the Knight of Faith is described as finding the infinite in the finite, we can see that Kierkegaard emphasizes the possibility of a transformation of the economy of subjectivity at the very point where God might otherwise be expected to enter the scene. Faith is more complex than simply 'belief in God'. What is crucial for Kierkegaard is that there be a form of individuality – or singularity – which can re-emerge *beyond universality*, i.e. beyond ethical generality. To find the infinite in the finite might seem paradoxical, but the example Kierkegaard gives in *Fear and Trembling* does have a certain coherence. Our knight dreams of the wonderful meal his wife has prepared for him, but when he gets home, he finds meagre fare. Instead of being disappointed, however, he is content. He is, it seems, able to be in the world (with ordinary desires) but not of the world, i.e. not tied to the satisfaction of those desires. Again, Kierkegaard is describing the religious life as a way of being-in-the-world.

It could be objected, of course, that this whole vein of interpretation extends no further than what Kierkegaard calls Religiousness A, a certain pathos of immanence, achievable even by paganism, and falling short of Religiousness B, paradoxical religiousness, which he calls dialectical to the second degree.[54] Religiousness A is a step beyond 'speculative philosophy' in that it understands truth inwardly, existentially. But it is limited by its telos of successful enactment of the infinite, whereas Religiousness B embodies the anxious impossibility of such a resolution. It is not clear that Kierkegaard's account of this distinction is entirely consistent. It is an achievement, says Kierkegaard, for us to understand our relation to God as a dimension of our subjectivity, a relation we have to ourselves rather than to an external object. But he believes, too, that we can understand Christianity as embodying a new dialectic, one in which our relation to God becomes again a relation to something external, although in a way different from the original naïve sense. Kierkegaard is clearly dealing here with the paradoxical historical reality of God made man in Christ. Religiousness B, paradoxical religiousness, seems intent on preventing us from achieving even the complacency of successful embodiment of God in our lives. Kierkegaard seems to be concerned that God as a structure of subjectivity might involve a loss of paradox, a loss of dialectical development.

I would like to end by suggesting that the idea of Religiousness B may indicate a misunderstanding on Kierkegaard's part of the implications already latent in his own account of subjectivity. If the significance of 'God' for subjectivity appears in the 'inwardness of passion', then we can understand the life of Christ as the inaugural performance of this (self-) sacrificial economy of life and gift of death. He opened up a world, which is preserved by the gospels and our reading of them. Christ may have shared with Religiousness B the belief in his relation to an actual external Being (God), but we need not share that view in order to acknowledge his significance. Perhaps Kierkegaard believed that the dialectic of doubt, perplexity, or paradox would cease if all relation to an exterior were removed – that interiority breeds complacency. But his description of *difference* in subjectivity is sufficient, perhaps, to keep the perils of good conscience at bay. If the self is a relation that relates itself to itself through the medium of its relation to the infinite, then this self-relation will never cease to be problematic.

To live in paradox is to be suspended in a space of contradiction. The 'external' paradox of Christ, of God-made-man, may be something we lose sight of at our spiritual peril, but perhaps we lose sight of its significance precisely to the extent that it continues to fascinate us, rather than becoming a challenge (and paradox) for our own lives. And if we were to dare to think that Christ never quite knew who he was or what he was for ('Father, father, why hast thou foresaken me?') we might come to see him as an exemplary instance of the gap between existence and knowledge.

We *are* invisible to ourselves – and there may be no one else who sees us either. The *way we are* constantly outstrips our knowledge of who we are. In that gap alone, there is dialectical ferment enough. And here there is a parallel with the limitations of Derrida's concept of absolute responsibility: he generates paradoxes by projecting infinite positive obligations into my habitual life, just as Kierkegaard opened up an external relation to God when he had already shown how to discard such topologies. In both cases, we may wonder whether the impulses that created the difficulties are not reasserting themselves. But my claim has been that the problems of religious discourse are modal, not substantive, so that 'God' may be understood as a disposition never to close the space of one's responsibilities. It is always a sign of the waning of insight to start up the engines of projection once again. There is no other realm, but there are radically different ways of inhabiting this one.

NOTES

1   Jean-Paul Sartre, 'Kierkegaard: The Singular Universal', in his *Between Existentialism and Marxism*, translated by John Matthews (NLB, London, 1974), pp. 141–69.
2   Jacques Derrida, *The Gift of Death*, translated by David Wills (University of Chicago Press, Chicago, 1995), p. 108.
3   Ludwig Wittgenstein, 'On Heidegger on Being and Dread', in *Heidegger and Modern Philosophy*, edited by Michael Murray (Yale University Press, New Haven, 1978), p. 80 [translation modified].
4   F. P. Ramsey, 'Last Papers of Philosophy', in his *Foundations of Mathematics and Other Logical Essays* (1931), quoted in Cyril Barrett, *Wittgenstein on Ethics and Religious Belief* (Blackwell, Oxford, 1991), p. 22.
5   Wittgenstein, 'On Heidegger on Being and Dread', pp. 80–1.

6 Ludwig Wittgenstein, *Tractatus Logico-Philosophicus*, translated by D. F. Pears and B. F. McGuinness (Routledge and Kegan Paul, London, 1966), 5.6 and 6.432.

7 Ludwig Wittgenstein, *Notebooks: 1914–1916*, translated by G. E. M. Anscombe (Basil Blackwell, Oxford, 1969), p. 73e.

8 *Notebooks: 1914–1916*, p. 74e.

9 *Tractatus Logico-Philosophicus*, 6.432.

10 Ibid., 6.45 [translation modified].

11 Martin Heidegger, *Being and Time*, translated by John Macquarrie and Edward Robinson (Basil Blackwell, Oxford, 1978), p. 176.

12 Compare Heidegger's reference to the ontico-ontological difference, the difference between (particular) beings, and Being.

13 'Kierkegaard: The Singular Universal', p. 167.

14 Ibid., p. 151.

15 Ibid., pp. 152–3.

16 Ibid., p. 146.

17 Another version of this claim may be found elaborated in Heidegger's distinction (which he insists is not a mere difference of category) between Being and beings, in *Being and Time*. It is well known that Heidegger subsequently came to rue this attempt at constructing a fundamental ontology, as if one could improve on traditional systematic metaphysics while keeping the constructive mode of exposition. His more allusive, 'poetic' later style is an attempt to form a new way of writing in keeping with the recognition that truth has the character of the *way*. Lacan claimed that Freud's hydraulic language (of libidinal flows and blockages) reflected a certain contingent restriction on available models, and that had Saussure's work been available to him, he might have found a linguistic model preferable. I am making an analogous argument about Kierkegaard's religious language, that it captures vital distinctions in a way that seems to preserve them, but actually sets up a different kind of struggle against their loss, one in which the struggle is more likely to be won, but the victory Pyrrhic. On this argument the institutionalization of religious thought against which Kierkegaard railed is already to be found in the very concepts that constitute religious discourse.

18 'Kierkegaard: The Singular Universal', p. 147.

19 Ibid., p. 146.

20 Ibid., p. 151.

21 Ibid., p. 163.

22 See *Fear and Trembling*, *The Concept of Irony*, and *Concluding Unscientific Postscript* (where the communication of inwardness is at stake).

23 'Kierkegaard: The Singular Universal', p. 163.

24 Ibid., p. 168.

25 Jacques Derrida, *The Gift of Death*, translated by David Wills (University of Chicago Press, Chicago and London, 1995), p. 6.

26 Ibid., p. 8.

27 Ibid., p. 54. See this volume p. 152.

28 Ibid., p. 57. See this volume, p. 154.

74 David Wood

29 Ibid., p. 58. See this volume, p. 155.
30 Ibid., p. 61. See this volume, p. 157.
31 Ibid., p. 66. See this volume, p. 161.
32 Ibid., p. 67. See this volume, p. 161.
33 See Jacques Derrida, *On the Name* (Stanford University Press, Stanford, 1995).
34 *The Gift of Death*, p. 68. See this volume, pp. 162–3.
35 Ibid., p. 68. See this volume, p. 162.
36 Ibid., p. 68. See this volume, p. 162.
37 Ibid., p. 69. See this volume, p. 163.
38 Ibid., p. 68. See this volume, p. 162.
39 Ibid., p. 71. See this volume, p. 164.
40 Ibid., p. 77. See this volume, p. 170.
41 Ibid., p. 77. See this volume, p. 170.
42 Ibid., p. 78. See this volume, p. 170.
43 [Matthew 6: 6].
44 *The Gift of Death*, p. 108.
45 Ibid., pp. 108–9.
46 Søren Kierkegaard, *The Sickness Unto Death*, translated by Howard V. Hong and Edna H. Hong (Princeton University Press, Princeton, 1980), p. 40 [translation altered].
47 *The Sickness Unto Death*, translated by Howard V. Hong and Edna H. Hong (Princeton University Press, Princeton, 1980), p. 14.
48 *Concluding Unscientific Postscript to Philosophical Fragments*, translated by Howard V. Hong and Edna H. Hong (2 vols, Princeton University Press, Princeton, 1992), vol. 1, p. 202.
49 *Concluding Unscientific Postscript*, p. 203.
50 Ibid., pp. 199–200.
51 Søren Kierkegaard, *Philosophical Fragments, Johannes Climacus*, translated by Howard V. Hong and Edna H. Hong (Princeton University Press, Princeton, 1985), p. 39.
52 *Concluding Unscientific Postscript*, p. 201.
53 *The Sickness Unto Death*, p. 40.
54 See *Concluding Unscientific Postscript*, pp. 555ff.

5
The Eyes of Argus: *The Point of View* and Points of View on Kierkegaard's Work as an Author

Joakim Garff

The religious is already decisively present from the very first moment, and definitely has precedence, but is patiently waiting a while, allowing the poet to finish speaking yet all the time watching with the eyes of Argus to ensure that the poet does not fool it and make of himself the whole.

It is from this point of view, I believe, that the significance of my work as an author shows itself most clearly for this age.[1]

One must be careful with metaphors. Consider the eyes of Argus, for example: Argus was a giant who, by order of the jealous Hera, watched over the beautiful Io. He had a hundred eyes, which took turns at keeping watch; when one of them closed, another immediately opened. Yet Argus's eyes saw only Io, and this was fortunate for Hermes. He lay in wait and, drawing his sword, plunged it suddenly into Argus.

This, then, is the myth behind Kierkegaard's metaphor. He is watching with a hundred eyes to ensure that 'the poet' will not fool 'the religious'. But although he watches 'sleeplessly', remaining 'awake, attentive, and obedient' – one could not 'demand more of a spy' – still he too is kept 'under the strictest surveillance': that of 'Divine Guidance' itself, in whose service Kierkegaard's espionage is being conducted.[2]

This chapter was first published in Danish in *Dansk Teologisk Tidsskrift* 4, 1989, and is translated here, with permission, by Jane Chamberlain and Belinda Ioni Rasmussen. Translation copyright © Jane Chamberlain and Belinda Ioni Rasmussen, 1998. References have been given to English-language editions, where available, although the translations have frequently been altered.

But there are other eyes looking on. We, the readers, are inspecting the hundred eyes in *The Point of View* and therefore find ourselves in the same position as Hermes: the reader is a hermeneut. But from what point of view should we regard *The Point of View*? What is the most effective way to spy on the spy? The answer must be: by allowing Kierkegaard himself to carry out the counter-espionage, though disguised, of course, as Climacus, author of the following note from the *Concluding Unscientific Postscript*:

> All ironic observation depends upon constantly paying attention to 'how', whereas the Honourable Gentleman with whom the ironist has the honour of dealing is attentive only to the 'what'. A man declares loudly and solemnly: this is my opinion; yet he does not restrict himself to reciting this brief formula, but explains himself further, venturing to vary his expressions. Yes, but variation is not so simple a matter as one thinks. More than one student would have gained Honours had be not varied, and many people possess the talent for variation which Socrates so much admired in Polos: they never say the same thing – about the same thing. The ironist, then, is keeping watch; he is naturally not concerned with what is written in capital letters, or with that which reveals itself, through the speaker's diction, as a formula (the Honourable Gentleman's 'what'), but is attentive to the little subordinate clause, a little beckoning predicate etc., which escapes the splendid attention of the Honourable Gentleman. And he sees now with astonishment, delighted by the variation (*in variatione voluptas*), that the Honourable Gentleman did not *have* that opinion or meaning [*Mening*]; not that he is a hypocrite – goodness no! – that would be too serious a matter for an ironist, but because the good man has concentrated on bawling it out rather than on having it within. Of course the Honourable Gentleman may be right in declaring that he has the opinion which he imagines he has with all his might; he can do everything for it . . . he can risk his life for it . . . and yet at the same time there might live an ironist who could not help laughing even when the unfortunate Honourable Gentleman was executed, because he knows from circumstantial evidence that the man was never clear about it himself.[3]

With a watchful eye on the significant meaning of details, the ironist inspects the individual variations, and can therefore deliver the mischievous judgement that 'the Honourable Gentleman did not *have* that opinion or meaning' which he – ironically enough – meant [*mente*] to have. For if it is true that variety is the spice of life, because it breaks out of banality, the fact that variety varies is equally banal. When our figure intensifies the production of meaning, he produces more signs and thereby increases the ambiguity, since the 'opinion' or 'meaning' originally put forward does not remain the same, unchanged by the intensification, but begins to displace itself in the various directions of the 'expressions'. To intensify the production of 'meaning' is – in other words – to produce another 'meaning'.

It is worth noting that this judgement has no ethical character – it is even emphasized that 'the Honourable Gentleman' was nothing so dishonourable as a 'hypocrite', although one might have expected such a verdict given that he was saying something *other* than what he meant. But the problem is not that 'the Honourable Gentleman' said something he did not mean, but rather that he meant something he could not say, which is why he always ended up saying something other than what he meant. And this contradiction seems to occur so utterly involuntarily that it could almost be a condition for all communication, which is why the heretical thought that no one ever succeeds in being entirely 'clear about it' themselves, even though they may pledge and risk their life for it, becomes obvious.

Were this 'no one' a text, then this little episode would reveal that a text is not always able to *accomplish* what it consciously aims to *mean*, and that – which is (as good as) saying the same thing – there is a difference between what a text *says* it does and what it *actually* does or, at least, does at the same time. Climacus has, one could say, revealed a strategy of reading which particularly interests itself in the (dys)functions of a text's attempt to convey its significance and express its opinion or meaning.

Given that *The Point of View* is precisely one of those texts which has an 'opinion' or 'meaning', it seems fair to adopt Climacus's subversive strategy. This will make it possible to read Kierkegaard with Kierkegaard against Kierkegaard. And Kierkegaard could hardly hope for a more Kierkegaardian reading.

Points of View Before *The Point of View*

If we want to adopt this point of view on *The Point of View*, we must begin by looking at the point of view in *The Point of View*; that is, at what Climacus calls its 'formula' and 'opinion'. And this is easy enough: 'The content of this little work is, then, what I really am as an author, that I am and always was a religious author, that the whole of my work as an author is related to Christianity, to the problem of becoming a Christian. [. . .] What I write here is for orientation and attestation, and is neither a defence nor an apology.'[4] This is the point of view in *The Point of View*. But the situation is complicated, somewhat, by the fact that a series of other points of view have been adopted earlier in the authorship 'for orientation and attestation', namely:

1   In an 'Appendix' in the *Concluding Unscientific Postscript* entitled
'A Glance at a Contemporary Effort in Danish Literature', Climacus
comments on the writings of a certain Magister Kierkegaard, from
Either/Or to *Stages on Life's Way*. Somewhat eccentrically, this 'Appendix' derives its dynamism from an indignant account of a literary ordeal.
For years this Magister, of whom Climacus knows nothing, had been
publishing all the works which Climacus himself had been planning to
write. With a mixture of disappointment and enthusiasm about his
strange synchronicity with the magical Magister, Climacus refers to and
comments on the published writings up to the *Fragments*, which he has
miraculously managed to complete under the very nose of the Magister.

2   However, in this same *Postscript* there is a final declaration,
signed S. Kierkegaard, claiming that it will be 'A First and Last Explanation',[5] although in fact it is neither of these, since the first explanation
is already given in the aforementioned 'Appendix', and the last explanation is still to come. Here Kierkegaard announces that, although it could
scarcely be of interest to anyone, he acknowledges the pseudonymous
production as his own, while emphasizing that his use of

> pseudonymity or polyonimity has not had an arbitrary basis in my *person-
> ality* . . . but is *essential* to the nature of the production itself. . . . What is
> written is therefore certainly mine, but only insofar as I, through the
> audibility of his lines, have put a life-view into the mouth of the poetically-
> real producing individual. My relation is even more external than that of
> a poet, who *poetically* fabricates characters yet is *himself* the author of
> the preface. For I am impersonally, or personally in the third person, a
> prompter who has poetically produced *authors* whose *prefaces*, indeed
> whose very *names*, are their own production. There is therefore in the
> pseudonymous books not a single word which is my own; I have no
> opinion of them except as a third party, no knowledge of their meaning
> except as a reader.[6]

Between the pseudonymous, individual authors and Kierkegaard himself, therefore, there is no connection at all, or at least only the remotest
one, 'whereas I am quite authentically and straightforwardly the author
of, for example, the edifying discourses, and of every word in them'.[7]

3   This account concurs with the text *On my Work as an
Author*, composed in 1849 but not published until the summer of 1851.
Here Kierkegaard once again focuses on the overall intention of the
authorship:

> The movement which the authorship describes is: *from* 'the poet' – from
> the aesthetic, from 'philosophy', from the speculative – *to* the suggestion of

the most profound categories of Christianity. . . . This movement has been traversed or described *uno tenore*, in one breath, if I dare say so, so that the authorship, viewed as a *whole*, is religious from beginning to end – something that anyone who has eyes to see must see, when he wants to see.[8]

Besides this, and a confused mass of variations on the same theme, *On my Work as an Author* plays a number of small improvizations around the dialectic of communication, and in a so-called 'Supplement' Kierkegaard indicates his position as a religious author in 'Christendom', as well as the tactics he has felt compelled to employ in order to give a fresh formulation to the radical demands of Christianity.[9]

4   Finally, there is *The Point of View for my Work as an Author*, composed in the summer of 1848 – that is, before *On my Work as an Author* but at roughly the same time as *The Sickness Unto Death* and the first edition of *Practice in Christianity*. For reasons which I will come back to, the book was set aside and published only posthumously, in an edition by Peter Kierkegaard, where it was accompanied by two 'Notes' whose connection with *The Point of View* had already been indicated by their author. All told, the number of pages corresponds to the number of Argus's eyes, and the original manuscript – almost symbolically – has been lost.

Each of these four pieces makes normative pronouncements about Kierkegaard's work and gives more or less explicit directions for its proper reading. The problem, of course, is that each piece does this separately from a different point of view, which not only undermines the normative status of each individual piece but also compromises the fourth point of view, which stubbornly claims that it is simply *The Point of View*.

If, for example, we try to determine the significance of the pseudonyms, we get rather contradictory results. Although in 'A First and Last Explanation', as we have seen, Kierkegaard renounces every connection with his pseudonyms, in *The Point of View* he claims that the pseudonymity has been a tactic of dissembling adopted by a religious author wishing to capture and retain the attention of the reader.[10] And if these statements are compared with those in Climacus's 'Appendix', we are not only confronted with the decidedly odd situation in which a pseudonym comments upon the significance of pseudonymity, but Climacus seems neither to be interested in pseudonymity as a maieutic strategy nor to have any idea that it is supposed to be a religious author's dissimulating form of presentation. Instead, Climacus fills out his

'Appendix' by thematizing the authorship's contraposition of the systematically objective with subjectivity as (un)truth.

Because the point of view on the authorship adopted in 'A First and
Last Explanation' differs from that in *The Point of View*, a special point
of view must be adopted in *The Point of View* on that adopted in the
former work. And without batting an eyelid, Kierkegaard makes a
pronouncement on the quality of Climacus's 'Explanation':

> this is pseudonym appraising other pseudonyms – that is, a third party who
> could not know anything about the intentions of a production which is
> foreign to him. The *Concluding Postscript* is not an aesthetic production,
> but neither is it religious in the strictest sense. It is therefore by a pseudo-
> nym, although I put my name on it as publisher, which I did not do with
> any purely aesthetic publication – a hint, to be sure, for those who concern
> themselves with and have a flair for such things.[11]

If we do, in fact, 'have a flair for such things', we will discover that this
account, too, does not hold up, for as late as 1846 Kierkegaard published
A Literary Review with his 'name on it as publisher', and this despite his
having classified the *Review* as an aesthetic work. Kierkegaard himself
discovered this discrepancy, however, and in a note added later
attempted to anticipate all possible objections.[12]

The four pieces are accompanied by a series of supplements which, on
closer inspection, reveal some disgraceful inaccuracies concerning the
extent of the authorship. In *The Point of View* the following titles are
mentioned: *First Group* (aesthetic productions): *Either/Or, Fear and
Trembling, Repetition, The Concept of Anxiety, Prefaces, Philosophical Fragments, Stages on Life's Way* – as well as eighteen edifying discourses.
Second Group: *Concluding Unscientific Postscript*. *Third Group* (purely religious productions): *Edifying Discourses in Various Spirits, Works of Love,
Christian Discourses* – plus a small aesthetic article: *The Crisis and a Crisis
in the Life of an Actress*.[13]

If this is supposed to be a definition of 'the totality of the authorship',
then this 'totality' is not identical with 'the total production'. For example, the youthfully libellous book about Hans Christian Andersen, *From
the Papers of One Still Living*, and the ironic dissertation *The Concept of
Irony*, are passed over in a telling silence, and one seeks in vain for several
journal articles that Kierkegaard acknowledged in 'A First and Last
Explanation'.[14] Most remarkable, though, is the omission of *A Literary
Review*, which cannot be a result of mere forgetfulness, as is clear from
the footnote where Kierkegaard carefully explained the place of the
Review in his production. The divergence between 'the totality of the
authorship' and 'the total production' is the consequence of a concern
for the evenness of the summary: the *Third Group* (purely religious

productions) is already burdened with one aesthetic work and therefore must not be further burdened – certainly not by anything so cumbersome as obviously aesthetic juvenilia.

One gets the impression that it was only by means of this reductive definition of 'the authorship' that Kierkegaard could establish a unity within which the mass of his writings could be symmetrically divided into two groups – the aesthetic and the religious – and this impression is strengthened by an examination of *On my Work as an Author*, which includes the following proclamation:

> The beginning was made, *maieutically*, with aesthetic publication, and the entire pseudonymous production is *maieutic* in this way. This production was therefore also pseudonymous, while the straightforwardly religious – which was present from the beginning in hints and glimpses – bore my name. The straightforwardly religious was present from the beginning, for *Two Edifying Discourses* of 1843 are of course contemporary with *Either/Or*. . . . The *Concluding Postscript* is the midpoint, and – although this of course only has interest as a curiosity – this is the case so precisely that even the quantity of achievement before and after is almost the same size if, as one should, one counts the 18 edifying discourses as part of the purely religious production. Even the time of the authorship before and after the *Concluding Postscript* is almost the same length.[15]

A curiosity, of course – especially when one considers that in *The Point of View* Kierkegaard placed those same eighteen discourses in the 'First Group', as part of the aesthetic production! If it can therefore seem paradoxical that the establishment of this *aesthetic* symmetry means that a text which is classified as *aesthetic* in one place has to be classified as *religious* in another, it is no less paradoxical that this symmetry is established precisely in order to prevent an *aesthetic* impression.[16]

So much for the audit of the various supplements to the accounts, whose mutual inconsistencies are due to the fact that Kierkegaard's transactions are heavily dependent on the goodwill of the reader, without which there would be an alarming disproportion between religious credit and aesthetic debt. For both himself and his reader, Kierkegaard must also, repeatedly, call the following to mind: 'There is one thing, above all, that he must not forget, namely, that the religious must be brought forth in a decisive way.'[17]

It can hardly be unreasonably belligerent to ask how and why such a reminder could be given in relation to an authorship which is religious from beginning to end. And why does not Kierkegaard – learning from Climacus – simply stay with his 'formula'? Why put forward arguments when this is not an 'apology', but something as down to earth as an 'orientation'? What is the meaning of all this? And where? Let us now turn to *The Point of View*.

The Point of View in *The Point of View*

The Point of View describes the writing which left its trace in Kierkegaard's earlier writings, the scattered writings seen as one writing, as 'the totality'. For the same reason, *The Point of View* asks its readers to see it as occupying a different level than the other texts – as the text of the other texts, the text of texts, a meta-text. As such, *The Point of View* wants to overwrite the other texts with *its* meaning. If there is, therefore, as stated in the work's own textual metaphor, a 'difference between writing on a blank sheet of paper – and bringing out, with the help of caustic means, a writing which is hidden under other writing',[18] then *The Point of View* itself is engaged in erasing this difference. The writing that is brought out as the true writing of the writings is not, in fact, an original, hidden, writing, for it is *The Point of View* that *generates* the true writing. Hence what becomes visible in *The Point of View* is not hidden writing, but rather the hidden intention of the visible writings. *The Point of View*, therefore, is far from being written on 'a blank sheet of paper', and if we are eventually to talk of 'caustic means' then some of the most effective must be those deceptions, tricks, and manoeuvres by which *The Point of View* tries to make *its* viewpoint into *the reader's*.

The Point of View wants the reader to share its point of view. And this is unfortunate. For in order to be in a position to present his religious concern, Kierkegaard has to resort to an excessively aesthetic discourse. Hence the incongruity between the 'what' and the 'how' of the expression, pointed out by the ironist Climacus, returns as a basic performative contradiction in the writing. Concerning the 'what': *The Point of View* wants to undertake the intricate task of making explicit the inwardness whose incommensurability is cited everywhere in the authorship as the real reason for communicating indirectly. And concerning the 'how': *The Point of View* wants to annul an aesthetic practice by means of its aesthetic practice; to 'make visible what it is to become a Christian', as it puts it, by bringing its reader to 'reflect himself out of the semblance of being a Christian.'[19]

The problem for the reader is that Kierkegaard seems to be aware of this to some extent, since he knows that it is the person who most energetically condemns 'the bewitchment of the aesthetic' who 'ends up becoming stuck in the aesthetic himself'. Kierkegaard's difficulty is that the reader might become aware of this as the fundamental problem of *The Point of View*, and this finds a quiet echo in the somewhat resigned instruction on the penultimate page of the book's 'Conclusion': 'do it or don't do it, stay silent or speak, it is wrong either way.'[20]

Rightly considered, then, *The Point of View* can neither stay silent nor speak, and if it cannot decide to do the former, neither can it bring itself to do the latter. It constantly breaks the silence, and even its 'Epilogue' is not the last word, but rather a prologue to the subsequent 'Conclusion', which in turn is not a conclusion, for it is followed by the 'Two Notes', which are introduced by a new 'Preface', which is followed by more writing, and then by a new 'Postscript', of which the true postscript is yet another 'Postscript', begging for 'Just one word more'. From this perspective it is therefore as symptomatic as it is farcical that Kierkegaard, roughly half way through *The Point of View*, allows himself to declare: 'The whole thing can be said in one word'.[21] If only it could.

But it cannot, of course, and if *The Point of View* goes on and on it is not only because the book has good reasons for being unable to keep silent, it is also and not least because the work wants to say *everything* – including, in particular, that which a critical reader might possibly want to say. This becomes clear when Kierkegaard proffers the following, rather teasing, invitation: 'Let the attempt be made; the attempt to explain the whole authorship on the assumption that it is by an aesthetic author'. This might perhaps sound tempting, but we soon understand that it is a temptation we ought to resist, since it invites us not to make one movement among several possible ones, but the most impossible one of all. If, by contrast, one 'tries to assume that it is a religious author, one will see that, step by step, it proves correct at every point'. Either/Or. *Tertium non datur.*[22]

And yet perhaps it is still best to arm oneself with a certain neutrality, for although the distance between the first, disingenuous proposal and the second, admonishing one initially seems quite considerable, they tacitly share the same hermeneutical premise. Both proposals take it for granted that there is a straight and unbroken line joining the declared intentions of an 'author' about his 'work', on the one hand, and the complete accomplishment of the intention, by that 'work', on the other. If one assumes that Kierkegaard is a 'religious author', this certainly does not establish that his 'work-as-an-author' must be religious, since that depends less upon 'the author' than on the 'work' – that is, on the text.

Learning from Climacus, Kierkegaard should have been content with the 'short formula', that the authorship was religious from beginning to end. But he is not – on the contrary, he 'explains himself further' and carries out an ocular proof in the 'First Section', by means of which he wants to prove the presence of the 'duplicity' which characterizes the authorship as a simultaneously aesthetic—religious whole. Kierkegaard has hardly announced this 'duplicity' before he identifies himself with the critical reader: 'But is that how it is?' he asks, 'is there such thorough duplicity? Can one not explain the phenomenon in a different way, so that an author, who began as an aesthetic author, *changed* over the years and became a religious author?' This solution sounds very plausible, but before long we will realize it is exceptionally naïve, and proposed only in order to give Kierkegaard the opportunity to show that 'it is impossible to explain the phenomenon in this way'.[23]

Here Kierkegaard seems to be launching into an 'apology', which is precisely what *The Point of View* was *not* supposed to be. He wants to *prove* the presence of a 'duplicity', and therefore 'The explanation: That the Author is and was a Religious Author'[24] soon creates the need for further explanation. However, since Kierkegaard is acquainted with the danger of perseverance – which, with its intensification of explanation, comes close to attacking the very reliability it wants to protect – he takes the following measure:

> It might seem as though a single assurance by the author in this respect is more than sufficient; for he must certainly know best which is which. However, I do not hold much with such assurances in relation to literary productions, and am accustomed to relating completely objectively to my own. If, in my capacity as a third party, as a reader, I cannot establish on the basis of the writings themselves that things are as I claim, and that they cannot be otherwise, then I could never dream of attempting to win a battle which I would have to regard as lost. If I begin, *qua* author, to give such assurances, it could easily alter the whole production, which is dialectical from beginning to end.[25]

Now is this an explanation or an assurance? It reminds one most of all of a performative contradiction of which the formula is: 'I assure you: I never give assurances.' If the reader's goodwill can stretch as far as accepting that Kierkegaard relates himself objectively, as a 'third party', to himself as author, then this same reader's memory must be as short as his goodwill is extensive, for his position as a 'third party' was, as we have seen, precisely what disqualified Climacus in relation to 'the intentions of a production which is foreign to him'. Hence, ironically enough: in order to avoid the intentional fallacy Kierkegaard must subscribe to the fallible intentionality of a pseudonym.

The quotation continues with the following assurance:

> Thus, I cannot give assurances on anything, at least not before I have made the explanation so evident in another way that the assurance in this sense becomes superfluous; for then it can be *allowed* as a lyrical satisfaction, insofar as I feel a need for it, and *demanded* as a religious duty. *Qua* human being, I am well within my rights in giving assurances, and it could be my

religious duty to do so. But this must not be confused with the authorship: *qua* author it helps little that I give assurance, *qua* human being, that I have wanted this and that.[26]

If the energy invested in the argument indicates that Kierkegaard was painfully aware of the conflict between 'explanations' and 'assurances', the argument also testifies to the painful difficulty of trying to escape that conflict. And scarcely two pages after his cool-headed comment that he does not care for literary 'assurances' he announces:

> This is how things are: In a strict sense *Either/Or* was written in a monastery, and . . . I can assure you that the author of *Either/Or* regularly and with monastic precision devoted a definite time every day, for his own sake, to the reading of edifying writings, and in fear and much trembling reflected on his responsibility. And he thought in that way in particular (oh, how strange!) about 'The Seducer's Diary'.[27]

Even the most generous reader will have to summon up extra generosity to conceive how such an assurance – which refers to circumstances which are, from a textual point of view, arbitrary – can guarantee the presence of a dialectical 'duplicity' in the authorship. However, it is not only 'oh, how strange!' that Kierkegaard imposed monastic restrictions on himself while preparing 'The Seducer's Diary' – it is also very interesting. Now a veil is lifted, just like in nineteenth-century confessions, revealing a hitherto hidden connection between the religious writings and the unedifying diary which endows Kierkegaard, seductively, with an interest of another order. And to maintain the religious character of the confession, Kierkegaard quickly adds the following penitent note: 'The book was a huge success – especially (oh, how strange!) "The Seducer's Diary". The world gave an extraordinary welcome to its admired author, who was not, however, "seduced" or transformed by all this – he was an eternity too old for that.'[28]

It is possible that Kierkegaard did not allow himself to be seduced, but it is certain that he was not transformed, for he was still a seducer. The unreflective innocence that the seducer presupposed in Cordelia is alarmingly similar to the uncritical seriousness that Kierkegaard presupposes in his reader. Step by step he renounces his epistemological pretentions and can therefore only imploringly declare that 'the true explanation is to be found by those who seek honestly',[29] by which the hermeneutic conditions have been exchanged for moral ones, and the reader called to account for his qualifications in that respect. It is therefore, as so often with Kierkegaard, the presupposed 'seriousness' of the presupposed reader that is to supply the presentation with its documentary validity, which means that the reader's 'seriousness' becomes

identical to a tacit approval of the fiction. It therefore follows quite
naturally that the confidence placed in the reader's perfectibility is significant and at times extremely demanding, as for example when
Kierkegaard puts himself in the reader's place and from there is able
to understand, without difficulty, the ambiguous situation that he himself had declared, shortly before, to be incomprehensible: 'Here the
reader can easily see the explanation of the duplicity of the entire
authorship, only that this was also incorporated in the consciousness of
the author.'[30]

If no 'seriousness' is to be found in the reader, then that which is
sought will not be found in the text, and the text must bring about that
true 'seriousness' in its reader. This often occurs in a series of rhetorical
fits and starts, for example when the aesthetic binds itself as intimately as
possible to the religious:

> As soon as the required seriousness takes hold, it can also release it [that
> is, 'the dialectical doubleness'], although always in such a way that the
> seriousness itself guarantees correctness: for just as a woman's coyness
> relates itself to the true lover, and then, but only then, surrenders itself, so
> in the same way a dialectical doubleness relates itself to true seriousness.
> The explanation therefore cannot be communicated to someone less seri-
> ous, for the elasticity of the dialectical doubleness is too great for him to
> master; it takes the explanation away from him again, and makes him
> doubtful about whether it really is the explanation.[31]

When a text lets a coy woman surrender to the true lover in order to
bring about the required 'seriousness' in its reader, that text not only
presupposes what it wants to bring about, but also risks losing any
'seriousness' there *could* be in the reader. What the woman loses, despite
her coyness, the reader loses through the text. And a reader's innocence
is no easier to restore that a woman's.

Documenta(fic)tion

Kierkegaard not only writes his own script in the writings, but he also
produces himself – (stage-)produces himself – in relation to that production, by which *The Point of View* becomes a fictive documentation, a
documenta(fic)tion. Kierkegaard presents his strutting involvement with
the writings in the second chapter of the piece under the title 'The
Difference in my Personal Mode of Existence Corresponding to the
Essential Difference in the Works'.[32] The chapter is divided into two
separate sections, explaining the techniques he employed as existential
support first for the aesthetic and then for the religious production. This

division obviously complicates the earlier claim about the simultaneous 'duplicity' of the authorship, but it also reveals some of the subtle (self-)deceptions at work in the author's presentation of his own work (as an author). Thus, during his account of his 'existence' in relation to the aesthetic production, Kierkegaard emphasizes that inverse deception has been the 'tactic' determining his maieutic activity: 'seldom has any author used so much cunning, intrigue, and ingenuity in order to win honour and respect in the world, to deceive it inversely as I have – to deceive it in the sense of truth.' For there is, Kierkegaard announces, a difference between deceiving someone out of the truth and deceiving someone *into* the truth, and one should therefore not let oneself 'be deceived by the word "deception".'[33] In short, the device is the complex performative: 'I deceive: believe me!'

As an individual example of this deception as a *fait accompli* – the correctness of which his friend Giødwad, incidentally, would be able to confirm – Kierkegaard cites how he was so busy during the proof-reading of *Either/Or* that he had no time for his daily posing as an 'Idler'. He would therefore rush to the theatre, after finishing his work, where he 'literally stayed only five or ten minutes', which was sufficient, however, to maintain 'the opinion: that he does nothing at all, he is a pure loafer.'[34] By providing the reader with such an insight into the intricate machinery of the deception, Kierkegaard involuntarily exposes himself to the suspicion that the virtuoso of deception is still master of his art and is now demonstrating his proficiency. And of course Kierkegaard defends himself against the obvious accusation that he lacks 'seriousness'. That is not at all the case, one understands:

> Melancholic, incurably melancholic as I was, with immense inner suffering, after having broken, in despair, with the world and all things worldly, brought up strictly from childhood in the understanding that truth must suffer, be insulted, be mocked, spending a certain part of every day in prayer and edifying meditations, myself personally a penitent. Because I was then who I was; yes, I do not deny it – I found a certain satisfaction in that life, in that inverse deception. . . .[35]

Here, as so often, the reader is tempted to ask whether Kierkegaard is writing in good faith, or whether he is the rather impious (stage-)producer of a pious deception. How can the reader know whether Kierkegaard, with his revelation of having spent 'a certain part of every day' in prayer and meditation, is not merely repeating the self-staged act he enacted – only a few pages earlier – by appearing for 'five or ten minutes' at the theatre? The two revelations stand side by side, the latter supporting the former, but what guarantees that this causality is not also an 'inverse deception', or that the 'inverse deception' which has brought Kierkegaard so much satisfaction is not inversely finding its own satisfaction in deceiving Kierkegaard?[36]

Just how much conscious intent there was in the poet's mind cannot be definitely determined, but one can confirm that there is *also* an element of retrospective reconstruction by looking at the second part of the chapter, in which Kierkegaard describes the correspondence between his own existential acting and the religious production which – as we have seen – is introduced on the second page of the *Postscript*. Kierkegaard repeats this information and mentions that he delivered the manuscript to Luno's printing-house in December 1845, but in the same breath he adds: 'the suspicious need not take my word for it, as it can be proved by Luno's journal'.[37] Why this sudden gesture? Because Kierkegaard, by appealing to the existence of 'Luno's journal', can divert the reader's attention from the fictional aspect in the construction of the correspondence between the authorship and his personal, existential acting. The reference to Luno, like the earlier reference to Giødwad, should endow the presentation with a documentary validity, which with regard to the *Postscript* is especially necessary since Kierkegaard had, as the title more than implies, actually considered concluding his authorship with this work. After that he wanted to establish himself as a minister.[38] Nevertheless, he *also* undertook the following on account of the publication of the *Postscript*:

> I immediately realized that my personal existence in relation to this had to be transformed, or that I must strive to provide those around me with another impression of my personal existence. I myself already had in view what must be done, when in a highly convenient way a little circumstance, in which I saw a sign from Divine Guidance, came to help me to act decisively in that direction.[39]

The circumstance which so very conveniently presented itself is the appearance of the *Corsair*[40] and its corrupting influence on the population of Copenhagen, which like 'a monstrous public, arm in arm, *in bona caritate*, [had] become as ironic as the devil'. The ironic craze of his contemporaries places Kierkegaard in the uncomfortable situation that he himself cannot make use of irony – as this would simply be taken as a 'newly invented extremely piquant form of irony' – and he must therefore, on the contrary, make himself 'the object of everybody's irony'.[41] The organization of the course of events is carried through here so thoroughly that the fiction becomes evident despite the intention, an impression strengthened when Kierkegaard establishes himself as the sovereign director of the play:

I had now calculated that dialectically the circumstances were appropriate for recovering the use of indirect communication. While I occupied myself with religious productions alone, I ventured to rely on the negative support of these daily showers from the rabble, which would be sufficiently cooling to ensure that the religious communication did not become too direct, or too directly supply me with supporters. And even those whom this would not deter would be frustrated by the fact that I had voluntarily exposed myself to all this, rushed into it, a kind of madness. . . . Ah yes, and yet again, ah yes, for this was dialectically exactly Christian self-denial. . . .[42]

There is no denial of self-assertion in Kierkegaard's Christian self-denial, which can confusingly resemble an aesthetic self-production which the many metaphors of disguise – 'costume', 'finery', 'clothing'[43] – among other things, contribute to. That such an arrangement is mainly a textual (stage-)production, the value of which should be endorsed and redeemed by the reader, is obvious and appears, for example, in the following erotic appeal:

When some day my lover comes, he will easily see that when I was regarded as an ironist, the irony lay by no means where the highly hon-oured public thought it was. . . . He will see that the irony lay precisely in the fact that in the aesthetic author, under this semblance or *Erscheinung* of worldliness, the religious author concealed himself. . . . My lover will see how it fitted to the letter, how my existence-relation transformed itself in precise correspondence with the change in the production.[44]

Who is Kierkegaard's lover? It is the reader who reads the fiction as non-fiction and who cannot see that Kierkegaard is not reproducing his own actions, but reproduces it exactly as a textual action which simulates itself as fact. What Victor Eremita says about textuality in 'The Seducer's Diary' can therefore be applied to *The Point of View* as a text: 'His diary is . . . not historically accurate or a simple narrative; it is not indicative, but subjunctive.'[45]
Only in this way, then, can everything fit to the letter.[46]

The Point of View as Bio-graphy

Through its construction of events the text produces a narrative about its narrator, a bio-graphy, in which the empirical self – rather ambiguously – is written off by the textual self. The desire to construct the text narratively or 'subjunctively' implies a destruction of the empirical or 'indicative' self, through which the bio-graphy takes on, in a double sense, the character of a deconstruction of the self. It is this bio-graphical condition that makes it impossible to give any final answer to the question of where Kierkegaard deceives with his text and where the text deceives Kierkegaard.

The relation between an indicative and a subjunctive self shows itself as a relation between the disclosure of the self and its concealment. Here one could refer to the function assigned to Regine in the confessional narrative, which is displayed in the last section of *The Point of View*. Kierkegaard refers to the event as a 'fact', the complex nature of which made him into a poet, but at the same time he emphasizes that 'that fact' was not of a religious nature. This serves to keep the story of the engagement within a purely aesthetic parenthesis, for only in this way can he insulate the broken engagement from an ethical evaluation of the relationship, which would involve events beyond the textual control of *The Point of View* and thereby threaten the religious teleology. The relationship with Regine, consistently and dispassionately called 'that fact', is concealed under other words to enable Kierkegaard to regain the moral self-justification that he lost through the disclosure.[47]

He stages this concealment, however, in a strategic dissimulation which is supposed to arouse the reader's curiosity in a kind of literary foreplay.[48] It is the law of raising the interesting to a higher power which is at work here, and it is also precisely that power – or rather, its loss – which is the theme of *The Point of View*'s dialogical 'Epilogue', where someone (an aesthete?) indignantly asks,

> But what have you done here now? I hear someone say, 'Do you not see what this information and proclamation have lost you in the eyes of the world?' Yes of course, I can see it all too well; through this I lose that which, from a Christian point of view, must be considered a loss to possess. . . . I lose the interesting, I lose being a riddle. . . . I lose the interesting, in place of which is substituted the no less interesting, the *direct communication* that the problem was and is: becoming a Christian.[49]

This is not really a particularly interesting communication, especially as it had already been expressed in the 'Introduction'. It is, rather, a deactivation of the maieutic function that claims to be the *raison d'être* of the aesthetic writings. And – as Kierkegaard was later to acknowledge – 'when something is to appear captivating, then it is certainly wrong to explain every trick. A fisherman would certainly not say to the fish about the bait: this is the bait.'[50] The interest Kierkegaard lost through his disclosure, however, he regains – only a few pages later – in the form of a concealment of his disclosure. First one reads: 'Now if, therefore, the sympathetic reader has read this small work with attention, then he will know what I am as an author.' But no sooner is this line read through to its end than a footnote sends the attentive and sympathetic reader down to another text set in small print. And here one reads: 'Of course, that I myself possess a purely personal, closer interpretation of my personal situation is something which is perfectly in order.'[51] So then. The most personal of the personal remains hidden, and perhaps it is hidden just here because the disclosure of the authorship as religious in itself was a loss of the interesting, which the person behind the work must compensate for by concealing himself and thus re-establishing the interesting.

It is entirely symptomatic of disclosure *qua* concealment that in his 'Conclusion' Kierkegaard gives the pen to 'an other, my poet', who concludes the bio-graphy, and thereby gives fiction the last word. Only in the fiction, the textual production of the self, can the Kierkegaard who is – as he frankly admits – before and after the writing 'an absence',[52] become present. But only present, of course, as a writer. As soon as he reads his bio-graphy, Kierkegaard becomes 'an absence' again.

Divine Guidance as the Pro-gramme of the Writing

As the hermeneutic manifesto of the authorship, *The Point of View* is programmatic; it wants to present the reader with the pre-scription [*for-skrift*] for a *correct* reading. But *The Point of View* is programmatic in another sense too, because it portrays the writing as a copy of a pre-existing text. And pro-gram here means pre-text [*før-skrift*]. Thus Kierkegaard maintains that there has been 'not even the slightest delay in the production; what was needed has always been to hand at precisely the moment it was needed. In one sense, the whole production has always had an uninterrupted smoothness, as if I had spent every day copying out a particular part of a printed book.' We should understand that Kierkegaard's work was not done for pleasure; it was, as he tells us, a 'simple work of duty', in relation to which he has 'lived like a scrivener at his desk'.[53]

This scrivener's desk is a metaphor for non-pleasure, for duty and punctuality; it ensures that the writing will be seen as the result not of aesthetic enthusiasm, but of an ethical command. Although Kierkegaard did not say what book it was that he copied out so diligently, it is fairly obvious that he was doing more than simply copying. But what? And to whose writing does Kierkegaard's relate as a copy?

These questions are answered with great originality in the third chapter of the work, under the title 'The Part of Divine Guidance in my Authorship'. He first confesses, to be sure, that he finds it 'rather embarrassing' to have to talk about himself, but that the embarrassment has been overcome is apparent in the following, which can very rightly be called Kierkegaard's confessional writing:

What hasn't this pen managed to expound, what boldness, enthusiasm, passion almost verging on madness is concerned! And now that I am to talk about my relationship to God; about what is repeated daily in my prayers, which give thanks for the indescribable things he has done for me, so infinitely much more than I ever had expected . . . now that I must talk about it, a poet's impatience awakens in my soul. I would, more decisively than that king who cried 'my kingdom for a horse', and blissfully decisive as he was not, I would give everything, including my life, to find 'the expression' – that which is more blissful for thought to find than when the lover finds the beloved – and then to die with that expression on my lips. And look, they present themselves, thoughts as enchanting as the fruits in a fairy-tale garden, so rich, warm, intense, the expressions, so soothing of the craving for gratitude in me, so cooling of the fervent longing – it seems to me as if I had a winged pen, yet even if I had ten pens I would not be able to follow fast enough the riches which present themselves. But as soon as I take my pen in hand, I cannot . . . move it. In this state not a line appears on the paper concerning the relationship. It is as if I heard a voice saying to me: stupid man, who does he think he is? Does he not know that obedience is dearer to God than the fat of the ram? Do the whole thing as a work of duty. Then I become quite calm. Then there is time to write every letter with my slower pen, almost painstakingly. And if that passion of a poet awakens in me again for a moment, then it is as if I heard a voice speaking to me as a teacher does to a boy when he says: Now, hold the pen properly and write each letter with equal precision. And then I can do it, almost ignorant of what the next word or line will be. And when I read it through afterwards it satisfies me in a completely different way. For though it may be that one or other glowing expression escaped me, the production is something else – the outcome not of the poet's or the thinker's passion, but of piety's, and for me it is a worship of God.[54]

The writing itself exhibits the point it wants to demonstrate. It seeks 'the expression' which in its profound singularity must be protected with quotation marks, but finds instead several 'expression*s*', and this – in a wild eruption of metaphoricity – makes Kierkegaard's confessional writing into an aesthetic writing about the religious. The text swarms with suspended allegorization, as if it really were the writing of a 'winged pen', perhaps of ten pens, which followed the 'passion of a poet' in their flight. And yet this is not quite the case. No less than twice the text gives voice to a 'voice' that rebukes Kierkegaard and orders him to hold on to the capricious pen 'properly', like a good pupil, and write each word with 'precision', which he then obediently does with a so-called 'slower pen'.

In this sudden change from monological to dialogical discourse, 'the voice' functions as a linguistic or grammatological authority, a *transcendental signified*: 'the voice' determines Kierkegaard's writing, just as 'Divine Guidance' directs it. And it is only by (re-)reading and

(re-)writing his texts from this perspective that Kierkegaard can characterize 'the aesthetic production' as 'a necessary discharge' and then in a
dialogical fragment recount how 'the religious put up with this discharge,
but urged incessantly as if to say: Won't you soon be finished with that?'
The text is silent about how and when Kierkegaard responded, but the
request was apparently repeated, and then Kierkegaard finally decided
'to satisfy the religious by becoming a religious author'.[55]

So in the middle of this metaphor, which connects aesthetic discharge
with religious satisfaction, God appears partly – in terms of text theory –
as the super-metaphor of the writing, which is to provide the writing with
consistency and evenness, and partly – in terms of instinct psychology –
as the super-ego that masters desire. Kierkegaard's confessional writing
is therefore handing it on a plate to every Freudian gourmet, and he
practically puts the words into the Freudian's mouth when he describes
his 'relationship to God' as the only happy 'love story'[56] in his unhappy
life. That he ends up aestheticizing his relationship to God in his attempt
to distinguish the religious from the aesthetic is no less paradoxical than
the fact that in order to erase all the distinctive signs of the artistic
experience, he makes God into the 'Muse' that he invokes 'every day to
defend myself from the wealth of thoughts. . . . I could sit down and
write uninterrupted day and night and yet another day and night, for
there is wealth enough. If I did it, I would burst. Oh, just the smallest
dietary carelessness and I am in mortal danger'.[57] Marvellous stamina in
1001 nights with writing. Anyone can see how the erotic desire for
Regine has here been sublimated and displaced onto God, who as a
(second) father watches over the son's uncontrollable desire for 'discharge' and therefore must time and again ask the wayward pen to
behave 'properly'.

But let us now leave Freud in peace. For the decisive point here is not
to explain 'the work' in terms of 'the author' but, on the contrary, to
explain 'the author' in terms of 'the work'; that is, to notice how the text
has guided its writer.

Auto-graphy

If it was fear of inconsistency that endowed Kierkegaard's account with
fictionality, and thereby revealed the factual as inconsistent, then, corre-
spondingly, the retrospective activity of (self-)interpretation seems to
force Kierkegaard into constant revision of *The Point of View*, which
therefore threatens to dissolve into a plurality of points of view. That
which is to be explained will not add up in the explanation without
remainder. The accuracy, 'the expression', will not present itself, and

this is not because it has not been sought, but because it has been sought too often. We recall that in Climacus's 'ironic observation' it was, among other things, 'the Honourable Gentleman's' desire to explain himself further, to define his 'opinion' or 'meaning' and 'vary his expressions', that provoked the ironist's laughter. And now Kierkegaard writes: 'Yet in a still more accurate sense I must enter into the account the part of Divine Guidance in the authorship. If I were to go and say that I had from the very first moment foreseen the whole dialectical construction of the authorship . . . this would be a dishonesty to God.' And, one could perhaps add, to the reader as well. Kierkegaard continues: 'No, I must truthfully say: I cannot understand the whole, precisely because I can understand the whole down to the smallest detail; but what I cannot understand is that I can understand it now, and yet can by no means dare to say that I understood it as accurately at the moment of beginning – and yet I am the one who has carried it out and taken every step with reflection.'[58]

If, at first glance, the idea of 'the Part of Divine Guidance in the Authorship' resembles rampant megalomania, then it seems here to be no less a declaration of limited independence. One understands that Kierkegaard considers himself the 'reader' of the authorship, rather than its author. Kierkegaard has not been directing the writing; on the contrary, the writing has been directing Kierkegaard – a direction that Kierkegaard interprets religiously as 'Divine Guidance'. It is, he explains,

> as categorically definite as possible. . . . Divine Guidance has educated me, and the education is reflected in the process of the production. In certain respects what has been set out in the foregoing is not quite true – that the whole of the aesthetic production is a deception; because this expression concedes too much to consciousness. However, it is not quite untrue either, for I have from the very beginning been conscious during my education.[59]

The dialectic between conscious and non-conscious text production is propelled by a compositional/confessional crisis in the writing. On the one hand, Kierkegaard has enthusiastically related how, in an 'almost possessed exuberance',[60] he managed to execute the complex tactic of the deception and thus allowed the aesthetic to function as an alluring mirror that would capture and hold the attention of his contemporaries. On the other hand, and later in the composition, 'Divine Guidance' is established as the highest authority of the production, and with that arises the crisis which stands out in the intentional dialectic between the conscious and the non-conscious and in the ethical dialectic between 'not quite true' and yet 'not quite untrue either'.

This double dialectic reveals the presence of two points of view in *The Point of View*, and if one casts a sidelong glance at the passage in the *Journals* where Kierkegaard comments on *The Point of View*, one can see that it is the conflict between the equality of these two points of view, and their mutual incompatibility, that made him hold the work back for posthumous publication. But writers always write *in* a language and *in* a logic, whose total system they cannot master in their own discourse. This may lead them to conceive the directing logic of this system as 'an inexplicable something, that indicates that I have been helped by another, as if I have come to perform and say something whose full significance I myself do not understand until afterwards.'[61] But Kierkegaard himself cannot understand precisely where this surplus comes from, not even 'afterwards'. It remains 'an inexplicable something', and for this same reason it must be understood as 'Divine Guidance'.

In both cases, however, the point is the same: to write is also to be written, and a writer who writes him or herself into a text, writes off the empirical 'I'. A textual 'I' is produced in and with this 'production', and Kierkegaard can therefore confess that he 'for a long time [has not] done anything except dialectical exercises with an admixture of imagination, experimenting with my spirit as one tunes an instrument: but *I* did not really live.'[62] When the subject, the 'I', lives off his writing in this specific sense, one can well understand why for Kierkegaard 'this solemn determination to put down a period [full-stop] is an extremely dangerous thing. . . .'[63]

That the textual 'I' is not identical with the 'I' who re-reads what has been written appears more or less explicitly from a journal entry where Kierkegaard (after writing 'NB' three times) records his impression of what he has just read by the writer Kierkegaard, who was writing about the author of the same name:

'The Point of View for my Work as an Author' must not be published, no, no!

(1) And this is the deciding factor (never mind all those ideas I had about endangering my future and my bread and butter): I cannot tell the full truth about myself. Even in the very first manuscript (which I wrote without any thought at all of publishing) I was unable to stress the primary factor: that I am a penitent, and that this explains me at the deepest level. But when I took the manuscript out with the thought of publishing it, I was obliged to make a few small changes, for in spite of everything it was cast too intensely to be published. . . .

(2) I cannot quite say that my work as an author is a sacrifice. It is true I have been unspeakably unhappy ever since I was a child, but I nevertheless acknowledge that the solution God found of letting me become an

author has been a rich, rich pleasure to me. I may be sacrificed, but my authorship is not a sacrifice; it is, in fact, what I unconditionally prefer to keep on being.

Thus I cannot tell the full truth here, either, for I cannot speak this way in print about my torment and wretchedness – when the pleasure is really predominant.[64]

The situation is wholly characteristic of the relationship between the writing and the reading of the written, and it shows how the textual 'I' has deconstructed the empirical 'I', which has become so foreign to itself that Kierkegaard cannot recognize himself. The hesitation in the textual monologue reveals the astonishment caused by the revision: Kierkegaard has brought to light the first draft, re-read it, and realized that 'the primary factor', namely the penitence, has been insufficiently described. He has then made minor interventions and corrections which, however, do not strengthen but, on the contrary, weaken 'the primary factor'. And why this weakening of something that is already too weak? Because the private, penitential motive for the text production does not converge with the text production itself, which has not been 'sacrifice' but, on the contrary, a 'rich, rich pleasure'. When the inner 'torment and wretchedness' are exposed 'in print', then the penitence of the penitent becomes interesting, which means that the religious is once again displaced by the aesthetic.

It is from this double point of view that Kierkegaard himself considers *The Point of View*: 'The book itself is true and in my opinion masterly', Kierkegaard writes in a self-confident journal entry in which he clearly has one eye on the religious and the other on the aesthetic. Without batting an eyelid, he continues: 'If my sin and guilt, my intrinsic misery, the fact that I am a penitent are stressed a bit more pointedly, then it will be a true picture.'[65] As a casual compositional sketch the journal entry shows how the confessional value of the writing rests on aesthetic premises. It is noted, almost technically, that something should be added concerning existential misery. But of course the question is how much can be added in that respect without also losing the documentary validity. In other words: If the book is to be 'true' then the documentary must be accompanied by a series of private declarations, but these would threaten to give the book the piquant character of confessional writing, making it an object of the insensitive gaze of an inquisitive public who will see the sensational in the confessional. The documentary validity is not only dependent on rhetorical efficiency, therefore, but also threatened by it. In short: 'All this about my person as author cannot be used at all, for it is clear that it will only involve me more in the interesting instead of getting me out of it, and this is also the effect it will have on my contemporaries.'[66]

Authenticity and Fictionality

This uncontrollable exchange between the penitent Kierkegaard and the interesting Kierkegaard corresponds to the text's transformation of the empirical Kierkegaard into the textual Kierkegaard. The latter seems 'literally' to marginalize the former, who as a *reader* is dissatisfied to see 'the primary factor' get lost in the text. And one such marginalization can be read – epigrammatically, so to speak – in a marginal note on a scrap of paper. Down one edge of the scrap, under the heading 'On the completed production and myself', is written 'The difficulty in publishing anything about the authorship is and remains that without my knowing it or knowing it positively, I really have been used, and now for the first time I understand and comprehend the whole – but then I cannot, after all, say: *I.*'[67]

Kierkegaard has been used or directed by the text to the extent of being written into the process of the production, such that when he turns and glances back he cannot say: 'I'. Despite this, or because of it, the marginal note continues: 'At most I can say . . . this is how I now understand the productivity of the past.'[68] But if this really is the 'most' Kierkegaard can say about his relationship to the completed production, then he has assigned himself the role of a 'third party' – and thereby written himself into a rather special dilemma. If he installs himself, that is to say, in the position of 'a third party', then his statements about the authorship acquire a fairly reassuring objectivity, but at the same time he must renounce his normal and obvious right to determine the total significance of the authorship, and hence *The Point of View* loses its singular status and becomes one among many – debatable – points of view. If, on the other hand, he insists on being the best qualified interpreter of the authorship, and justifies this by reference to the indisputable fact that he is, after all, the author, then he must relinquish his (self-)constructed grasp of 'The Part of Divine Guidance' in the production. In short: only by turning himself into a fictive 'third party' can Kierkegaard relate himself interpretatively to an authorship in relation to which he, as the factual 'first person', cannot say 'I'.

Almost paradoxically, but yet with an inner logic which more than suggests that the absence of authenticity and authority finds its compensatory expression in the fiction, Kierkegaard – who otherwise fervently vows that he will not risk a 'bewildering poetic confusion'[69] – considers publishing *The Point of View* under the pseudonym Johannes de Silentio! He soon realizes, however, that then 'it is no longer the same book at all. For the point of it was my personal story.'[70] The point is therefore the problem that the closer Kierkegaard gets to himself, the less self he is able to see. It is, as a consequence, not despite but by virtue of this crisis in the personal 'point' that the idea of a pseudonymous publication presents itself once more. Indeed Kierkegaard composed a 'Foreword' to *The Point of View* supposedly written by a certain 'A-O', which concluded with, among other things, the following:

> I have now ventured to make this poetic experiment. The author himself speaks in the first person; but one will, I hope, remember that this author is not Magister K but my poetic creation. – I must apologise to Mr Magister K that I have ventured, right under his nose, so to speak, to understand him poetically or to poeticise him in this way. However, not more than . . . this apology. For I have, poetically, completely emancipated myself from him. Yes, even if he were to declare that my understanding was factually untrue in some particular, it certainly would not follow that it was poetically untrue. For the conclusion could also be turned around: ergo Magister K has not corresponded to or realised what would have been the poetically correct.[71]

The attempt to organize epistemological material and mount an effective strategy of argument is here superseded by a rhetorical game which is certainly dialectical but at the same time destructive, because with its mischievous double use of factual untruth and poetic truth it removes every trait that distinguishes 'A-O' from Magister K. Transparency has had to give way to opacity, authenticity to fictionality, subject to writing. The inverse logic makes it clear that if the fictive figure has completely emancipated itself from Kierkegaard, nevertheless a corresponding emancipation has not been completely carried through by the Kierkegaard who – as we have seen – had to conclude *The Point of View* by turning its 'Conclusion' around and then 'letting another speak, my poet'.[72]

The authoritative codification of 'the totality of the authorship' cannot, then, be realized in a unified fashion *in propria persona*, but must be dispersed into a series of fictive techniques, which is why the work that should have been 'A Direct Communication' and 'Report to History' – as is so boldly announced in the subtitle – has become anything but direct and seems most of all to report on a plurality of points of view: the eyes of Argus.

And at this point we can let our ironist burst into some perhaps well-deserved laughter, for it has now become clear that 'the man was never clear about it himself', and it was precisely such a diagnosis that 'the ironist' found so amusing. The 'serious reader' might perhaps have more difficulty finding an appropriate grimace, and therefore ought to (re-)read the passage which Climacus, prompted by the author, wrote in his *Postscript*, for it is a weighty passage. It takes the reader's part against the author – 'as if an author were, in a purely legal sense, the best interpreter of his own words, as if it helps a reader that an author "wanted this and that" when it was not realised, because the author himself said so in the preface'.[73]

Presumably it hardly improves matters when an author first says what he has wanted in 'the Epilogue', and Climacus's comment can therefore be an appropriate 'Preface' to a further reading of Kierkegaard. New readers start here.

NOTES

1   Søren Kierkegaard, *The Point of View for my Work as an Author: A Report to History*, translated by Walter Lowrie and edited by Benjamin Nelson (Harper and Row, New York, 1962), pp. 73–4.

2   *The Point of View*, pp. 66n., 95, 87. [The Danish word *Styrelse* has been translated here as 'Divine Guidance', although this deviates from common practice and is the subject of some debate. See, for example, Walter Lowrie's note: 'I translate the word *Styrelse* by 'Governance', hoping that this word may distinguish the providence which *rules* from the providence which *provides* (which in Danish is denominated by a different word), and that it may direct attention to the fact that S.K. has in mind a divinity which shapes our ends from *without*, by the providential ordering of events, not by a mystical 'guidance' from *within*. I persist, with some diffidence, in using this word, in spite of the fact that at least one of the translators with whom I should like to be in agreement is unwilling to adopt it.' (*The Point of View*, p. 64n.)]

3   Søren Kierkegaard, *Concluding Unscientific Postscript*, translated by Howard V. Hong and Edna H. Hong (Princeton University Press, Princeton, 1992), pp. 614–15.

4   *The Point of View*, pp. 5–6.

5   *Concluding Unscientific Postscript*, pp. 625–30.

6   Ibid., pp. 625–6.

7   Ibid., p. 627.

8   *The Point of View*, pp. 142–3.

9   Cf. *The Point of View*, pp. 153–8.

10 Cf. *The Point of View*, pp. 38–9.

11 *The Point of View*, p. 13.

12 Kierkegaard notes: 'The *Literary Review* of the "two ages" is no objection against this – partly because it is not aesthetic in the sense of a poet-production but critical, and partly because it has a whole religious background in its understanding of the present' (*The Point of View*, p. 13n.). After this explanation one must surely ask why Kierkegaard includes the review in the so-called 'aesthetic production' when it is so obviously anything but aesthetic.

13 *The Point of View*, p. 10n.

14 Cf. *Concluding Unscientific Postscript*, p. 625.
15 *The Point of View*, pp. 144–7.
16 In connection with 'the Accounting', Kierkegaard thought of marking the difference between the aesthetic and the religious purely typographically: 'It will therefore be printed with different typefaces on half Pagina, in order to indicate that it is God's cause' (*Søren Kierkegaards Papirer*, second edition (Gyldendal, Copenhagen, 1909–48), X 2 A 377). Unfortunately, he later abandoned this help to the reader.
17 *The Point of View*, p. 33. Cf. p. 39.
18 Ibid., p. 40.
19 Ibid., pp. 90, 96.
20 Ibid., pp. 29, 26, 90–91.
21 Ibid., pp. 100, 107, 136, 137, 138, 38.
22 Ibid., p. 17. The attentive reader familiar with the theory of the stages as key to the interpretation of the authorship cannot fail to note that there is no attempt to effect an *ethical* reading. Either aesthetic or religious: *tertium non datur* [no third alternative].
23 *The Point of View*, pp. 10–11.
24 Ibid., p. 15.
25 Ibid., p. 15.
26 Ibid., p. 15.
27 Ibid., pp. 18–19.
28 Ibid., p. 19.
29 Ibid., p. 16.
30 Ibid., p. 84.
31 Ibid., p. 17.
32 Ibid., p. 44.
33 Ibid., pp. 49, 39.
34 Ibid., pp. 49–50. [Garff's comment about Giødwad refers to Kierkegaard's rather offhand remark that this strategy was 'known to my friend Giødwad, the proof-reader of *Either/Or*'.]
35 *The Point of View*, p. 52.
36 Kierkegaard confesses that his strategy of deception was so successful that it could have become 'a dangerous temptation'. The danger was not that he would seek 'flattery, admiration, etc.', but rather that he would revel in the 'satisfaction' of accomplishing the perfect deception (*The Point of View*, p. 52.). The very choice of words suggests seduction, and may remind the reader of the following in 'The Immediate Erotic Stages': 'That which will occupy us here . . . is the art, the thoroughness, the profound subtlety with which he seduces. . . . The musical *Don Juan* enjoys the satisfaction, the reflective *Don Juan* enjoys the deception, enjoys the stratagem. The immediate enjoyment is over, and it is more reflection on the enjoyment that is enjoyed' (*Either/Or*, translated by Howard V. Hong and Edna H. Hong (2 vols, Princeton University Press, Princeton, 1987), vol. 1, p. 108).
37 *The Point of View*, p. 53. If we are going to doubt Kierkegaard's word, we can consult that Journal entry in which he informs us that 'The entire

manuscript, lock, stock, and barrel, was delivered to the printer *medio* December, or thereabouts, 1845 – "A First and Last Explanation" was dashed off on a piece of paper in the original manuscript, but was laid aside to be worked out in detail and was delivered as late as possible lest it lie around and get lost in a print shop' (VII 1 A 2; *Søren Kierkegaard's Journals and Papers*, translated by Howard V. Hong and Edna H. Hong (7 vols, Indiana University Press, Bloomington, 1978), 5871, vol. 5, p. 309).

38   Cf. *The Point of View*, p. 86.

39   *The Point of View*, p. 53.

40   [The *Corsair* was a satirical journal which singled out Kierkegaard for savage and relentless mockery throughout 1846. Walter Lowrie provides a full account of the affair in his *A Short Life of Kierkegaard* (Princeton University Press, Princeton, 1942).]

41   *The Point of View*, pp. 55, 57.

42   Ibid., p. 58.

43   Ibid., pp. 59f.

44   Ibid., pp. 62–3.

45   *Either/Or*, vol. 1, p. 304.

46   Kierkegaard liked to quote Lichtenberg: 'Such works are mirrors: if an ape peers in, no apostle can see out' [see, for example, *Concluding Unscientific Postscript*, pp. 285–6n]. And when one considers the development of critical judgement that *The Point of View* has undergone over the years, the apostle seems to have yielded more and more to the ape. The apostle Geismar writes that *The Point of View* is a 'singularly reliable document . . . an objective, reliable account' (*Søren Kierkegaard* (Gad, Copenhagen, 1926), vol. 3, p. 74). Rubow believes that Kierkegaard has 'mythologised' (*Kierkegaard og hans Samtidige* [*Kierkegaard and his Contemporaries*] (Gyldendal, Copenhagen, 1950), p. 46). Aage Henriksen maintains: 'We cannot simply adopt Søren Kierkegaard's view of Søren Kierkegaard's production' (*Methods and Results of Kierkegaard Studies in Scandinavia* (Munksgaard, Copenhagen, 1951), p. 10). Bejerholm describes *The Point of View* as '*ex poste* construction' and as 'polemical self-interpretation', but nevertheless believes that one ought to try 'to unify statements of different logical type' (*Meddelelsens Dialektik* [*The Dialectic of Communication*] (Ohlssons, Lund, 1962), pp. 270, 273, 277). With Bertel Pedersen the ape begins to become visible: 'a more careful reading of this text will reveal its dominant theme as another fiction. . . . The text exhibits all the familiar literary entrapments of a confession and the fictions of an autograph. . . . Thus we see in POV [*The Point of View*] a curious combination of truly penetrating insights and a pathetic blindness' (*MLM Comparative Literature*, vol. 89, no. 6, 1974, pp. 950, 955). Henning Fenger, source criticism's answer to Sherlock Holmes, endorses this point of view: 'The book contained many concrete inaccuracies, but is especially curious in its blending of the will to honesty and naïve self-suggestion' (*Kierkegaard-myter og Kierkegaard-kilder* [*Kierkegaard Myths and Kierkegaard Sources*] (Odense Universitetsforlag, Odense, 1976), p. 32).

The apes have seen what the apostles have been unable to see: *The Point of View* is, as an interpretation of texts, itself a text that can be interpreted.

47   Cf. Christopher Norris, 'Fictions of Authority: Narrative and Viewpoint in Kierkegaard's writing', in *The Deconstructive Turn: Essays in the Rhetoric of Philosophy* (Methuen, London and New York, 1984), pp. 93f.

48   What Paul de Man wrote about Rousseau could therefore refer here to Kierkegaard: 'The more there is to expose, the more there is to be ashamed of; the more resistance to exposure, the more satisfying the scene, and, especially, the more satisfying and eloquent the belated revelation, in the later narrative, of the inability to reveal' (*Allegories of Reading* (Yale University Press, New Haven and London, 1979), p. 285).

49   *The Point of View*, p. 93.

50   *Papirer*, X 1 A 117.

51   *The Point of View*, p. 98.

52   Ibid., pp. 100, 99.

53   Ibid., pp. 72, 69.

54   Ibid., pp. 66–8.

55   Ibid., pp. 73, 84, 86.

56   Ibid., p. 64.

57   Ibid., p. 68.

58   Ibid., p. 72.

59   Ibid., p. 73.

60   Ibid., p. 52.

61   *Papirer*, X 5 B 168.

62   *The Point of View*, p. 80.

63   X 1 A 510; *Journals and Papers*, 6431, vol. 6, p. 173. Elizabeth Sewell formulates the dialectic in the briefest form imaginable: 'To make any work of art is to make, or rather to unmake and remake one's self', quoted in Wayne C. Booth, *The Rhetoric of Fiction*, second edition (University of Chicago Press, Chicago, 1983), p. 71 n.7. Cf. J. Hillis Miller, *Fiction and Repetition* (Harvard University Press, Cambridge, 1982), pp. 11f.

64   X 1 A 78; *Journals and Papers*, 6327, vol. 6, p. 108.

65   X 1 A 78; *Journals and Papers*, 6327, vol. 6, p. 109.

66   X 1 A 510; *Journals and Papers*, 6431, vol. 6, p. 173.

67   X 2 A 89; *Journals and Papers*, 6505, vol. 6, pp. 231–2.

68   X 2 A 89; *Journals and Papers*, 6505, vol. 6, pp. 231–2.

69   X 2 A 110; *Journals and Papers*, 6511, vol. 6, p. 235.

70   X 1 A 78; *Journals and Papers*, 6327, vol. 6, p. 110.

71   *Papirer*, X 2 A 171.

72   *The Point of View*, p. 100.

73   *Concluding Unscientific Postscript*, p. 252.

6

The Wound of Negativity:
Two Kierkegaard Texts

George Steiner

It is difficult to write about Søren Kierkegaard. He has written about himself with a mixture of immediacy and indirection, of confessional urgency and ironizing distance so vivid, so diverse as to beggar commentary from outside. Famously, Kierkegaard's pseudonyms, the *dramatis personae* he alleges to be the begetters of some of his exemplary works (while assuming that the reader will detect the figure beneath the mask), enact a system of self-mirroring. But the aim is in no straightforward sense autobiographical. Sharp-edged as are the assumed guises of S. K., they also achieve effects of dispersal, of dissemination. (At key points, current deconstructive notions of 'dissemination' and of the 'abolition of the author' go back to Kierkegaard.) Kierkegaard purposes to remain elusive also to himself, to be opaque and in motion as he traverses successive 'stages on life's way'. Pseudonyms, the division of the self into contradictory voices (the 'dialectic'), the brusque pendulum swing between prayer and sophistry, gravity and play, keep open (in Kierkegaard's memorable phrase) 'the wound of negativity'.[1] They prevent the frozen certitudes of the dogmatic, the inertia of the canonic. If music, notably that of Mozart, was to Søren Kierkegaard a touchstone of the pulse of meaning, the reason is clear: he sought in his reflexes of argument and sensibility, in his prose, to translate out of music its capacities for counterpoint, for plurality of simultaneous moods and

This chapter was originally published as the Introduction to the Everyman edition of *Fear and Trembling and The Book on Adler* (David Campbell, London, 1994) and is reproduced here with permission, copyright © George Steiner, 1994, 1997.

movements, for self-subversion. Like no other major thinker, perhaps, Kierkegaard is polyphonic.

We must, in consequence, respond with a provisional, questioning lightness matching his own to even those fundamental aids to understanding to be found in his writings. The Kierkegaardian 'triad' is well known. It proceeds from an aesthetic stance to one of ethics; from ethics to religion. The aesthetic modulates into the ethical; from the ethical the 'leap of faith', the quantum jump 'into absurdity' (which twentieth-century existentialism took from Kierkegaard), conveys a chosen or afflicted few into the transcendent adventure of God. Kierkegaard often insists on the tripartite construct of his life and labours. The early *Either/Or* dramatizes the conflictual temptations of the aesthetic and the ethical conditions of spirit. The leap across the abyss of mundanity and of reason – ethics is still a worldly, a calculable strategy – which makes accessible the religious sphere, is carefully prepared for and plotted in successive meditations and pseudonymous tracts. Yet Kierkegaard lays traps both for himself and for us. In such texts as the *Edifying Discourses*, as the enigmatic but probably decisive treatise on *Repetition*, as the teasing reflections on Kierkegaard's own 'authorship', the interwoven triplicity of voices and points of view is manifest. There is, from the outset, a moralistic malaise in the paradoxes and avowals of the aesthete, of the romantic dandy and seducer. Kierkegaard's ethical 'scenarios' and self-scrutiny are charged with poetic, rhetorical display and the disinterested exuberance in stylistic experiment of a literary master. The 'transgression' into sacrificial, uncompromising faith, the tormented acceptance of the demands of the absolute in 'imitation of Christ' is latent throughout Kierkegaard. As I read and re-read this extensive, kaleidoscopic body of work, the 'decision for God' in the image of Jesus seems to me discernible, like the flash of a distant lighthouse, as early as Kierkegaard's doctoral dissertation on Socratic irony, with its subtle but unmistakable critique of even the loftiest of pre-Christian souls. The three strands are interwoven almost to the very end. The 'credal' totality prevails only near that very end, in those polemic indictments of the imperfection of the established church which so clearly spell out Kierkegaard's own imminent death.

Furthermore, an external factor obtrudes. In mid-October 1843, Kierkegaard, at one simultaneous stroke, published three books: *Fear and Trembling*, signed Johannes de Silentio; *Repetition*, under the name of Constantine Constantius; and *Three Edifying Discourses* by Søren Kierkegaard.[2] In one sense, we are confronted by a single 'speech-act'. In another, these three texts qualify, scrutinize and even ironize each other. But all three arise immediately from a crisis at once intimate and strangely public (Copenhagen was a small city addicted to censorious gossip). They enact Kierkegaard's torment and analytical apologia in respect of his broken engagement to Regine Olsen. The drama of self-alleged infidelity and philosophic licentiousness had already been played out, all too transparently, in *Either/Or*. Now two occurrences precipitated Kierkegaard's anguish: Regine had nodded to him in church, suggesting forgiveness and a true understanding of her 'betrayer's' motives (the root incompatibility of the philosophic and the married state). Then he learnt of her betrothal to another. The psychological effect was both ruinous and liberating. Wild energies of argumentative, allegoric self-dramatization and social satire erupted in Kierkegaard. His henceforth aloneness turned to strategy. He took his stance at the frontiers of his community and of his own psyche. Each of the three treatises published in that *mirabilis* month bore on Regine Olsen's conventional retreat from what might have been a solitude, a symbolic apartness concordant with S. K.'s. Allusions to intimate episodes and storms of sensibility are encased in the psychological, metaphysical and theological motions of argument even where these appear to be most abstract and general. Kierkegaard, in manoeuvres of rhetoric not always attractive, strips himself naked while advocating uttermost reticence and the burial of the heart. The very pen-names advertise: 'the constant one' and the 'apostle of silence', itself a reference to a fairy-tale by the brothers Grimm in which a lover turns to stone rather than betray his secret despair.

As a rule, I find current modes of 'psycho-biography' fatuous. The fibres which relate a man to his work are, where anyone of Kierkegaard's dimensions and refinement go, of a tautness and complication which rebuke our indiscretions. But in the case of *Fear and Trembling* (and the two masterpieces which closely accompany it), the private domain compels notice were it only because Nietzsche, indirectly, and Wittgenstein, in plain awareness, were attentive to Kierkegaard's precedent when they conducted their own spiky lives and when they failed at or rejected certain 'normal' human relations (such as marriage).

Regine Olsen's is not the only biographical presence in *Fear and Trembling*. The black persona of Kierkegaard's dead father looms. The vacant, sombre heath invoked at the outset of chapter one is not that of biblical Canaan, but of Jutland. It was there that Søren's father, in starved and despairing childhood, had cursed God. This distant malediction became a lifelong obsession. It was revealed by the father to his son. In moods of 'Lamarckian Calvinism', Kierkegaard persuaded himself that he had inherited this scar of anathema and was, ineluctably, an object of God's retribution. Again, a certain willed cultivation of terror and of a psycho-doctrinal tragic drama is palpable. But the ensuing *Angst* was none the less graphic, nor the trembling any less feverish. In the double shadow of his 'infidelity' and pariahdom on the one hand, and of the sin inherited from his father's blasphemy on the other, Kierkegaard was able, as has been no other imaginer or exegete, to make his own Genesis 22.

The subtitle is exactly challenging. 'A dialectical lyric'. The tensed interplay between philosophic propositions and poetic–dramatic means of expression dates back to the pre-Socratics and, supremely, to Plato's dialogues. It is instrumental in Wittgenstein's *Tractatus*, itself heir to the rhetorical genius of Lichtenberg and of Nietzsche. A great philosophy is always 'stylish': this is to say that its impact on the listener or reader, the force of coherence which it generates, its music of persuasion, are necessarily cognate with its performative means (those of language). Søren Kierkegaard was a craftsman of prose of the very first order. We can locate his tonality, the darting, intensely personalized dynamics of his presentations, within the more general context of European romanticism. He comes after Rousseau, after the early Goethe no less than does, say, Carlyle. It was in Schiller, in Novalis, that Kierkegaard could find full justification for the coexistence, in the same work, of philosophic and poetic components, of technical meditation and fictive–dramatic genres. Kierkegaard's fascination with the theatre and the ambiguous authenticity of the actor's trade never ceased. He writes incomparably of Mozart. His critical reviews of contemporary drama or novels are maliciously informed. He observed a rival in Hans Christian Andersen. Only towards the end are his philosophical and theological books, essays, sermons, unmarked by quotations from, by analogies with, literary examples. *Fear and Trembling* draws, among others, on Plato, Euripides, Shakespeare, Cervantes and Goethe as well as on the brothers Grimm and Andersen. *Don Quixote* is the subtext to the Bible.

Hence the concept of a 'dialectical lyric', or a narration of thought. The logical contradictions posited, the psychological and philosophic-religious endeavours to resolve them – the 'dialectic' in the Platonic sense, as this sense is taken up and modified by Hegel – are set out in what appears, at moments, to be an arbitrary, fictive manner. But the play of possibilities and of voices has its own severe logic, as do the successions of myths and of seeming digressions in a Platonic dialogue. *Fear and Trembling* is, above all, a fable of insight.

*

In a technique which anticipates the semiotic games of Umberto Eco and of today's deconstructionists, S. K. sketches a set of variants on the parable of Abraham and Isaac. Each variation on the given theme of the scriptural narration raises further psychological, moral and credal dilemmas. Immanuel Kant had opined that God, so far as we can attach to that concept and presence within us any intelligible meaning, *could not* order a father to slaughter his own beloved, miraculously conceived son. For Kant, the commandment heard by Abraham is daemonic. It stems from the voice of absolute evil. Abraham is the victim of infernal deceit. A degree of culpability attaches to his confusion. (How could he possibly have taken this to be a message from God?) Kierkegaard's reading is rigorously antithetical to Kant's. *Only* the true God can demand of Abraham the sacrifice of Isaac. It is in the (sickening) unreason, in the incomprehensible enormity of precisely such an injunction that the believer will recognize God's authentic summons. It is the profound error of Kant and of Hegel to seek to identify the God of Abraham, Isaac and Jacob, the God who ordains the hideous death of His Son on the cross, with categories of human understanding and reasoned ethics. In intimate echo to Pascal, Søren Kierkegaard would have us discriminate unflinchingly between the *dieu des philosophes* and the living God, into whose hands it is indeed 'terrible to fall'.

There follows the harsh yet exultant eulogy of Abraham. Kierkegaard spirals characteristically around one pivot, probing now from one angle of incidence, now from another. No aesthetic of tragic heroism, no rational morality, however high they are pitched, will bring us in reach of Abraham's journey to Mount Moriah. When men of war or guardians of civic virtue such as Jephthah and Brutus sacrifice their children to the Lord of Hosts or to the laws of the state, they do so with intelligible, albeit mistaken or fanatical, motivations. The barbaric sacrifice of Iphigenia ensures the departure to Troy of the Greek fleet. Creon the despot sacrifices his son so as to ensure the salvation of Thebes from murderous and blaspheming foes. Such exemplary acts and the devastating consequences which they have on their agents are the very stuff of heroic chronicles, sagas and tragic dramas. (S. K. had toyed with the project of composing his own version of *Antigone*.) But they throw no genuine light on the matter of Abraham and Isaac.

Nor does ethics. It is here that Kierkegaard's analysis is most arduous. Ethically considered, Abraham's acquiescence in God's commandment or indeed that of any man enjoined to carry out human sacrifice, is indefensible. Obedience may arise from fear of supernatural retribution, from superstition, from atavistic usages (the history of blood-offerings is immemorial and has its unsettling survival into periods which we associate with mature civilization). None of these categories is moral. Where morality is at its most elevated, in a Socrates, in a Kant, inhumanity and irrational absurdity have no place. Confronted with God's demand, the response of the ethical must be one of counter-challenge. How can God justify the order to slay Isaac? Is such a behest not *prima facie* a trap, a means of testing human courage and compassion (i.e. God waits for man's refusal)? Should divine coercion be so impervious as to make any such refusal finally impossible, morality and reason have a further resource. There are those who have chosen suicide rather than injustice, self-destruction rather than manifest criminality.

Kierkegaard is acutely cognizant of these arguments. He dwells with loving irony on their dialectical strengths. They are, he rules, wholly irrelevant to the *akedah*, to the overwhelming enigma and interpretation of Abraham's obedience. The sole pertinent rubric is that of absolute faith, of a faith which transgresses against and thus transcends all conceivable claims of intellectual accountability and of ethical criteria. Abraham's readiness to sacrifice Issac, his son, to enact God's prescription unquestioningly, lies beyond good and evil. From any point of view other than that of total faith, of total trust in the Almighty, Abraham's conduct is appalling. There can be no intellectual or ethical excuse for it. If we are to grasp Genesis 22, we must apprehend 'enormity' (a term whose etymology points, precisely, towards transgression, towards a sphere of meaning outside any reasoned legality). The cardinal notion is that of *the absurd*. Fixing on this crux, S. K. looks back to certain legacies of mystical illumination, of self-abolition in God, and forward to modern 'surrealism' and existentialism. Abraham's actions are radiantly absurd. He becomes the 'Knight of Faith' riding forth like Don Quixote as God's champion in the face of humanist revulsion and ridicule. He dwells in paradox. His quantum leap of and into blinding faith isolates him completely. The heroic and the ethical can be generalized. They belong to arguable systems of values and representations. Faith is radically singular. The encounter with God as experienced by Abraham is, eternally, that of an individual, of a private being in the grip of infinity. Only to a 'Knight of Faith', in his unbearable solitude and silence, is the living God simultaneously unfathomable and so close as to eradicate, to burn away, the limits of the self. No synagogue, no *ecclesia* can house Abraham as he strides, in mute torment, towards his appointment with the Everlasting.

★

Do such appointments come to pass in modern times? This question is, theologically envisaged, vexatious. Judaism, in its orthodox vein, holds Elijah to have been the last mortal man sanctified by a direct meeting with God. In non-mystical Christianity, the divine epiphany does disclose itself, miraculously, to certain men, women or children; but does so via the figure of the Son or of the Blessed Virgin. Islam, if I interpret its position correctly, does not look to any face-to-face encounter with Allah after the time of the Prophet. In December 1842, in Copenhagen, Adolph Peter Adler, clergyman and *Magister* in theology (Kierkegaard had attended his academic *viva* in June 1840), experienced a direct visitation and revelation from Christ. The Son of God had bidden Adler to burn all the manuscripts of his Hegelian writings and had dictated to him, in complete immediacy, the true doctrine concerning the origins of evil. On 12 June 1846, *Magister* Adler published simultaneously no less than four books. One consisted of sacred verse; the other three set out Adler's revealed insights as granted to him by Jesus. S. K. seems to have been among the very first buyers of these four titles.

The result was *The Book on Adler*.[3] Whereas *Fear and Trembling* is among the best-known and influential works in nineteenth and twentieth-century philosophic theology and literature, the treatise on Adler has remained almost unknown to the general reader. This obscurity inheres in its genesis. Kierkegaard began composition in the summer of 1846, immediately after perusing the *Magister*'s revelations. The polemicist in Kierkegaard aimed at rapid publication. Dissatisfied with his first version, S. K. withdrew the manuscript in 1847, completing a third and more or less definitive version late that same year. Again, he chose not to publish. Having extracted from *The Book on Adler* two major essays on the relations between 'genius' and the apostolic and on the dilemma of whether or not a Christian has a right to solicit martyrdom, to offer his life for his faith, S. K. left the book itself among his *Papirer* (the diaries, the fragments, the voluminous notes). It appeared after his death.

Why this withholding? Plainly, Kierkegaard found himself in an exceedingly awkward personal situation in regard to Adler. They were acquainted. Adler had called on S. K., informing him that he, Kierkegaard, was in some sense the John the Baptist to the *Magister* whom the Lord had chosen as His special messenger. Kierkegaard pondered the probability that Adler (whom the ecclesiastical authorities had suspended from his ministry in 1844) was quite simply mentally deranged. Why, moreover, draw further public attention (and derision) to a wretched business soon forgot? But substantive as they may have been, these inhibitions do not touch on the heart of the problem. Adler's conviction that mundane, rationalistic, officious Christianity in Denmark must be electrified into authentic crisis, was exactly Kierkegaard's. The *Magister*'s readiness to suffer ridicule and ostracism on behalf of his 'absurd', existentially enforced certitudes, must have struck a deep, unsettling chord in S. K. himself. As we will see, Adler's claims, however suspect and, indeed, pathological, embroiled Kierkegaard in psychological–theological dilemmas which even his acutest dialectical means failed to unravel convincingly. The Adler 'case' might well prove trivial and wholly ephemeral. The issues which it raised would not go away. Thus there is a perspective in which the wretched Adler defeated his grand inquisitor.

As so often in Kierkegaard's speculations and dialogues, the 'third presence' is that of Hegel. S. K.'s ironies sparkle: the *Magister* no doubt committed his Hegelian lucubrations to the fire, but he remains arch-Hegelian in his confusions. Incapable of discriminating between subjective phenomena and objective truths, Adler, like so many of Hegel's uncritical adepts, makes naïve use of the Hegelian concept of synthesis between the self and the external world. As it were, he 'hallucinates reality'.

But S. K. is after bigger game. The crux of the Adler affair is that of 'calling', in the very strongest sense of the term. How does a human being *know* that he/she is being summoned by God? How can human sensibility and intellect differentiate between an ecstatic, deeply felt intimation of divine solicitation, whose actual sources are those of personal need or emotion, and the authentic voice of God? The enigma is not one of possible psychic disorder (as it may have been in *Magister* Adler's instance); nor is it one of calculated self-deception or public falsehood (as in the case of innumerable gurus and market-place mystics). What, asks Kierkegaard, could be the conceivable criteria by which to determine the roots and verity of God's summons to any individual human person? Even visible excellence of moral conduct, even sacrificial suffering, such as is endured by martyrs, provides no *proof* for the spiritual validity of a vocation from God. As T. S. Eliot has it in his meditation on the possibly opportunistic martyrdom of Beckett, 'doing the right thing for the wrong reason' may, especially in respect of the religious, be 'the subtlest form of treason'.

Nothing is more fascinating to note than Søren Kierkegaard's almost despairing attempts to clarify, to unravel a conundrum whose intricacies, whose scandalous implications, seem to ebb from his ardent grasp. The focus is not, of course, poor Adler: it becomes Kierkegaard himself and his most deep-buried anguish and hopes.

The dialectical motions of proposal and qualification, of imaginative thrust and self-deconstruction, are of a complexity, indeed of a fragility, which make any outline crass. Neither intellectual lucidity and analytical rigour ('genius') nor ethical, sacrificial engagement, necessarily lead towards the 'hand-to-hand' encounter with God. Here the image burning between the lines is that of Jacob wrestling with the Stranger. It may well be that genius and reasoned morality of even the loftiest order – say in Kant – inhibit the mystery of a veritable calling. There is, and S. K. touches at this point on an elusive paradox, a self-sufficiency in moral excellence, a harmonic finitude at the heart of goodness, which in some manner excludes or renders marginal the dread, the devastating nearness of God. Only the Apostle is *called*. He alone embodies, literally, the act of possession by God and is authorized to enunciate, to translate into mortal speech, the message which he has – there is no other way of putting it – become. Does this election glorify the Apostle? On the contrary, argues Kierkegaard. The authenticating mark of the apostolic is an existential humility of the most radical kind. The true Apostle is humbled beyond all other humilities known to man. Hence the rebellious terror, the surge of refusal, with which Old Testament prophets respond to the charge which God puts upon them. An Apostle is, at any given moment – be it in a street in nineteenth-century Copenhagen – in a synchronic correspondence with the *humilitas* of Jesus, of the mocked, scourged, spat-upon and done to death Jesus of the Passion. (Adler's evident satisfaction in consequence of his 'visions', the vanity in his resolve to make them public, disqualify him at once from any claim to being an instrument of God's purpose.) Only the man or woman contemporaneous with, 'synchronized with', the suffering Christ and compelled to speak, to exemplify the meaning of that suffering, can be held to reveal God, to be – McLuhan knew his Kierkegaard – the medium made message.

Yet, at once, perplexities bristle. Whence, then, the power and the glory of the apostolic, its imperative hold on human acquiescence and imitation? How, moreover, can we reconcile Kierkegaard's insistence on the kerygmatic obligations of the apostolic, on the necessity of the declared revelation, with an emphasis on secrecy, on an ultimate inwardness? Kierkegaard grapples subtly, tenaciously, with these formidable questions. He sets himself nakedly at stake. Once again, the logic of contradiction, of the paradox (so Hegelian in essence, whatever S. K.'s protestations), is instrumental. Where it attains the requisite pitch of lived intensity, where it is fully analogous to that of Jesus, humility is total powerlessness, a finality of impotence. But it is precisely this impotence which constitutes, exactly in the sense of Jesus' revaluation of values, a greater power, very nearly an impotence of the absurd. Kierkegaard's thesis remains opaque. It helps, I suggest, to remember the 'powerless force' of such literary personae as Don Quixote or of Prince Muishkin, Dostoevsky's 'holy idiot'. Something of this sort is in Kierkegaard's mind when he wrestles with the contrarieties of the apostolic. Nor does he resolve the irreconcilable demands for silence, for humble self-effacement in the carrier of God's calling with the ministry entailed by that very calling. No thinker, no writer, is more illuminating than Kierkegaard on the motif of moral–metaphysical discretion, on the sacrament of secrecy which makes efficacious the love, the suffering of an Antigone or a Cordelia. S. K. is a celebrant of inward withdrawal, of absolute silence. He is, at the same time, a publicist of rare vehemence, one who bears witness loudly, self-revealingly, in public places. The satiric journal, *The Corsair*, had lampooned him cruelly. Kierkegaard had been made an object of open derision in his native city. This condition was the very demonstration of the burden borne by a witness ('a martyr', in Greek, signifies 'witness'). To shuffle off this burden, to leave God's discourse unproclaimed, would be nothing less than apostasy. In the pseudonym, 'Petrus minor', under which Kierkegaard planned to issue *The Book on Adler*, these unresolved contradictions are inherent.

From any systematic point of view – philosophical systems being S. K.'s bugbear – the demolition of Adler is flawed. We have seen that Kierkegaard neither hammers out a clear delineation of the nature of the apostolic in a modern context, nor can he harmonize the antithetical demands on the chosen spirit of self-concealment and of public witness. But even in direct reference to Adler's pretences, Kierkegaard's indictment remains, finally, dogmatic. The *Magister*'s account of divine encounter, the 'revelations' he alleges, are indeed shown to be wholly implausible and even risible. The inference of deranged vanity and mental confusion lies to hand. But nothing in S. K.'s pitiless diagnosis elucidates any formal and substantively definitive criteria whereby we may discriminate between hysterical or hallucinatory illusion and a 'God-experience' in any verifiable sense. The leap into the absurd, the abolitions of pragmatic causality and of logic which would characterize such an experience, remain, by Kierkegaard's own criteria of 'necessary impossibility', issues of trust. Ineluctably, the possibility that Adolph Peter Adler has received direct communication from Christ (however garbled, however unworthy his modulation of the message into his own words and person) survives Kierkegaard's negation. How could it be otherwise if, in S. K.'s own phrase, the 'wound of negativity' is to be kept open?

It is precisely these flaws, these knots in the argument, which generate the fascination of our text. The mercurial *finesse* of Kierkegaard's psychological probing, its adumbration (literal 'foreshadowing') of Freudian theories of the subconscious, where Freud, however, flinches from any serious analysis of religious convictions, make of *The Book on Adler* one of the dark jewels in the history of philosophic psychology. As an examiner of the lives of the mind, of the associative pulses of the imagination at those points in which the anarchic yet somehow ordered energies of the unspoken are brought to bear on rational proposals, Kierkegaard has only two peers. His inquisition into Adler stands beside those descents into the deeps of the human psyche performed by Dostoevsky and by Nietzsche. In these three cases, we are dealing with dramatists of the abstract, with analysts of surpassing penetration, capable of circumscribing frontier zones of unreason, of ecstatic and mystical flashes, even of madness. Modern psychoanalytic and psychotherapeutic knowingness has sometimes deepened, but often flattened, the geology of consciousness explored by *The Possessed*, by Nietzsche's *Genealogy of Morals* and by *The Book on Adler*. But here already lies the essence of our psychological modernity.

There is as well a direct link. Throughout his tracking of Adler, S. K. is spiralling around himself. The *Magister* threatens to be his faithful though parodistic shadow. In short, he turns out to be Kierkegaard's double. The *Doppelgänger* theme obsesses western interest from E. T. A. Hoffmann, Poe and Gogol all the way to Kafka. It enacts an urgent intimation as to the schizophrenic potential in the ego, as to the dangers of self-splitting inherent in a certain vivacity of thought and of fantastication. Dostoevsky's novel, *The Double*, marks only one among numerous invocations of this theme in his fictions. Nietzsche and his Zarathustra circle around each other in a complex figure of rival mirrorings. On almost every page of the Adler book, we observe Kierkegaard labouring, sometimes with satiric confidence, but more often in barely muffled *Angst*, to shake off the intimacy of his scandalous familiar, of the 'house-demon' who is also his twin. A particular terror emanates from these pages.

NOTES

1   Søren Kierkegaard, *Concluding Unscientific Postscript*, translated by Howard V. Hong and Edna H. Hong (2 vols, Princeton University Press, Princeton, 1992), vol. 1, p. 85.
2   [Steiner is referring to the 'Three Discourses' in *Eighteen Upbuilding Discourses*, translated by Howard V. Hong and Edna H. Hong (Princeton University Press, Princeton, 1990), pp. 49–101.]
3   [*The Book on Adler* was completed by Kierkegaard in 1847, but he left it among his unpublished papers. He completed three drafts of this text: one as *The Book on Adler*, with himself as author; the second as *The Confusion of the Present Age*, by Petrus Minor with a preface by Kierkegaard; and the third as *A Cycle of Ethico-Religious Treatises*, again signed by himself. It was first translated into English, by Walter Lowrie, as *On Authority and Revelation: The Book on Adler* (Princeton University Press, Princeton, 1941).]

7
Kierkegaard and the Novel

Gabriel Josipovici

My intention is not to write here about Kierkegaard as novelist, though
that would be an interesting subject. After all, each of his pseudonymous
works is in a sense an attempt to extend the range of fiction, and
I can see no good reason why they should be dumped in a box
marked 'Philosophy', while Sterne's *Tristram Shandy*, for example, or
Dostoevsky's *Notes from Underground* are dumped in one marked
'Literature'.

However, to write about Kierkegaard as novelist implies that we know
what a novel is, and what is really interesting about Kierkegaard is that
he raises questions about that very issue, and does so by reminding us
that we cannot begin to understand what novels are, what fiction is, until
we recognize that how we think about fiction depends on how we think
about ourselves. In other words, if the concept of fiction cannot be taken
for granted, it is because story-telling is intimately bound up with what
we are, not in any absolute sense but in our concrete social and historical
reality. Kierkegaard's critique of his time ('the present age'), his struggles
to understand himself and his experiments with form are part of one
single enterprise, and there is no easy way to separate the different
strands from each other. But if that makes matters difficult it also ensures
that the investigation will at least be dealing with serious, not to say
fundamental matters.

A good place to start is Kierkegaard's Introduction to *The Book on
Adler*.[1] The book turns on the question of authority: what authority do I
have for what I say and write? What authority do authors have in general
and in the present age in particular? Artists are fond of referring to their
'calling', but in what sense have they been called? In the same sense as

the Apostles were called by Jesus? And, if not, are they justified in using such a term?

Kierkegaard begins his Introduction in a typically offhand way with a reference to the world of the barber-shop, where rumours and gossip fly and which acts in small communities as a kind of informal newspaper. Then with no apparent change of gear, he plunges into the heart of the matter: 'It is not improbable that the lives of many men go on in such a way that they have indeed premises for living but reach no conclusions. . . . For it is one thing that a life is over and a different thing that a life is finished by reaching its conclusion.' The ordinary man, he goes on, the one whose life has no conclusion, may, if he finds he has talent, decide to become an author. But, says Kierkegaard, though

> he may have extraordinary talents and remarkable learning . . . an author he is not, in spite of the fact that he produces books. [. . .] No, in spite of the fact that the man writes, he is not essentially an author; he will be capable of writing the first . . . and also the second part, but he cannot write the third part – the last part he cannot write. If he goes ahead naïvely (led astray by the reflection that every book must have a last part) and so writes the last part, he will make it thoroughly clear by writing the last part that he makes a written renunciation to all claim to be an author. For though it is indeed by writing that one justifies the claim to be an author, it is also, strangely enough, by writing that one virtually renounces this claim. If he had been thoroughly aware of the inappropriateness of the third part – well, one may say, *si tacuisset, philosophus mansisset* [If he had kept quiet he would have remained a philosopher!].

And he concludes with a pregnant aphorism: 'To find the conclusion it is necessary first of all to observe that it is lacking, and then in turn to feel quite vividly the lack of it.'[2]

It is not too much to say that those who have felt the full force of Kierkegaard's argument here will be forever separated from those – the bulk of writers, readers and reviewers of fiction in Kierkegaard's day and our own – who have not. And I hasten to add that one does not need to have read Kierkegaard to feel it, only to be aware of the possibilities of art in the post-Romantic age. For Kierkegaard is merely articulating, with great humour but also great power and acumen, what has been felt and struggled with by Hölderlin and Mallarmé, Kafka and Proust, Rilke, Eliot and Wallace Stevens: that since the writer has no authority for what he is saying, to go on writing as if he had is the greatest sin, for it falsifies the way things are instead of helping to clarify it.

The argument turns on the question of the difference between endings and conclusions: 'For it is one thing that a life is over and a different thing that a life is finished by reaching its conclusion.' In the first case a man goes through life and then dies. His life has not had any meaning, it has simply consisted of a series of actions and reactions, and his death does not have any meaning either. It is like a line which goes along the page for a while and then stops. To say that line goes from A to B implies that there is a shape to it, a certain kind of progression. But the line does not 'go' anywhere. It exists for a while and then stops. Clov and Hamm, in Beckett's *Endgame*, wind up an alarm clock and then listen to it ringing. When it stops Clov says: 'The end is terrific!' 'I prefer the middle', replies Hamm.[3] This is both funny and disturbing. Funny because Hamm and Clov, by treating, or pretending to treat the undifferentiated sound of an alarm clock as they would a piece of music, make fun of concert-goers. Disturbing, because behind the concert-goer stands the critic of art in general, and its practitioners, and we ourselves, who insist on seeing meaning and value in our lives when we know full well that in the end there is none. As Kierkegaard puts it: all we ever have in life are gossip and rumours; our world is the world of the newspaper and the barber-shop, it is not the world of Jesus and his Apostles. A person seduced by our culture's admiration for art into becoming a writer embarks on a more dangerous enterprise than they may realize. If they embark on a work of fiction they imply that they have escaped the world of rumour, that instead of living horizontally, as it were, they live vertically, in touch with some transcendental source of authority. And we who read them do so because we feel that this must indeed be the case. But the closer they get to the end the clearer it becomes that there is no vertical connection. And should they try to bring their work to a close the contradiction between what the novel implies and the truth of the matter will become quite obvious. The only way for some semblance of truth and clarity to emerge is for the author to recognize that the conclusion, that which would finally give authority to the book, is lacking, to feel this quite vividly and make us feel it as well.

I have been moving indiscriminately between the terms 'fiction', 'the novel' and 'the story-teller', but it is time to try to distinguish them. Kierkegaard himself does not do so explicitly, but it is clear that in the passage above he is thinking of novels, and elsewhere he makes it clear that there is a historical dimension to the problem, that earlier writers, such as the authors of fairy-tales and the ancient Greek tragedians, were not faced with the same problems as those who write in the age of the barber-shop and the newspaper. It may be helpful, though, to turn first to a writer who, our of the same concerns as Kierkegaard, *has* attempted to define the difference between the story-teller and the novelist. That writer is Walter Benjamin.

In one of his finest essays, 'The Storyteller', Benjamin notes that the earliest symptom of a process whose end is the decline of storytelling is the rise of the novel at the beginning of modern times. [. . .] What differentiates the novel from all other forms of prose literature – the fairy-tale, the legend, even the novella – is that it neither comes from oral tradition nor goes into it. [. . .] The storyteller takes what he tells from experience – his own or that reported by others. And he in turn makes it the experience of those who are listening to his tale. The novelist has isolated himself. The birthplace of the novel is the solitary individual, who is no longer able to express himself by giving examples of his most important concerns, is himself uncounseled, and cannot counsel others.[4]

And Benjamin finds the authority of the story-teller to rest in death: 'Dying was once a public process in the life of the individual and a most exemplary one. . . . In the course of modern times dying has been pushed further and further out of the perceptual world of the living.' As we live isolated and alone, so we die, 'stowed away in sanatoria or hospitals.' But 'not only a man's knowledge or wisdom, but above all his real life – and this is the stuff that stories are made of – first assumes transmissible form at the moment of death.' A public death surrounded by traditional customs is what once gave 'authority which even the poorest wretch in dying possesses for the living around him.' 'This authority', concludes Benjamin, 'is at the very source of the story.'[5]

There may be something romantic and mystical in Benjamin's formulation, but it is easy to see that he is on to something serious and substantial. The story-teller is part of a tradition: he acquires his wisdom from others and in turn passes it on to others. The novelist, by contrast, is isolated, 'is himself uncounseled and cannot counsel others'.

Kierkegaard, unfortunately, did not write about story-telling as opposed to novel writing, but he did touch on the issue in a diary entry from 1837, before, that is, he had published any of his works. He is meditating on the telling of stories to children, and he puts forward the view that there are

two recommended ways of telling children stories, but there is also a multitude of false paths in between. The *first* is the way unconsciously adopted by the nanny, and whoever can be included in that category. Here a whole fantasy world dawns for the child and the nannies themselves are deeply convinced the stories are true . . . which, however fantastic the content, can't help bestowing a beneficial calm on the child. Only when the child gets a hint of the fact that the person doesn't believe her own stories are there ill-effects – not from the content but because of the narrator's insincerity – from the lack of confidence and suspicion that gradually develops in the child.

The second way, he goes on, 'is possible only for someone who with full transparency reproduces the life of childhood, knows what it demands, what is good for it, and from his higher standpoint offers the children a spiritual sustenance that is good for them – who knows how to be a child, whereas the nannies themselves are basically children.' And he concludes that '*false paths* crop up by coming beyond the nanny position but not staying the whole course and stopping half-way.'[6]

The movement here is typical of Kierkegaard's method. First we have an original, 'natural', situation; then a series of false intermediary positions, positions which fail to take account of the new situation; and, finally, a radical solution which does take the new situation fully into account. The story-teller in Benjamin's argument, we could say, is like the nanny, who, deeply convinced of the truth of what she is saying, bestows a beneficial calm on the child. The novelist is like the nanny who can no longer quite believe what she is saying, and thus leaves the child uneasy and suspicious. The 'essential writer', the one who senses that a conclusion is lacking, feels quite vividly that lack and makes the reader feel it too; by so doing he 'from his higher standpoint offers the children a spiritual sustenance that is good for them.' The 'essential writer' thus in a sense 'knows how to be a child, whereas the nannies themselves are basically children'.

The same pattern is to be found in an essay in the first part of *Either/Or*, 'The Tragic in Ancient Drama Reflected in the Tragic in Modern Drama'. Here it is drama, not fiction, that Kierkegaard is concerned with, but the parallels with Benjamin's essay are striking. In ancient Greek culture, says Kierkegaard, 'even if the individual moved freely, he nevertheless rested in substantial determinants in the state, the family, in fate.' Modern man, on the other hand, is alone, and takes all decisions for himself. Thus tragedy is alien to him, for by throwing 'his whole life upon his shoulders as his own deed,' he turns tragic guilt into ethical guilt.[7] The tragic hero becomes merely bad, and badness and goodness have no aesthetic interest. Thus writers who persist in trying to write tragedy merely produce banality and confuse instead of clarifying our relation to the world. There is, however, he goes on, a truly modern kind of tragedy, but it cannot form the subject of drama because it does not belong to the realm of the aesthetic at all. This is a totally inward kind of tragedy, and its paradigm is Christ, who lived a life of absolute obedience without any outward evidence that he was doing so. The modern writer who wishes to write tragedy must do so then in a roundabout way, by showing us that tragedy is no longer possible and making us intuit what cannot be said. In other words, he must force us to recognize that the conclusion, that which would finally give authority to his play, is lacking, and make us feel vividly the lack of it.

That of course is what Beckett does in *Endgame*. 'What's happening? What's happening?' Hamm asks at one point. 'Something is taking its course,' replies Clov.[8] Something, somewhere, is taking its course, which is quite a different thing from the ringing of the alarm clock having a beginning, middle and end. But the sense of lack, of modern story-telling as false coinage, pseudo-nutrition, is to be found in all the great modernists, and notably in Kafka, where it reaches its clearest expression in one of his last stories, *A Hunger Artist*, in which the fasting showman confesses, as he is dying, that he only fasted 'because I couldn't find the food I liked. If I had found it, believe me, I should have made no fuss and stuffed myself like you or anyone else.'[9] It is already there in Kafka's outburst, in an early letter to his friend Oskar Pollack:

> I think we ought to read only the kind of books that wound and stab us. If the book we're reading doesn't wake us up with a blow on the head, what are we reading it for? So that it will make us happy, as you write? Good Lord, we would be happy precisely if we had no books, and the kind of books that make us happy are the kind we could write ourselves if we had to. But we need the books that affect us like a disaster, that grieve us deeply, like the death of someone we loved more than ourselves, like being banished into forests far from everyone, like a suicide. A book must be the axe for the frozen sea inside us. That is my belief.[10]

For Kierkegaard, trained as a theologian and a philosopher, however, the quarry was only incidentally the novel. He simply wanted to bring out the striking similarity between the false aura of authority that surrounds the novel and all the other fraudulent assertions of authority with which 'the present age' bombards us. Chief among these is the fraudulent authority of Hegel and the Hegelians. 'I nurture what is for me at times a puzzling respect for Hegel', he writes in his journal in 1845, for all the world like Nietzsche trying to come to terms with his own terribly mixed feelings towards Wagner. 'I have learned much from him, and I know very well that I can still learn much more when I return to him again. [. . .] His philosophical knowledge, his amazing learning, the insight of his genius, and everything else good that can be said of a philosopher, I am willing to acknowledge. [. . .] But nevertheless, it is no less true that someone who is really tested in life, who in his need resorts to thought, will find Hegel comical despite all his greatness.'[11]

What is it that is so comic about Hegel? It is that he forgets the one essential thing: that each of us has a single, unique life and each of us must die, and that this is not a mere contingent fact about us, but the most important thing. 'Now, all in all, there are two ways for an existing individual', he says in the *Postscript*, that massive work he thought would cap his pseudonymous production and lay the ghost of Hegel once and for all:

> Either he can do everything to forget that he is existing and thereby manage to become comic . . . because existence possesses the remarkable quality that an existing person exists whether he wants to or not; or he can direct all his attention to his existing. It is from this side that an objection must first be made to modern speculative thought, that it has not a false presupposition but a comic presupposition, occasioned by its having forgotten in a kind of world-historical absentmindedness what it means to be a human being, not what it means to be human in general, for even speculators might be swayed to consider that sort of thing, but what it means that we, you and I and he, are human beings, each one on his own.[12]

What Kierkegaard objects to in Hegel's system (leaving aside the question of how right his critique of Hegel may be and how far he is simply attacking Hegelianism, the dominant philosophy of the age) is this: that in asking us to think of history and of individual lives from the end, backwards, it misses what is central to life: that it is lived forwards.[13] As far as history is concerned this means that it will always be an account of the winners, never of the losers, since in world-historical terms it was necessary for the losers to lose. As far as the individual is concerned it leaves out of account the fact that we live our lives forward, that for us there is no pattern, only the moment with its choices. For Kierkegaard, Hegel's System and the bland Hegelian Christianity trumpeted from pulpits every Sunday are not simply wrong on that score: in their insistence that a pattern is known to the speaker (that Abraham sacrificed his son as a prefiguration of Christ's sacrifice for us, for example) it falsifies both the past (it ignores Abraham's anguish as he went to Mount Moriah) and the present (since it treats its audience as though they were already dead and in heaven).

Sartre, perhaps influenced by his reading of Kierkegaard, makes the same point about the novel in his *Nausea*. We start a novel, he says, and read about a man walking down a road. The man seems free, the future open before him. At once we identify with him, for that is how our existence seems to us. We too are walking down the road of life, unsure of what is to come. But the pleasure of reading the novel lies in the fact that we know that the man is in fact the subject of an adventure that is about to befall him. How do we know this? Because he is there at the start of the novel and he would not be there if nothing were going to happen to him. 'But the end is there. For us, the fellow is already the hero of the story.'[14] The extraordinary power of the traditional novel lies in this fact, that it makes us feel that our lives are both free *and* meaningful. It does not say this, for it neither needs to nor is fully aware of it, but nevertheless that is its essence, the secret of its power.

How to wake people up? How to bring them back to a sense that their own lives are infinitely precious as their own and not as part of some large pattern? Not, at any rate, by presenting them with another system, for the whole point is that

> a system of existence cannot be given. Is there, then, not such a system? That is not at all the case. Neither is this implied in what has been said. Existence itself is a system – for God, but it cannot be a system for any existing spirit. System and conclusiveness correspond to each other, but existence is the very opposite. . . . In order to think existence, systematic thought must think it as annulled and consequently not as existing. Existence is the spacing that holds apart; the systematic is the conclusiveness that brings together.[15]

Kierkegaard has a model for his method, which depends not on what is said but on the tension between what is said and the person speaking, and that model is Socrates. In his earliest book, *The Concept of Irony*, he contrasts the irony of Socrates with the System of Hegel, and shows how little Hegel understands Socrates. Hegel does not understand, says Kierkegaard, that the 'self' of Socrates in not a plenum, but only the sense the 'I know nothing.' Hegel sees Socrates as a part of his System, as the triumph of the individual and subjectivity over the Gods and external authority, whereas, says Kierkegaard in a wonderful image, Socrates 'placed individuals under his dialectical vacuum pump, pumped away the atmospheric air they were accustomed to breathing, and left them standing there'.[16] The discourse of Socrates, he says, 'does not have the powerful pathos of enthusiasm; his bearing does not have the absolute authority of personality; his indifference is not a blissful relaxation in his own repletion. [. . .] What bears him up is the negativity that still has engendered no positivity.'[17] And if the contrast drawn here between Socrates and his opponents strikes us as more like that between, say, Kierkegaard himself and Goethe, or Kierkegaard and Beethoven, rather than anything in the Greek world, that would not be the first time a philosopher has dramatized his own relation to his age in his portrait of an earlier thinker.

Kierkegaard comes back to this point about negativity in the *Postscript*. As ever, he is aware of the traps that lie in wait for even the most rigorous thinker: 'The subjective existing thinker who has the infinite in his soul has it always, and therefore his form is continually negative,' he says. 'When this is the case, when he, actually existing, renders the form of existence in his own existence, he, existing, is continually just as negative

as positive, for his positivity consists in the continued inward deepening
in which he is cognizant of the negative.' He goes on to say that,

> among the so-called negative thinkers, however, there are a few who, after
> gaining an inkling of the negative, succumb to the positive and go roaring
> out into the world in order to recommend, urge, and offer their beatifying
> negative wisdom for sale. These hawkers are scarcely more sagacious than
> the positive thinkers, but it is rather inconsistent of the positive thinkers to
> become angry with them, for they are essentially positive. The hawkers are
> not existing thinkers. Perhaps they were so once, until they found a result;
> from that moment they no longer exist as thinkers, but as hawkers and
> auctioneers.[18]

We have seen many such in modern times. Indeed, the entire movement known as Postmodernism can be seen as a prime example of
Kierkegaard's dictum. Instead of a struggle to 'hold apart', came a new
system, which 'brings together', even if it was a system based on some
theory of apartness. Kierkegaard, by contrast, remains aware that 'the
genuine subjective existing thinker is always just as negative as he is
positive', and that 'he is always that as long as he exists, not once and for
all in a chimerical mediation.' Such a thinker, he says, is conscious of
'the negativity of the infinite in existence; he always keeps open the
wound of negativity, which at times is a saving factor.'[19] The others let
the wound heal over and become positive; they cease to be learners and
become teachers.

How to stop oneself becoming a teacher? How to think against thinking? For that is what it amounts to, since thinking, even thinking that
existence is always more and other than thinking, is still always thinking.
That is Kierkegaard's central insight and his central preoccupation, as
the Journals show, from the beginning to the end of his writing life.
Thus, in a series of diary entries from 1837 (before, that is, he had
written any of his books), he notes that 'the humorist' can never become
'a Systematizer', since 'the systematizer believes he can say everything,
and that whatever cannot be said is wrong and unimportant,' whereas
the humorist 'lives in life's fullness and so feels how much is always left
over, even if he has expressed himself in the most felicitous manner
possible (hence his disinclination to write).' This leads him into a powerful meditation on the difference between the indicative and the subjunctive, between, that is, the mode of existence and the mode of
possibility: 'The indicative thinks something as actual (the identity of
thinking and the actual). The subjunctive thinks something as think-
able.' The writer sensitive to the difference between thinking and living
will reflect this distinction by choosing the subjunctive, the mode of
possibility, not the indicative, the mode of actuality: 'One should be able

to write a whole novel in which the present tense subjunctive was the invisible soul, as light is for painting.' The true writer, conscious of the precious nature of the actual, will use the subjunctive precisely because the indicative means so much to him: 'That is why one can truthfully say that the subjunctive, which enters as a glimpse of the individuality of the person in question, is a dramatic line whereby the narrator steps aside and makes the remark as being true of the character (poetically), not as factual, not even as if it might be fact; it is presented under the illumination of subjectivity.'[20]

This is why Kierkegaard uses pseudonyms: not to confuse his readers, nor to play games with them, but to bring out the subjunctive nature of what is being said. It is not Kierkegaard saying this but Johannes de Silentio or Johannes Climacus; saying that which Kierkegaard *imagines* them to say, were they to speak, to write. And that is why so many modern novelists emphasize, in their writing, that their novels are novels. Not to play games on their readers and not to trick them (though of course some do this for these banal reasons), but to bring out the gap that will always exist between lived life and written-about life.

Kierkegaard is still struggling with the problem in 1850, five years after the publication of the *Postscript*, which was supposed to have settled it once and for all. ' "Actuality" cannot be conceived,' he writes in his journal for that year:

Johannes Climacus (in the *Postscript*) has already shown this correctly and very simply. To conceive something is to dissolve actuality into *possibility* – but then it is impossible to conceive it, because conceiving something is transforming it into possibility and so not holding on to its actuality. As far as actuality is concerned, conception is retrogressive, a step backward, not a progress. Not that 'actuality' contains no concepts, by no means; no, the concept which is come by through conceptually dissolving it into possibility is also inside actuality, but there is still something more – that is actuality. To go from possibility to actuality is a step forward . . . to go from actuality to possibility is a step backward. But there's this deplorable confusion in that modern times have incorporated 'actuality' into logic and then, in distraction, forgotten that 'actuality' in logic is still only a 'thought actuality', i.e. it is possibility.[21]

Everything would be fine if works like Hegel's *Phenomenology* presented their ideas as hypotheses, not as actuality, but does this happen? No. And it is the same with history:

But isn't history actual? Certainly. But what history? No doubt the six thousand years of the world's history are actuality, but one that is put behind us; it is and can exist for me only as thought actuality, i.e. as possibility. Whether or not the dead have actually realised existentially the tasks which were put before them in actuality has now been decided, has been concluded; there is no more existential actuality for them except in what has been put behind them, which again, for me, exists only as ideal actuality, as thought actuality, as possibility.[22]

In other words, I can think of history as actuality, but the very thinking of it robs it of its actuality.

This is so difficult to grasp precisely because 'to grasp' means to understand and Kierkegaard is arguing that there will always be a gap between understanding and lived actuality. We can get a purchase on his argument by turning to one of Beckett's finest stories, *Dante and the Lobster*. There the protagonist, Belaqua Shua, a Dublin intellectual and layabout, having bought a lobster for dinner with his aunt, is appalled when he discovers that the creature is alive and that the aunt is about to cook it by dropping it alive into boiling water. He tries to placate his feelings of guilt and horror with the cliché: 'It's a quick death, God help us all.' But the narrative will not let him get away with this: 'It is not', the story ends.[23] Here the distinction between the subjunctive and the indicative is a gulf which divides those – the aunt, Belaqua, the reader – who are only asked to *imagine* what it is like to die by being plunged alive into boiling water, and the lobster, for whom this is actuality. Of course 'It is not' is still part of the story, and even the reader's recognition that 'it is not' a quick death is still only an imaginative recognition, still, for us, a possibility among others. So Beckett will have to start again and, as he says elsewhere, fail again, fail better, if he is to get at the truth.[24]

We can now begin to see why Kierkegaard said that the more an inessential writer writes the more they reveal that they are no writer. For they write as though system and existence were one, and, not noticing that anything is amiss with their method, they therefore merely perpetuate confusion and misunderstanding. In *Fear and Trembling*, on the other hand, Kierkegaard brings out powerfully how impossible it is for narrative and even for language ever to convey what the individual is going through as he faces the choices life puts before him. For both narrative and language generalize and so lose what is unique to the individual. All the narrator, Johannes de Silentio, can say is: I understand only that I do not understand Abraham. Thus he can bring us to the point where we too understand that we do not understand, and then leave us there.

In *Either/Or* Kierkegaard set two life-views against each other by means of collage, forcing us to make our choice between them and then to recognize that both are right and neither is, so that we go round and round, warming to the young man of the first part, with his wit and his melancholy and his vulnerability, then recognizing that the older man is right when, in the second half, he criticizes the young Aesthete for wallowing in his condition, for wanting to have all women, all lives, instead of committing himself to one. Yet we also come to see that the older man is a complacent and self-satisfied bore who has no inkling of the impossibility of choice for one who has begun to question the values of a bourgeois existence of marriage and children and getting on in life. Still, tiresome as he is, is the older man not perhaps right? Would things not perhaps change decisively for the young man were he to take the plunge and commit himself? Perhaps the older man has been through the same thing and simply found it in himself to make his choice.

In *Fear and Trembling* the question is no longer to set two life-views against each other, but to ask how it is possible to become a Knight of Faith, like Abraham. The narrator can make us feel vividly that he – and we – cannot really understand Abraham, but the implication remains that so long as he goes on writing about Abraham he himself will never be a Knight of Faith. This is Kierkegaard's problem. He cannot remain simply ironical, like his beloved Socrates. Times have changed. Christianity, with its new imperatives, has come into the world and, besides, there is no Plato to write down his words. He is committed to writing in order to make people see the lies they are telling themselves, but so long as he goes on writing he remains in the subjunctive mode and so cuts himself off from the life he most desires. He feels that if only he could make the leap he would himself become a Knight of Faith, quietly going about his tasks in the world, unknown to men but in a meaningful relationship to God and to himself. But what does it mean to make the leap? To stop writing? To take Holy Orders? He has in a sense already made the leap by devoting himself to his vocation. But what is this vocation? Has God in fact called him? Is this what God really wanted of him? Did he not perhaps rather want him to marry Regine and lead a quiet, unadventurous life, far from the temptations of authorship? There is, of course, no answer to these questions, yet they will not go away. If only, he thinks, he could quiet his intellect, put to sleep his febrile imagination, then perhaps he would, finally, *be* a kind of Abraham. But he cannot. This is the sort of person he is and the sort of person his upbringing has made him, and all he can do is go on writing about the difficulty, the impossibility, the desirability, of that leap.

The trouble is that Abraham does not need to make a leap. He just is – Abraham. Kierkegaard understood this well, and seeks to explain the difference by arguing that since Christ's Incarnation matters have changed totally. To be natural is no longer enough, for what Christ teaches is that nature must be redeemed by faith:

Voltaire is said to have remarked somewhere that he would refuse to believe in the hereditary nobility until there was historical proof of a child being born with spurs. Similarly I would say: I propose for the time being to keep to the old view that the Christian and the human, the humane, are qualitative opposites; I propose keeping to that until we are informed that a naturally, in other words innately self-denying child has been born.[25]

As no child is born with spurs, so no child is born a Christian. And baptism is of course merely the Church's way of fitting spurs on to the child and pretending they are now a natural part of him. For Kierkegaard, for this radical Protestant, the logic of his position is simply this: 'To love God is . . . impossible without hating what is human.'[26]

At other times though he is less certain of his ground. Perhaps this Manichean view is not the truth but only his own biased perspective on things: 'If I look at my personal life, am I a Christian or isn't this personal existence of mine a pure poetic existence with a dash of the demonic? . . . Is there not an element of despair in all this, starting a fire in a kind of betrayal, just to throw oneself into God's arms? Maybe, since it might turn out that I didn't become a Christian.'[27]

Such torments can be replicated in the letters and diaries of Kafka and in the utterances of many of the great modernist writers. They, however, seem to have been able to develop and grow through an innate trust in the act of writing itself as a way out of the impasse, in their willingness to embrace confusion and uncertainty and find a new voice in the process. But a very narrow line divides such trust from the bad faith of becoming a 'hawker' and so failing to keep 'the wound of negativity' open. One could say that Kierkegaard's personal tragedy lay in the fact that he was not enough of a writer to take pleasure in the writing process itself, but too much of one ever to be a Knight of Faith. But then that too could perhaps be seen as the best way of defining all those modern writers whom, like Kierkegaard, we may call 'essential writers' to distinguish them from the scribblers, even the highly talented scribblers, who will always be with us.

NOTES

1 Søren Kierkegaard, *Fear and Trembling and The Book on Adler*, translated by Walter Lowrie (David Campbell, London, 1994).
2 *Fear and Trembling and The Book on Alder*, pp. 113–14.
3 Samuel Beckett, *Endgame* (Faber and Faber, London, 1964), p. 34.
4 Walter Benjamin, 'The Storyteller', in his *Illuminations*, edited by Hannah Arendt and translated by Harry Zohn (Jonathan Cape, London, 1970), p. 87.

Kierkegaard and the Novel 127

5 'The Storyteller', pp. 93–4.

6 II A 12; *Papers and Journals: A Selection*, translated by Alastair Hannay (Penguin Books, London 1996), pp. 73–7; or, for the standard translation, see *Søren Kierkegaard's Journals and Papers*, translated by Howard V. Hong and Edna H. Hong (7 vols, Indiana University Press, Bloomington, 1967–78), 265, vol. 1, pp. 113–19.

7 Søren Kierkegaard, *Either/Or*, translated by Howard V. Hong and Edna H. Hong (2 vols, Princeton University Press, Princeton, 1987), vol. 1, pp. 143–4.

8 Samuel Beckett, *Endgame*, p. 17.

9 Franz Kafka, 'A Hunger Artist', translated by Willa and Edwin Muir, in *The Complete Short Stories of Franz Kafka*, edited by Nahum N. Glatzer (Reed International, London, 1992), p. 277.

10 Franz Kafka, *Letters to Friends, Family, and Editors*, translated by Richard Winston and Clare Winston (John Calder, London, 1978), p. 16.

11 VI B 54 12; *Papers and Journals: A Selection*, p. 195; cf. *Journals and Papers* 1608, vol. 2, p. 221.

12 *Concluding Unscientific Postscript*, p. 120.

13 [See IV A 164: 'It is quite true what philosophy says: that life must be understood backwards. But then one forgets the other principle: that it must be lived forwards. Which principle, the more one thinks it through, ends exactly with the thought that temporal life can never properly be understood precisely because I can at no instant find complete rest in which to adopt the position: backwards.' (*Papers and Journals: A Selection*, p. 161; cf. *Journals and Papers*, 1030, vol. 1, p. 450.)]

14 Jean-Paul Sartre, *Nausea*, translated by Robert Baldick (Penguin Books, Harmondsworth, 1965), p. 62.

15 *Concluding Unscientific Postscript*, vol. 1, p. 118 [translation altered].

16 Søren Kierkegaard, *The Concept of Irony*, translated by Howard V. Hong and Edna H. Hong (Princeton University Press, Princeton, 1989), p. 178.

17 *The Concept of Irony*, p. 196.

18 *Concluding Unscientific Postscript*, pp. 84–5.

19 Ibid., p. 85.

20 II A 140, 156, 160, 161; *Papers and Journals: A Selection*, pp. 90–1; cf. *Journals and Papers*, 1702, vol. 2, p. 259 and 2310, 2314, 2315, vol. 3, pp. 4, 5.

21 X 2 A 439; *Papers and Journals: A Selection*, p. 470; cf. *Journals and Papers*, 1059, vol. 1, p. 461.

22 X 2 A 439; *Papers and Journals: A Selection*, p. 470. Cf. *Journals and Papers*, 1059, vol. 1, p. 461.

23 'Dante and the Lobster', in Samuel Beckett, *More Pricks than Kicks* (Calder, London, 1993), p. 21.

24 That is why all his work could bear the title of one of his fragments, 'Imagination Dead Imagine', just as Wallace Stevens's remark that 'Yet the absence of the imagination had/Itself to be imagined' is merely the articulation of the imperative he had always set himself (Wallace Stevens, 'The Plain Sense of Things', in *Collected Poems* (Faber and Faber, London, 1955), pp. 502–3).

25   X 4 A 258; *Papers and Journals: A Selection*, p. 525; cf. *Journals and Papers*, 3647, vol. 3, p. 689.

26   XI 1 A 445; *Papers and Journals: A Selection*, p. 606; cf. *Journals and Papers*, 6902, vol. 6, pp. 526–7.

27   X 1 A 510; *Papers and Journals: A Selection*, p. 392; cf. *Journals and Papers*, 6431, vol. 6, pp. 172–3.

8
We Are Not Sublime:
Love and Sacrifice,
Abraham and Ourselves

Sylviane Agacinski

When I started re-reading *Fear and Trembling*, a few years after I had written *Aparté*,[1] I found myself fascinated once again by what Johannes de Silentio calls the *sublimity* of Abraham's sacrifice, and my reflections here still bear the mark of that fascination.[2] The 'here I am' with which Abraham replied to the God who was demanding the death of his son was always, for me, a paradigm of faith, of utter devotion, of the absolute risk of religious love. It seemed to offer a glimpse of a mysterious heroism that surpassed not only our understanding, but that of the religious poet too, or rather the poet of the religious.[3] But now, returning to *Fear and Trembling* after a long absence, I am more suspicious of this exaltation of greatness, immensity and the absolute, and I have suspicions about the idea of the formless and the faceless too. The sublime and the sentiment of the sublime presuppose some absolute greatness in comparison with which, as Kant says, 'all else is small'.[4] However much they may differ amongst themselves, all thoughts of the sublime, all eulogies to it, necessarily proceed by reference to some conception of sacrifice, a conception for which the idea of sacrificing a tiny remnant, the little one, will always be possible or conceivable.

'Nous ne sommes pas sublimes' was first published in this version in Sylviane Agacinski, *Critique de l'égocentrisme* (Galilée, Paris, 1996), pp. 107–32. An earlier version appeared in the special Kierkegaard edition of *Les Cahiers de Philosophie*, 8–9, Autumn 1989, pp. 167–85. It has been translated for this volume by Jonathan Rée and is published with permission of Galilée and the author. Copyright © Editions Galilée. Translation Copyright © Jonathan Rée 1998.

For me, the question raised by the theme of the sublime affects any way of thinking which either takes itself to be somehow capable of infinity, or else suffers as a result of its incapacity for it.[5] The sublime call or demand that issues from the infinite or the absolute involves a condemnation of finitude, a condemnation which is present in all forms of nostalgia for the incommensurable.

In this respect the legacy of Kierkegaard is at the very least twofold. As a thinker of existence, he recalls existing individuals to their finitude, blocking off all access to the point of view of the absolute, and forcing us back to our first responsibility, our primary task: namely, to have our being in the mode of existence. He confronts existing individuals with the unappeasable responsibility which requires that an arch-decision be made: the decision to exist as a singularity in time.

But on the other hand, to the extent that existence is derived and created, it also reveals itself as difference. The other – in the shape of the father or God – will always have gone before it and marked it in advance. Existence is always infinitely indebted to this absolute antecedence, this inconceivable origin. In order to take up the burden of this originary debt, the existing individual must take up the passion and panic of thought itself (of intelligence), and learn to vindicate or even love the fact that, in relation to God, it is always *in the wrong*. Thus Kierkegaard not only calls on us to think from within finite existence; he also insists on the absolute wrongness of finitude.

It is the same as Antigone: the existing individual is primarily an inheritor, that is to say a child; but the choice of existence may also be that of sacrifice, of a sacrificed existence. The child wants to remain 'hidden within its father'.

Let me also comment on the first word of my title: *We* are not sublime. It could be the *we* of a single epoch or it could be the *we* of several: Kierkegaard's and our own, for example. Or it could be the *we* of those who are simply *bewildered* by Abraham's faith – those who, regretfully or not, have (so to speak) lost their capacity for the sublime: for instance, those who can no longer sustain any relationship with the absolute, the great and the eternal; or perhaps those who no longer need to sustain it, because they have moved beyond the contradiction between the finite and the infinite (a Hegelian *we*, as it might be).

Or it might be a *we* by which I speak to someone indirectly, as Søren spoke to Regine in so many of his writings. It might, for example, be a way of saying 'we ought to be able to love each other eternally following our loss – if only we were sublime . . .'. Or again, to say to another: 'We know we lack eternity, but this knowledge means that we do not lack it after all. We have time; but we have nothing else. We are not sublime.'

Which would imply: above all let us avoid being sublime, for everything that exists is *finite*.

Fear and Trembling is all about the question of trembling in the face of sacrifice. Did Abraham tremble? And who is it in us that fears Abraham and trembles before him? It is about silence as well. Abraham stayed silent: after all what could he have said? And it is also about reason – the kind of rationality that seeks to ward off the ever-present threat of criminality, by setting up laws and the universality of law in the hope of eliminating the risk that the individual will be led astray by faith, led into an aside [*aparté*] with God. So was Abraham sublime? Can the question make any sense for us? Surely not: we have no way of getting the gods to speak. There is nothing for us to listen for. But Abraham was the man who listened to God.

Johannes de Silentio was a poet, a poet of the religious. And Johannes tells us: 'Look at Abraham, he is sublime.' But he also says, in effect: 'I myself am incapable of faith, I am only the poet of the Knight of Faith.'[6] Thus we are already within the field of aesthetics.

So can the sublime be understood other than as an aesthetic category? If we described Abraham's religious faith by means of the category of 'sublimity', would this not signal a forgetting of religiosity? But perhaps Johannes never speaks of anything else except this irrevocable forgetting.

Abraham's duty was both secret and scandalous. He was the man who would not allow himself to be tempted by moral duty, his duty as a father – a duty that anyone could understand, whereas no one could share in the unique unreason of his obedience. His madness, the madness of faith, lies in this absolute singularity: Abraham's relationship with God is that of one absolute to another. It cannot be confined to the moral order or the universality of law: morality has to be 'teleologically suspended'. There is no language to express the uniqueness of this relationship. So Abraham cannot speak, and he cannot be understood: otherwise he would inhabit 'generality' – alongside Agamemnon, the tragic hero who could still be understood by Iphigenia. But why speak on Abraham's behalf? Perhaps only in order to say: 'I am not sublime.' If Kierkegaard can be said to have spoken to Regine in the voice of Johannes, surely it was simply to tell her: 'I am not sublime.' And also, perhaps: 'What a shame that we are not sublime, you and I, that unlike Abraham we cannot resign ourselves infinitely to loss – without weakness, without suffering, and without uncertainty – and then continue to believe that nothing is impossible and we will be restored to each other.'

Faith is not necessarily madness, but it always *might* be. In this respect, Kant and Kierkegaard were in agreement: where reason gives out, madness may always take over. Hence the terror that Abraham strikes into us, and our trembling before his crime. The crime must be faced unflinchingly, and that is what Johannes forces himself to do by means of the stories he tells and retells four times over: the preparations, the journey to Mount Moriah, the Knife: 'Silently he arranged the firewood and bound Isaac; silently he drew the knife.'[7]

He did not have time to use the knife. But still he bound Isaac. The name of this episode – the *akedah* – is derived from this binding and these bonds: it is the story of a son being *bound*. The son was bound hand and foot by his father; and Sarah might have died merely to hear tell of it. Oedipus too was bound at the feet.

Genesis docs not give Abraham a moment for hesitation. God told him: 'Take now thy son, thine only son Isaac, whom thou lovest, and get thee into the land of Moriah; and offer him there for a burnt offering upon one of the mountains which I will tell thee of.

'And Abraham rose up early in the morning, and saddled his ass. . . .'[8]

The Night of Abraham

Abraham's ability to respond immediately and without hesitation makes his action all the more bewildering. But the idea that he did not really hesitate is itself an interpretation, projected on to Abraham's silence, in the text of Genesis, in the period between hearing God's command and setting off for Moriah.

What can that night have been like? We have no way of knowing. Did Abraham manage to get any sleep? Are we to imagine him calm, steady and fearless? Are we to suppose that he made up his mind immediately? No doubt Abraham responded to God's call without delay. But what happened during that night? And if Abraham had doubts then, can we be sure he was not assailed by further doubts when the final moment came? How does one embark on a crime? Where is the 'beginning' when it comes to inflicting or giving death [*donner la mort*]?

God allowed Abraham to tie up his son on the altar. He did not provide the lamb for the sacrifice except *in extremis*. The four tales told by Johannes – 'it was early in the morning' – have the appearance of repetitions or repeats, different versions of a single scene. You take a step back, and then start over again, in slow motion. The purpose is to *represent* the incident to oneself, rather than simply to 'think' it, since thought is always hastening towards an ending: we know it was only a test, and that Isaac will be spared *in the end*. But knowing the ending would efface the entire trial.

And if Isaac really was spared (but could he really be spared, after having seen his father raise the knife above him?), then did Abraham ever really embark on his crime? If you are engaged in a criminal act, at what point does it become impossible to turn back? If Abraham made all the preparations but then stayed his hand, if he hesitated at the final second, the last moment, then surely he would remain, for himself, completely guilty of the crime?

But as we know, the angel intervened: 'Abraham stretched forth his hand, and took the knife to slay his son.' But the angel of the Lord called to him out of heaven, and said, 'Abraham, Abraham.'[9]

How much time remained before the slaughter itself, before Isaac would actually have died? A second would be enough, or even less, for Abraham to cast aside the knife.

I like to think that Abraham might not have gone through with the sacrifice anyway, but that he did not know it. He had made all the preparations, organized everything meticulously, and resigned himself to the death of his son – the son who was a gift from God himself. Mourning had already entered his heart. That is what Johannes describes as the movement of 'infinite resignation'.

The interminable moment began with Abraham's preparations, and it lasted till the very end of his journey. Throughout this time – three whole days – Abraham was forced to contemplate the imminent death of Isaac, the death which was already on its way, and already present to Abraham: for it was Abraham who was going to inflict it, and who must therefore have 'willed' and accepted it. But the 'courage' of Abraham need not, I think, be seen as expressing a straightforward 'decision', based on a faith untouched by doubt. Nevertheless Johannes writes: 'But he did not doubt, he did not look in anguish to the left and to the right.'[10]

But one might also imagine a trembling, agitated Abraham, filled with uncertainty and anguish: for one thing – though this only touches the surface – because Abraham's 'will' and 'resolution' can never be known, given the intervention of the angel. Or rather, it may be a mistake to see it in terms of resolution or an 'act of will' at all – unless will is understood, following Hobbes, in the sense of a 'will and testament'. When death arrives, calling an absolute halt to any alterations of our arrangements, inclinations and desires, then the last inclination and arrangement are regarded as the 'will of the deceased'. It is always the '*last* appetite' or the '*last* fear' which, in retrospect, acquires the status of our 'will', with all the assurance and mastery of execution that this term implies. But in reality, the will is more commanded than commanding; an event has interposed itself and put an end to the succession of our desires and fears, a succession which continues, according to Hobbes, 'till the action be either done, or some accident come between, to make it impossible.'[11]

On the other hand, Abraham's exemplary obedience presupposes a classical conception of resolution, decision, and execution: the act of resolution must be independent of all external forces. It would appear that Abraham showed no sign of hesitation, nothing that might suggest the slightest doubt. The time he spent on the preparations testifies to the nature of his obedience to God. But the intervention of the angel was going to *halt* the sacrifice all the same, in several senses. The incident which was going to occur would mean that Abraham's hand would be stayed as it lifted the knife, halted in a kind of freeze-frame. God would have exacted the pledge he required; the sacrifice would have taken place in that the death sentence had been pronounced. But at the same time, God will have stopped the sacrifice, substituting a lamb for Isaac, and the sacrifice will actually not have taken place. A death sentence [*arrêt de mort*] in a different sense of the word.

The intervention of the angel of Jehovah was an astonishing marvel; but somehow Abraham seemed to have been expecting it all along: 'My son, God will provide himself a lamb for a burnt offering.'[14]

But Abraham's reply to Isaac suggests, I suspect, that as well as Abraham being tested by God, God was being put to the test by Abraham. 'Just how far will you let me go? Behold: I do as I am commanded, but are you really going to let me slaughter my son?' Johannes tries to demonstrate Abraham's faith by saying that he 'believed that God would not demand Isaac of him'. But the point could also be expressed negatively: Abraham did *not* believe that God would demand the sacrifice of Isaac. And this formulation can itself be read in two different ways: either 'he did not *believe* that God would demand Isaac' or 'he did not believe that *God* would demand Isaac'. In other words, did Abraham really believe in a God who would have required Isaac to be sacrificed?

Did he put God to the test? This interpretation would imply, paradoxically perhaps, that the relationship between Abraham and God was marked by a certain sense of humour: 'So you want my son? Sure. But I bet you don't really want me to go through with it.' In that sense, Abraham's faith would reside not in blind obedience, but in scepticism. 'Let's see if God is really asking me to sacrifice Isaac. But I don't believe it. . . .'

Utter Devotion

And Abraham would have been right: God did not want Isaac slaughtered. But if Abraham was putting God to the test, it is not clear what he

would have done if the angel had not intervened. Admittedly the supposition that Abraham was testing God takes us a long way from what
Johannes calls Abraham's madness. It means crediting Abraham with a
kind of free relationship to God, and imagining that one can sit in
judgement on divine justice while remaining within the limits of reason
alone. And the supposition that Abraham did *not* believe that *God* was
really asking him to give up his son certainly takes Abraham a long
distance from the text of the Bible (which of course Johannes did as well,
thought in a different way). Abraham himself does not seem to have
considered any such questions, at least not in Genesis: he was in the
hands of God, and belonged to him utterly. He could not assume that
God was going to return Isaac to him 'on the basis of the absurd' since
if God then appeared to break his promise, it would not be for Abraham
to judge him. To Johannes, the faith of Abraham was comparable to that
of Job.

Abraham accepted immediately what Job slowly came to acknowledge. For Job finally realized that there was an absurd pride in wanting
to be in the right against God, or even in merely wanting to understand
God's reasons, or demanding that God be 'fair'. God's response to Job
did not consist in giving him arguments or 'reasons', but in presenting a
sublime vision of his power, so that no one could ever again hope to
grasp anything of this power or greatness. Faced with the incommensurable and the absolute, Job realized that his protestations were ridiculous. In the end he fell silent. One is never in the right against God. No
one is ever in the right against the Creator.

To fear God is to accept this absolute failure in advance. God alone
can judge.

And perhaps what Kierkegaard added to this fearful humility,
so powerfully present in the Old Testament, was an element of sheer
joy.

There is a fearful happiness in being able to lose onself immediately in
the desire to *respond* by saying, simply and absolutely: 'Here I am.' And
by saying it in silence. Passionate love always tends towards this kind of
devotion, a cheerful accession, faithful and unguarded, to the desire of
the other.

If there is such a thing as love, can it refuse to take this absolute risk?
Could there be a love that was not sublime?

But it seems to me that philosophy – the claim of reason and the claim
to reason, the need to be in the right and always to judge for oneself –
necessarily implies, in various ways, the end of this devotion. It implies
the end of passion in general, the end of religion as well as love, the end
of the sublime devotion which says to the other: 'Thy will be done.' The
question would then be whether there can be a conception of love that

does not depend on the sublime: could there be a love that owes nothing either to aesthetics, or ethics, or religion?

The Sublime Law

One thing that never varies in the uses of the word 'sublime', Kierkegaard's included, is its reference to something incommensurable and absolutely vast, something which could not be represented at all, except perhaps through what Kant called a 'negative representation'. The same definition also applies to Hegel's use of the term in his *Aesthetics*.[13]

When we speak of an 'end of the sublime', we mean something like the end of Abraham's faith, or the end of the conception of an omnipotent creator, or, more generally, the end of our fear of something absolutely *external* to us which might be capable of exciting either devotion or respect. But there is also a different kind of sublimity: the moral sublime, which came into existence with the interiorization of absolute immensity. That is why the *sentiment* or *feeling* of the sublime became, for Kant, 'a feeling of a supersensible faculty within us'.[14] In Kant, the fear was exorcized: the absolute was no longer external. It is as if it had been turned inward so that we need no longer bow down before anything external, but only before the moral law *within*.

Religion can thus be brought within the limits of 'reason alone'. If the Old Testament retained some archetypal value for Kant, it was only as an illustration of the idea that every representation necessarily falls short of absolute immensity, which meant that it was mere vanity to wish to represent the absolute, when this absolute had been dislodged, and the moral law had taken the place of divinity. As Kant wrote: 'the veiled Goddess before whom we kneel, is the moral law within us'. Or again: 'Perhaps there is no more sublime passage in the Jewish Law than the commandment: "Thou shalt not make unto thee any graven image, or any likeness of any thing that is in heaven above, or that is in the earth beneath, or that is in the water under the earth." . . . The very same holds good of our representation of the moral law and of our native capacity for morality.'[15]

When the law has been turned inwards, so that immensity becomes human and religion is reduced to morality, then only two things can still be sublime: the person who respects the moral law, and this respect itself. As Kant says: 'Even *freedom from affection* . . . in a mind that strenuously follows its unswerving principles is sublime.'[16]

But Abraham was not following any principles. And he was not sublime. From Kant's point of view, there was nothing in Abraham apart from his crime, his isolation, and his waywardness.

Hegel's *Aesthetics* retained the Kantian idea of the sublime as the attempt to represent the unrepresentable, but the reference to the sublime as the moral law was abandoned. The sacred art of the sublime was now seen as testifying that the absolute had been conceived inadequately, as an absolutely remote divinity, separate from its creatures and its creation. Hegel's thought implied the end of the sublime, in both its religious and its moral forms. Only the aesthetic category of sublimity remained.

That is why Hegel found sublimity in Hebrew poetry: 'God is the creator of the universe. This is the purest expression of the sublime itself.'[17] For the sublime is the affirmation that the works of spirit are absolutely external to it – God's works primarily, but human works as well. According to Hegel, the art of the sublime can be regarded as uniquely holy, and – since such an art would have to express the relationship between God and the world he had created, while avoiding 'representing' him or portraying any particular image of him – it could only take the form of poetry. The relationship between creation and creator then appears as one of absolute dependence and remoteness. The created world is not regarded as the 'true manifestation' of God, but remains *external* to him: a finite world, emptied of God, but testifying directly to his power and his glory. God's creatures can then experience nothing but their own finitude and the 'impassable gulf' that separates them from God.[18] Their unworthiness before God makes them 'tremble before God's wrath', but nevertheless leaves it open for the individual to adopt an affirmative relationship to God by obeying the divine law and attributing every misfortune to some violation of it. Thus the sublime could be said to refer both to the absolute otherness of God – the relationship without relationship to this absolute – and to the sacred art which attempts to express this 'relationship', or rather this separation.

For Hegel, a symbol always expresses the discrepancy between form and meaning, the inadequacy of the perceptible exterior to the interiority which it represents. And the relationship between created reality and its creator is marked by the same discrepancy: God transcends and exceeds the reality in which he is manifest. Thus the sublimity of God resides in his transcendence of works that testify to his glory without being able to contain it.

The sublimity of sacred art is meant to 'express' the sublimity of God, who remains the reference point of all creation, and its constant allusion, even though he is withdrawn from the world, invisible, and beyond representation. Sacred art can therefore do nothing but express an impossible 'relationship' to God, to a God removed from the world, and it can never display his essence.

It will be noted that the art which corresponds to a God who has withdrawn into lonely isolation is a sacred art in which the plastic or visual arts can have no place, since God can be given neither shape nor form. The only way to evoke the relationship between the visible and the invisible is through words. In Hegelian aesthetics, the sacred art of the sublime can only be the art of poetry.

. And the same applies to pantheism: 'where pantheism is pure, there is no visual art for its representation.'[19] Any form of expression which would limit God to some permanent, precise and individual shape would be ruled out by the omnipresence (or immanence) of God just as effectively as it is by his separation from the world. For the visual arts present precise shapes: they 'bring to our vision only as existent and static the determinate and individual thing.' If, as pantheism asserts, substance is constantly passing from one determination to the next, 'abandoning it in order to proceed to another', controlling all contingencies but not confining itself within them, then God cannot possibly take on any one individual shape.[20] Either way (the absolute transcendence of God or his absolute immanence), all individual shapes have to be obliterated.

There is another example of sublimity, already mentioned by Longinus and taken over by Hegel, for which the word of God appears as a condition of his withdrawal from the world: 'God said, Let there be light: and there was light.'[21] Here is Hegel's commentary: 'The Lord, the one substance, does proceed to manifestation, but the manner of creation is the purest, even bodiless, ethereal manifestation; it is the word, the manifestation of thought as the ideal power, and with its command that the existent shall be, the existent is immediately and actually brought into being in silent obedience.'[22] The withdrawal and transcendence of God are possible only to the extent that creation is *spiritual*, that things are not brought forth by natural procreation from the breast of God. God's spiritual authority has the form of command over bodily creatures. The words of God are commands: the created world, finite and emptied of God, can have no relationship with God except by listening to his law, as the only true manifestation of his power.

The withdrawal of God from the world means that his creatures are left with only one form of relationship to him: that of *listening* or attentive obedience. Having removed himself from the world, God is present only through his law, his voice: listening to this voice is our only possible relationship to the Creator. If God's word of command is the condition of creation and hence of the world's relationship to God, then conversely the relationship of creatures to their Creator must consist in listening – and listening in silence.

But sacred poetry is not poetry for poetry's sake. Rather it is part of religion, and the concept of a sublime *art* could not arise unless 'we' had already lost our 'relationship' to the God of the Old Testament. The term *sublime* belongs to a philosophy which was seeking to locate Jewish religion within a theory of symbolism in general: the category of the sublime belongs to a form of thought which supposes that concrete spirituality has 'transcended' the abstract hebraic vision of infinity. To call the sublime by its name is to transcend it, and so to have lost it. More specifically, to call creation 'sublime' is to use an aesthetic concept in order to proclaim that a representation is inadequate to what it is supposed to represent or embody.

The Bible says: God is *not* his creation, and the distinctive character of Jewish thought lies in this discrepancy. It is a way of thinking which dwells on the non-correspondence between Spirit and the world which it has created. But according to Hegel this conception of God does not measure up to the real and concrete divine substance. Such sublimity falls short of God. The conception of God as removed from the world is inadequate, and therefore *merely* symbolic. Poetry, mere poetry.

Religion and poetry merge into each other here, and distance themselves from any conceptual grasp of Spirit in and for itself. It is only 'for us' that such a conception can be 'sublime', or such poetry symbolic: by reference to 'our' concept of symbolism and the Kantian concept of the sublime in the *Critique of Judgement*, that is to say to the theme of the non-correspondence or *inadequacy* of representation to an infinite which it nevertheless strives to represent. Hegel's use of the category of the sublime presupposed that he had *already* succeeded in transcending, overcoming and transforming the *inadequate* conception of God as creator, and thus reducing religion to a mere representation (an *inadequate* representation) of the truth. 'We' – we dialecticians – have negated the idea of God as the negation of the phenomenal world. And this negation of the negation enables us to conceive of the reconciliation of the spiritual and the sensible, the subjective and the objective. Sublimity is born in this reconciliation, but dies in it too, in the retrospective naming of the unrepresentable.

Those who sustained a relationship with the absolute in the form of the moral law could still be sublime. But we dialecticians have no wish to be sublime, so we are able to make the claim: 'we are not sublime'. Religious sublimity, dialectically transcended, mutates into aesthetic sublimity.

If Abraham's sacrifice, or his devotion, can be described as aesthetically sublime, then they are no more than the transcended shapes of a transcended form of religious thinking: 'consciousness of an impassable gulf between the being of God and the being of men', as Hegel said of

Judaism in 'The Spirit of Christianity and its Fate.'[23] But if philosophical aesthetics always associates the sublime with an 'impassable gulf', it can only do so *after* the gulf has supposedly been bridged. Religiosity as such can never think of itself as *sublime*, any more than sacred art can think of itself as *art*.

And Abraham's faith could only be 'sublime' to those for whom it had been transcended or lost for ever. That is why Johannes's poetic meditations on Abraham's sacrifice will never constitute a religious text, or imply a genuine return of faith: perhaps they are only representations of its obliteration. And it is not only God that is hidden: the image of a man who believed in God is concealed from us too. Hegel denied the withdrawal of God from the world, in a dialectical negation of the *negative* God of creation. For the poet of the sublime, however, there could only be a forgetting of this divine withdrawal: a withdrawal of the withdrawal, perhaps.

But if Hegel's philosophy transcends the sublimity of Hebrew religion and poetry, that of Kant denies the sublimity of Abraham altogether. Why should that be?

The Madness of Abraham

For Kant, nothing can be absolutely immense except the voice of Reason. Only the law of Reason can impose absolute and universal obligations on *humanity*, and nothing else could be truly sublime. This turning inward of the religious toward the moral, which we have already mentioned above, was achieved by means of the Kantian conception of *rational faith* as providing the only criterion for judging religious observances and beliefs; and it completely destroyed the religious value and greatness of Abraham's obedience. Abraham could not possibly be sublime; moreover Judaism itself could not even be a genuine religion if it permitted such a clash between religion and morality.

But Abraham had to choose between religion and morality, or at least he thought he had to: on this point at least, the author of *Religion Within the Limits of Reason Alone* is in complete agreement with the author of *Fear and Trembling*.

Johannes observes that the temptation which Abraham was called upon to resist was no ordinary one. It was not a temptation to fail in his moral duty. On the contrary: moral duty is precisely what tempted Abraham to disobey God's command. Hence the religious trial of Abraham entailed the 'teleological suspension' of the ethical. It required the individual whom God was putting to the test to place himself above the universal. That is the paradox. And Kant and Johannes both used the same words to describe Abraham's 'choice': it makes you tremble, and it fills you with horror. The whole of *Religion within the Limits of Reason Alone* was designed to denounce Abraham and banish such acts of reason-blind faith from the sphere of religion. This exclusion was needed in order to avoid any possibility of error concerning what is 'truly agreeable to God', and to preclude any relationship to a God whose law was not simply the moral law, and capable of being comprehended by Reason. Any religious language that involved vision, revelation, imagination, or feeling was contaminated with empiricity, and was merely the expression of singularities: it was neither instructive nor edifying. It could always err and mislead: 'It is at least possible that in this instance a mistake has prevailed.' It was precisely the *possibility* of this false and misleading voice that Kant invoked in connection with the command that Abraham should 'slaughter his own son like a lamb'. To Kant this command was not only monstrous but absurd, in view of God's promise concerning Abraham's descendants. To obey such a commandment, such a 'terrible injunction', would necessarily be to act without conscience, or unconscientiously. 'This is the case with respect to all historical and visionary faith; that is, the *possibility* ever remains that an error may be discovered in it. Hence it is unconscientious to follow such a faith with the possibility that perhaps what it commands or permits may be wrong, i.e. with the danger of disobedience to a human duty which is certain in and of itself.'[24]

Johannes knew it too. He knew that Abraham must be 'either a murderer or a man of faith', and that is why he wrote that 'one approaches him with a *horror religiosus*, as Israel approached Mount Sinai'.[25]

But the Kantian identification of religion with rational faith and a purely ethical religion raises a problem: for it is not clear that Christianity – which for Kant was the only religion – really is a purely ethical religion.

When Kant wrote that 'steadfast diligence in morally good life-conduct is all that God requires of men, to be subjects in His kingdom and well-pleasing to him',[26] he deliberately ignored the problems of faith, of belief in the incarnation, the demand for love addressed to all of us by Christ, and the irreducibility of this love – or any other love – to reason. Love is an individual response to a unique call: a call addressed directly to me. Anyone who answers this call by saying 'Here I am' is acting like Abraham and overstepping the limits of reason alone.

Kant's 'pure rational faith' may well be genuinely pure; but in that case it can no longer be faith. By reducing Christianity to a purely ethical religion, Kant was abstracting from faith in Jesus Christ, and from the mystery of the trinity and the incarnation, and hence from the absolute risk which inheres in the belief that God was *this particular man*, an empirical and historical reality. He abstracted from love for the God-become-man who gave the infinite such a specific face. And yet Abraham was a man of faith only to the extent that his faithfulness – his 'answer' to God's call: 'here I am' – was a leap into danger. (Can it really be *God* who is asking this of me; can *this* really be what he wants?) And faith in Christ is another absolute risk: could this particular man really be the son of God? Thus *Religion Within the Limits of Reason Alone* cannot comprehend either the faith of Abraham or that of the apostles: neither obedience to the God who hides his face, nor love for the God incarnate.

The philosopher of 'reason alone' was not addressing himself to a singularity: he was concerned with humankind in general, universal humanity. The Kantian conception of religion is inseparable from a discourse in which 'humanity' has already been defined.

The preface to the second edition of *Religion Within the Limits of Reason Alone* specifies that its author speaks as 'a teacher of pure reason'.[27] For Kant, education was 'perverted' as soon as it became priestly, mystagogical, or aristocratic. This kind of teaching drew on the authority of mysterious voices and visions, secrets handed down through obscure traditions, and poetical, cryptic language. . . .

Anything that could not be said unequivocally by the voice of reason belonged to empirical singularity, to the private sphere, and had nothing to do with genuine education. The reason why the teachable coincided with the rational lay in the very nature of education, whose only possible goal was the improvement and general good of *humanity* as such. The teachable was confined to the universalizable, and reason – as the faculty for knowledge of the unconditioned absolute – was the only true master. Outside it there was no education. Religion *unsettles* us by abandoning us all to our singularity; but philosophy reassures us by identifying the true with the universal. Kantian humanity has a horror of going mad, and it would never risk sharing the madness of Abraham.

The only way religion could become universal, therefore, was by being incorporated into philosophy. If all of us must, in virtue of our humanity, be capable of honouring God, then God's laws must be purely moral, and accessible to all of us solely in virtue of our own reason: '*Pure religious faith* alone can found a universal church; for only rational faith can be believed in and shared by everyone.'[28]

It was not impossible for an 'ecclesiastical faith' – a historical faith based merely on facts – to coincide with the true rational faith, but it would be a pure coincidence, or the grace of a benevolent providence. Hence there was only one religion, one teaching, one voice, and one language (a language which should, if possible, be spoken without a hint of artifice or style).

Abraham, however, exalted individuality into an absolute. He put an absolute human singularity into a direct relationship with the absolute of his God: a necessarily secret relationship. Abraham could not even understand himself, since to do so would be to stray into the sphere of universality. And this lack of mediation cut him off from any use of language that might *constrain* his singularity. He responded to the voice that said 'Come', by saying 'Here I am.' But he did not answer it. At least that is how Johannes saw it.

'Here I am' is not exactly an answer. Nor is it an indication of servile obedience. To say 'Here I am' is to speak protectively, like a mother: – 'I'm here.' As if to say, 'don't worry, you're not alone'. The figure of a maternal Abraham. . . . Maybe God wanted to make sure that he could take the place of the child? A jealous God.

The Withdrawal of Abraham

The words 'Here I am' could never be spoken out of duty, and they could not possibly be addressed to 'humanity in general'. Nevertheless they speak of something absolute: whatever happens, whatever you wish, here I am. It is an unconditional *yes*, and it is neither moral nor fair. The experience of this *yes* does not arise from any kind of knowledge. It is not even an experience: those who give themselves up to their *yes* are not the kind of classical subjects in relation to whom empirical knowledge is defined, but neither are they the subjects of a mystical experience that presupposes some direct communion with the absolute.

Faith cannot be taught, and neither can love (perhaps they are the same). And that is why Johannes was neither a philosopher nor a believer, but a poet. He did not speak the language of philosophy, and neither was he able to say 'yes'. He simply said he could not understand Abraham – that was the point he wanted to emphasize. Of course he referred to the 'Here I am' – but only as an *impossibility* for him, and no doubt for us too. For us, Abraham has disappeared into the night, into his night, and for us it remains as dark as ever. We have no knowledge to shine upon his shadowed face.

'I can only admire him', says Johannes. It is as if we were left with absolutely nothing, except perhaps our admiration for Abraham as a man of faith. And if we can still see him as sublime, it is only because we cannot understand either his God or his devotion: his obedience and his *yes* are now beyond our measure.

Johannes's text bears witness to a gap between religious poetry and the poetry of the religious.[29] The sublimity of the creator and his creation have been replaced by the sublimity of Abraham's ability to enter into a relationship with God, and it is this figure of Abraham that is now unrepresentable, erased, withdrawn. To say that Abraham is sublime is to say that he has become a stranger to us. We tremble before the man of faith just as he trembled before his God. Abraham encountered the mystery of God, but we only encounter the mystery of Abraham.

Human Loves

Religious devotion may be closely connected with erotic love, but Kierkegaard never equated the two. Adoration and unconditional obedience belong to our love for God, not for each other.

> Erotic love is still not the eternal; it is the beautiful dizziness of infinity; its highest expression is the foolhardiness of riddles. This explains its attempting an even dizzier expression, 'to love a person more than God.'[30]

Erotic love is all too human, it is love by predilection – love according to preference and choice. It is quite unlike the adoration and obedience that God inspires, and also unlike the love of our neighbour that God requires of us in the Gospels: 'Thou shalt love thy neighbour as thyself.'

The second chapter of *Works of Love* is called 'Thou *shalt* love.' Writing now under his own name, Kierkegaard insists on the need to give up the immediacy of human love – the precariousness and danger, the jealousy and anguish – in favour of eternal love, which owes nothing to either luck or chance. The love that binds us to each other cannot achieve peace, eternity, or truth, unless it can detach itself from the contingencies of individual tenderness and subject itself to the medium of law. Freed from the whims of inclination, our love for our neighbour comes to resemble a Kantian sublime respect for principles. But love cannot be 'reunited' with the principle of law unless it breaks away from the singularity of its object and occasion. It achieves eternal certainty by becoming a duty. 'Thou shalt love. *Only when it is a duty to love, only then is love eternally secured against every change, eternally made free in blessed independence, eternally and happily secured against despair.*'[31]

This 'thou shalt' serves to shelter love from change. And the unconditional 'duty to love' grants love both peace and independence: 'that love has the law for its existence in the relation of love itself to the eternal'.[32]

If the one I love tells me: 'I cannot love you any longer', my pride would probably make me say: 'Then it's all over between us' – which shows that my love was not independent. But if I replied 'I must still love you all the same' then my love would be eternally free and independent – a love '*sheltered by despair*'.[33] In this way, the law of love can be said to reintroduce the safety net of a universal imperative.

Kierkegaard knew that love, even when it is happy, loves with '*the power of despair*'. He knew that despair never takes us by surprise in our unhappiness but simply reveals that we were in despair already.[34] What hands us over to despair is not unhappiness, but our lack of the eternal – a lack which marks all human loves.

The power of love is surely the same as the power of despair. But if this despair really is inextricably linked with our lack of the eternal, it can also be understood, I suspect, as a means of freeing ourselves from vain optimism and foolish notions about eternity and immortality. Without this essential lack, and our acceptance of it, we would never be able to form any conception of giving, or conceive of love as a gift. What more can I give than my time – that is to say not my life or death, but my essential mortality. Lovers dream of dying in each other's arms, dying for each other, and watching each other die, like Romeo and Juliet, as if they wanted to make a gift to each other of their own mortality.

For Kierkegaard, however, the command to love draws its sustenance from eternity, responding to the primordial duty *not to despair*:

> When it is made impossible to possess the beloved in time, eternity says, 'Thou shalt love' – that is, eternity saves love from despair by making it eternal.[35]

It saves it from despair by preserving it: 'Thou shalt preserve love and thou shalt preserve thyself and by and in preserving yourself preserve love.'[36]

No doubt it is necessary to have dwelt in absolute despair in order to understand the force of the commandment which strikes it down and says: 'You must not despair.' One might say: preserve yourself from despair, preserve yourself by preserving your love, your own love, unconditionally and for all eternity. Do not die to your own love, do not die to yourself: preserve yourself. But if lovers take such precautions, then surely they are simply seeking their *own* survival. And this passion for eternal preservation through dutiful love is precisely what separates us from the other as such, what separates us from the *event* of the other, of time, of randomness, of luck, of finitude – and of love. Or at least, of love in its essential precariousness, the love which is directed towards an empirical mortal individual, on whom it knowingly depends; and lovers surrender themselves to such individualities only because giving oneself away is always dangerous, or rather because one is bound to lose every time. How could we ever make a gift, if we did not know that we are destined to grow old and die, if we were not giving something that can be reckoned up, something that we know will *pass away*? Of course the eternal does not rush past us, but it does not come up to meet us either. How could eternity ever belong to what happens, to events? And how should we conceive of love, except as an event that comes upon our mortal existence and takes it by surprise – entrusting everything we thought we were, everything we thought we possessed, to the unsafe keeping of another mortal, and taking the other into our own keeping as well.

No doubt the injunction to preserve love in order to preserve oneself could make me independent of the other, if not indifferent: I would no longer be prey to either anguish or jealousy, even if I ceased to be loved, even if I were abandoned. I would love for eternity. Thus Søren could say to Regine: 'I have abandoned you, but I shall love you for ever, and that is the standard by which my love should be measured. What more could you ask for?' But we may have our doubts about the humility of those who make it their duty to love for all eternity: they abase themselves before the 'thou shalt', but not before the other. That is how they are able to be 'independent'.

For what is left of love, after the madness of religious devotion, and after the ethical injunction to love eternally? Surely the humblest love is what occurs when one individuality simply attends to another, finitude inclined toward finitude. In a case of ethical respect or dutiful loving, my relationship flows from a requirement which is indifferent to the individuality of the other, and what I owe to the other is inextricable from what I owe to myself: keeping myself, keeping myself free, and keeping myself free of despair. Love as a duty will always be egocentric. But what distinguishes love at its humblest from devotion is that it does not treat the finite individuality to which it attends as if it were an absolute; it sustains and affirms its finitude through a tenderness which is as singular – as random and unfair – as existence itself.

This kind of tenderness is therefore *neither* ethical *nor* religious, and it has no interest in freedom as classically conceived, or in law. It is an attachment, the link which makes one existence necessary for another, and which allows existences to depend upon and suffer through each other. If love is a duty, however, then it can free itself from its object and adhere only to the law. Without law, as Kierkegaard writes, there can be absolutely no freedom.[37] And the theme of freedom as autonomy crops up just when you would least expect it: in love, but in love understood as a commandment: 'Thou shalt love.' This is a paradoxical love, to be sure: the love that frees me from its object: it frees me from the object by freeing me from the risk of losing it, the risk of mourning. 'Such a love neither stands nor falls with the contingency of its object.'[38] What Kierkegaard referred to as the courage of loving in eternity is in fact the 'courage' of giving up in advance whatever might be taken away from us – in the hope of getting it back again. But surely there is another kind of courage: the courage of accepting the event of loss, and enduring it without anticipation. Why should we *not* have to suffer? By what right? As Freud put it in his essay 'On Transience': 'What is painful may none the less be true.'[39]

Losing in order to win: it would seem that this is the law of the spirit as well as the spirit of the law, of the law of detachment: losing the finite in order to keep it, and anticipating the loss. A tactic of sacrifice. Making a sacrifice of the instant, the ephemeral, the unique, and the immediate. That is also the law of memory, of memorial interiorization, of recollection. Mourning everywhere, and the anticipation of mourning. Merely by thinking, the existing individual strains to avoid suffering. And Kierkegaard was not exempt from this law.

Law always requires the same thing, whatever its source and however it may be defined (divine law, moral duty, unconditional love for our neighbour); it requires a dissolution of ties – of the ties that attach us to finite individualities, the ties that bind individual bodily existences together. How did God refer to Isaac? He called him: *thy son, thine only son, whom thou lovest*. Isaac was to be sacrificed so that the most natural of physical bonds should be broken. Otherwise there could be no access to spirituality, or law, or freedom.

To love in eternity, in conformity with the religious movement of the infinite, would be to fulfil the requirements of law in a sublime sacrifice of the finite. But existing can also mean being able to love the finite, and being capable of finitude, of saying yes to finitude, that is to say, to time. To subject oneself to the ephemeral, to suffer it, to suffer loss without suffering it *in advance*, to accept the time of the wound and the wound of time; and to accept the event of the other.

NOTES

1 [Sylviane Agacinski, *Aparté: Conceptions et morts de Sören Kierkegaard* (Aubier Montaigne, Paris, 1977), translated by Kevin Newmark as *Aparté: Conceptions and Deaths of Søren Kierkegaard* (Florida State University Press, Gainesville, 1988.]

2 [Johannes de Silentio – the pseudonym in whose name *Fear and Trembling* was published – remarks for example that 'to change the leap into life into walking, absolutely to express the sublime in the pedestrian – only that knight can do it, and this is the one and only marvel.' See *Fear and Trembling, Repetition*, translated by Howard V. Hong and Edna H. Hong (Princeton University Press, Princeton, 1983), p. 41.]

3 [Cf. *The Sickness Unto Death*, translated by Howard V. Hong and Edna H. Hong (Princeton University Press, Princeton, 1980), p. 78: 'He becomes a poet of the religious in the same way as one who became a poet through an unhappy love affair and blissfully celebrates the happiness of erotic love.' See also n. 29 below, p. 149, and n. 7 to Ricoeur, p. 24 above.]

4 [Immanuel Kant, *Critique of Judgement*, translated by James Creed Meredith (Oxford University Press, Oxford, 1952), Part One, Section One, Book Two, §25, p. 97.]

5 Nevertheless I feel quite close to an essay by Jean-Luc Nancy which strikingly argues that a 'sublime sacrifice' can never provide the 'sovereign satisfaction of a spirit capable of infinity'. The sublime does not lie *beyond* the limit; rather it is the emotion of a subject *at the limit*. But his highly original approach to the sublime and to freedom (a freedom which is both sacrificing and sacrificed) is not the one I shall be adopting here. [See Jean-Luc Nancy, 'L'offrande sublime' in *Du Sublime* (Belin, Paris, 1986).]

6 [Cf. two statements from Problema III of *Fear and Trembling*: 'no poet can find his way to Abraham', and 'I am not a poet, and I go at things only dialectically.' See *Fear and Trembling, Repetition*, pp. 118, 90.]

7 [Cf. the section of *Fear and Trembling* entitled 'Stemning' ('Attunement' or 'Exordium'). See *Fear and Trembling, Repetition*, translated by Howard V. Hong and Edna H. Hong (Princeton University Press, Princeton, 1983), pp. 9–14, p. 12.]

8 [Genesis 22: 2–3.]

9 [Genesis 22: 11.]

10 ['Eulogy on Abraham', *Fear and Trembling*, p. 22.]

11 Thomas Hobbes, *Humane Nature: Or, the Fundamental Elements of Policie* (1650), in William Molesworth, *The English Works of Thomas Hobbes* (11 vols, London, 1839–45), vol. IV, p. 68. Hobbes continues as follows: 'In deliberation, the last appetite, as also the last fear, is called *will*, viz. the last appetite, will to do, or will to omit. It is all one therefore to say *will* or *last will*; for, though a man express his present inclination and appetite concerning the disposition of his goods, by words or writings; yet shall it not be counted his will, because he hath still liberty to dispose of them otherways; but when death taketh away that liberty, then it is his will.'

12 [Genesis 22: 8.]

13 [See G. W. F. Hegel, *Aesthetics: Lectures on Fine Art*, translated by T. M. Knox (2 vols, Oxford University Press, Oxford, 1975), vol. 1, p. 363.]

14 [*Critique of Judgement*, Part One, Section One, Book Two, §25, p. 97.]

15 [*Critique of Judgement*, Part One, Section One, Book Two, §29, p. 127; see also Exodus 20: 4.]

16 [*Critique of Judgement*, Part One, Section One, Book Two, §29, p. 124.]

17 ['The Art of the Sublime' in G. W. F. Hegel, *Aesthetics: Lectures on Fine Art*, vol. 1, p. 373.]

18 [See 'The Spirit of Christianity and its Fate' in G. W. F. Hegel, *Early Theological Writings*, translated by T. M. Knox and Richard Kroner (University of Chicago Press, Chicago, 1948), p. 265.]

19 [Hegel, *Aesthetics*, p. 366.]

20 [Hegel, *Aesthetics*, p. 366.]

21 [See Genesis 1: 3, and Longinus, *On the Sublime*, ix 10.]

22 [Hegel, *Aesthetics*, pp. 373–4.]

23 [Hegel, *Early Theological Writings*, p. 265.]

24 [Immanuel Kant, *Religion Within the Limits of Reason Alone* (1793), translated by Theodore M. Greene and Hoyt H. Hudson (Harper and Row, New York, 1960), p. 175.]

25 ['Problema I', *Fear and Trembling*, pp. 57, 61; cf. Exodus 19: 24.]

26 [*Religion Within the Limits of Reason Alone*, p. 94.]

27 [*Religion Within the Limits of Reason Alone*, p. 11.]

28 [*Religion Within the Limits of Reason Alone*, p. 94.]

29 ['The reason a religious poet is a dubious category in relation to the paradoxical–religious is that, esthetically, possibility is higher than actuality, and the poetic consists in the ideality of imaginative intuition. This is why we not infrequently see hymns that, although stirring and childlike and poetic through a tinge of imagination verging on the fantastic, are not, viewed categorically, Christian.' See *Concluding Unscientific Postscript*, translated by Howard V. Hong and Edna H. Hong (2 vols, Princeton University Press, Princeton, 1992), p. 580; see also pp. 351, 357. See also n. 3 above and n. 7 to Ricoeur, p. 24 above.]

30 [*Works of Love*, translated by Howard V. Hong and Edna H. Hong (Princeton University Press, Princeton, 1995), p. 19.]

31 [*Works of Love*, p. 29. This and other translations have been amended to read 'thou shalt' for 'you shall' in order to accord with Matthew 22: 39 in the Authorized Version.]

32 [*Works of Love*, p. 38.]

33 [Agacinski here paraphrases Kierkegaard. 'If when another person says, "I cannot love you any longer," one proudly answers, "Then I can stop loving you" – is this independence? Alas, it is dependence, because whether he will continue to love or not depends upon whether the other will love. But the person who answers, "In that case I *shall* still continue to love you" – that person's love is made eternally free in blessed independence. He does not say it proudly – dependent on his pride – no, he says it humbly, humbling himself under eternity's "Thou shalt"; and for that very reason he is independent./ *Only when it is duty to love, only then is love eternally and happily secured against despair.*' *Works of Love*, pp. 39–40.]

34 ['When spontaneous love despairs over misfortune, it only becomes manifest that it was in despair, that in its happiness it had also been in despair.' *Works of Love*, p. 40.]

35 [*Works of Love*, p. 41.]

36 [*Works of Love*, p. 43.]
37 ['Without law, freedom does not exist at all, and it is law that gives freedom.' *Works of Love*, pp. 38–9.]
38 ['en saadan Kjerlighed staaer og falder ikke med sin Gjenstands Tilfældighed' – a passage mistranslated by Hong and Hong (*Works of Love*, p. 39) as 'love stands and does not fall'.]
39 ['Auch das schmerzliche kann wahr sein.' Sigmund Freud, 'Vergänglichkeit' (1915), translated by James Strachey as 'On Transience' in Albert Dickson, ed., *Art and Literature* (Pelican Freud Library, vol. 1, Penguin, Harmondsworth, 1985), pp. 267–90.]

9
Whom to Give to
(Knowing Not to Know)

Jacques Derrida

Mysterium tremendum. A frightful mystery, a secret to make you tremble.

Tremble. What does one do when one trembles? What is it that makes you tremble?

A secret always *makes you tremble.* Not simply quiver or shiver, which also happens sometimes, but tremble. A quiver can of course manifest fear, anguish, apprehension of death; as when one quivers in advance, in anticipation of what is to come. But it can be slight, on the surface of the skin, like a quiver that announces the arrival of pleasure or an orgasm. It is a moment in passing, the suspended time of seduction. A quiver is not always very serious, it is sometimes discreet, barely discernable, somewhat epiphenomenal. It prepares for, rather than follows the event. One could say that water quivers before it boils; that is the idea I was referring to as seduction: a superficial pre-boil, a preliminary and visible agitation.

On the other hand, trembling, at least as a signal or symptom, is something that has already taken place, as in the case of an earthquake [*tremblement de terre*] or when one trembles all over. It is no longer

This piece was originally Chapter 3 of Derrida's *Donner la mort*, first published in *L'éthique du don, Jacques Derrida et la pensée du don*, edited by Jean-Michel Rabaté and Michael Wetzel (Métailié-Transition, Paris, 1992). It was published in English as Chapter 3 of Jacques Derrida, *The Gift of Death*, translated by David Wills (University of Chicago Press, Chicago, 1995) and is reprinted here with permission.

preliminary even if, unsettling everything so as to imprint upon the body an irrepressible shaking, the event that makes one tremble portends and threatens still. It suggests that violence is going to break out again, that some traumatism will insist on being repeated. As different as dread, fear, anxiety, terror, panic, or anguish remain from one another, they have already begun in the trembling, and what has provoked them continues, or threatens to continue, to make us tremble. Most often we neither know what is coming upon us nor see its origin; it therefore remains a secret. We are afraid of the fear, we anguish over the anguish, and we tremble. We tremble in that strange repetition that ties an irrefutable past (a shock has been felt, a traumatism has already affected us) to a future that cannot be anticipated; anticipated but unpredictable; *apprehended*, but, and this is why there is a future, apprehended precisely *as* unforeseeable, unpredictable; approached *as* unapproachable. Even if one thinks one knows what is going to happen, the new instant of that happening remains untouched, still inaccessible, in fact unliveable. In the repetition of what still remains unpredictable, we tremble first of all because we don't know from which direction the shock came, whence it was given (whether a good surprise or a bad shock, sometimes a surprise received as a shock); and we tremble from not knowing, in the form of a double secret, whether it is going to continue, start again, insist, be repeated: whether it will, how it will, where, when; and why *this* shock. Hence I tremble because I am still afraid of what already makes me afraid, of what I can neither see nor foresee. I tremble at what exceeds my seeing and my knowing [*mon voir et mon savoir*] although it concerns the innermost parts of me, right down to my soul, down to the bone, as we say. Inasmuch as it tends to undo both seeing and knowing, trembling is indeed an experience of secrecy or of mystery, but another secret, another enigma, or another mystery comes on top of the unliveable experience, adding yet another seal or concealment to the *tremor* (the Latin word for 'trembling', from *tremo*, which in Greek as in Latin means *I tremble, I am afflicted by trembling*; in Greek there is also *tromeō*: I tremble, I shiver, I am afraid; and *tromos*, which means trembling, fear, fright. In Latin, *tremendus*, *tremendum*, as in *mysterium tremendum*, is a gerundive derived from *tremo*: what makes one tremble, something frightening, distressing, terrifying).

Where does this supplementary seal come from? One doesn't know *why one trembles*. This limit to knowledge no longer only relates to the cause or unknown event, the unseen or unknown that makes us tremble. Neither do we know why it produces this particular symptom, a certain irrepressible agitation of the body, the uncontrollable instability of its members or of the substance of the skin or muscles. Why does the irrepressible take this form? Why does terror make us tremble, since one can also tremble with cold, and such analogous physiological manifestations translate experiences and sentiments that appear, at least, not to have anything in common? This symptomatology is as enigmatic as tears. Even if one knows why one weeps, in what situation, and what it signifies (I weep because I have lost one of my nearest and dearest, the child cries because he has been beaten or because she is not loved: she causes herself grief, complains, he makes himself complain or allows himself to be felt sorry for – by means of the other), but that still doesn't explain why the lachrymal glands come to secrete these drops of water which are brought to the eyes rather than elsewhere, the mouth or the ears. We would need to make new inroads into thinking concerning the body, without dissociating the registers of discourse (thought, philosophy, the bio-genetico-psychoanalytic sciences, phylo- and ontogenesis), in order one day to come closer to what makes us tremble or what makes us cry, to that *cause* which is not the final cause that can be called God or death (God is the cause of the *mysterium tremendum*, and the death that is given is always what makes us tremble, or what makes us weep as well) but to a closer cause; not the immediate cause, that is, the accident or circumstance, but the cause closest to our body, that which means that one trembles or weeps rather than doing something else. What is it a metaphor or figure for? What does *the body mean to say* by trembling or crying, presuming one can speak here of the body, or of saying, of meaning, and of rhetoric?

What is it that makes us tremble in the *mysterium tremendum*? It is the gift of infinite love, the dissymmetry what exists between the divine regard that sees me, and myself, who doesn't see what is looking at me; it is the gift and endurance of death that exists in the irreplaceable, the disproportion between the infinite gift and my finitude, responsibility as culpability, sin, salvation, repentance, and sacrifice) As in the title of Kierkegaard's essay *Fear and Trembling*,[1] the *mysterium tremendum* includes at least an implicit and indirect reference to Saint Paul. In the Epistle to the Philippians 2: 12, the disciples are asked to work towards their salvation in fear and trembling. They will have to work for their salvation knowing all along that it is God who decides: the Other has no reason to give to us and nothing to settle in our favour, no reason to share his reasons with us. We fear and tremble because we are already in the hands of God, although free to work, but in the hands and under the gaze of God, whom we don't see and whose will we cannot know, no more than the decisions he will hand down, nor his reasons for wanting this or that, our life or death, our salvation or perdition. We fear and tremble before the inaccessible secret of a God who decides for us although we remain responsible, that is, free to decide, to work, to assume our life and our death.

So Paul says [. . .]:

Wherefore my beloved, as ye have always obeyed, not as in my presence only, but now much more in my absence (*non ut in praesentia mei tantum, sed multo magis nunc in absentia mea / mē hōs en tē parousia mou monon alla nun pollō mallon en tē apousia mou*), work out your own salvation with fear and trembling (*cum metu et tremore / meta phobou kai tromou*).[2]

This is a first explanation of the fear and of the trembling, and of 'fear and trembling'. The disciples are asked to work towards their salvation not in the presence (*parousia*) but in the absence (*apousia*) of the master: without either seeing or knowing, without hearing the law or the reasons for the law. Without knowing from whence the thing comes and what awaits us, we are given over to absolute solitude. No one can speak with us and no one can speak for us; we must take it upon ourselves, each of us must take it upon himself) (*auf sich nehmen* as Heidegger says concerning death, our death, concerning what is always 'my death', and which no one can take on in place of me).[3] But there is something even more serious at the origin of this trembling. If Paul says 'adieu' and absents himself as he asks them to obey, in fact ordering them to obey (for one doesn't ask for obedience, one orders it), it is because God is himself absent, hidden and silent, separate, secret, at the moment he has to be obeyed. God doesn't give his reasons, he acts as he intends, he doesn't have to give his reasons or share anything with us: neither his motivations, if he has any, nor his deliberations, nor his decisions. Otherwise he wouldn't be God, we wouldn't be dealing with the Other as God or with God as *wholly other* [*tout autre*]. If the other were to share his reasons with us by explaining them to us, if he were to speak to us all the time without any secrets, he wouldn't be the other, we would share a type of homogeneity. Discourse also partakes of this sameness; we don't speak with God or to God, we don't speak with God or to God as with others or to our fellows.) Paul continues in fact:

For it is God which worketh in you both to will and to do of his good pleasure.[4]

One can understand why Kierkegaard chose, for his title, the words of a great Jewish convert, Paul, in order to meditate on the still Jewish experience of a secret, hidden, separate, absent, or mysterious God, the one who decides, without revealing his reasons, to demand of Abraham that most cruel, impossible, and untenable gesture: to offer his son Isaac as a sacrifice. All that goes on in secret. God keeps silent about his reasons. Abraham does also, and the book is not signed by Kierkegaard, but by Johannes de Silentio ('a poetic person who exists only among poets', Kierkegaard writes in the margin of his text[5]).

This pseudonym keeps silent, it expresses the silence that is kept. Like all pseudonyms, it seems destined to keep secret the real name *as* patronym, that is, the name of the father of the work in fact the name of the father of the father of the work. This pseudonym, one among many that Kierkegaard employed, reminds us that a meditation linking the question of secrecy to that of responsibility immediately raises the question of the name and of the signature. One often thinks that responsibility consists of acting and signing *in one's name*. A responsible reflection on responsibility is interested in advance in whatever happens to the name in the event of pseudonymity, metonymy, homonymy, in the matter of what constitutes *a real name*. Sometimes one says or wishes it more effectively, more authentically, in the secret name by which *one calls oneself*, that *one gives oneself or affects to give oneself*, the name that is more *naming* and *named* in the pseudonym than in the official legality of the public patronym.

The trembling of *Fear and Trembling* is, or so it seems, the very experience of sacrifice. Not, first of all, in the Hebraic sense of the term, *korban*, which refers more to an approach or a 'coming close to', and which has been wrongly translated as 'sacrifice', but in the sense that sacrifice supposes the putting to death of the unique in terms of its being unique, irreplaceable, and most precious. It also therefore refers to the impossibility of substitution, the unsubstitutable; and then also to the substitution of an animal for man; and finally, especially this, by means of this impossible substitution itself, it refers to what links the sacred to sacrifice and sacrifice to secrecy.

Kierkegaard/Johannes de Silentio recalls Abraham's strange reply to Isaac when the latter asks him where the sacrificial lamb is to be found. It can't be said that Abraham doesn't respond to him. He says God will provide. God will provide a lamb for the burnt offering ['*holocauste*'].[6] Abraham thus keeps his secret at the same time as he replies to Isaac. He doesn't keep silent and he doesn't lie. He doesn't speak non-truth. In *Fear and Trembling* (*Problema III*) Kierkegaard reflects on this double secret: that between God and Abraham but also that between the latter and his family. Abraham doesn't speak of what God has ordered him alone to do, he doesn't speak of it to Sarah, or to Eliezer, or to Isaac. He must keep the secret (that is his duty), but it is also a secret that he *must* keep as a double necessity because in the end he *can only* keep it: he doesn't know it, he is unaware of its ultimate rhyme and reason. He is sworn to secrecy because he is in secret.

Because, in this way, he doesn't speak, Abraham transgresses the ethical order. According to Kierkegaard, the highest expression of the ethical is in terms of what binds us to our own and to our fellows (that can be the family but also the actual community of friends or the nation). By keeping the secret, Abraham betrays ethics. His silence, or at least the fact that he doesn't divulge the secret of the sacrifice he has been asked to make, is certainly not designed to save Isaac.

Of course, in some respects Abraham does speak. He says a lot. But even if he says everything, he need only keep silent on a single thing for one to conclude that he hasn't spoken. Such a silence takes over his whole discourse. So he speaks and doesn't speak. He responds without responding. He responds and doens't respond. He responds indirectly. He speaks in order not to say anything about the essential thing that he must keep secret. Speaking in order not to say anything is always the best technique for keeping a secret. Still, Abraham doesn't just speak in order not to say anything when he replies to Isaac. He says something that is not nothing and that is not false. He says something that is not a non-truth, something moreover that, although *he doesn't know it yet*, will turn out to be true.

To the extent that, in not saying the essential thing, namely, the secret between God and him, Abraham doesn't speak, he assumes the responsibility that consists in always being alone, entrenched in one's own singularity at the moment of decision. Just as no one can die in my place, no one can make a decision, what we call 'a decision', in my place. But as soon as one speaks, as soon as one enters the medium of language, one loses that very singularity. One therefore loses the possibility of deciding or the right to decide. Thus every decision would, fundamentally, remain at the same time solitary, secret, and silent. Speaking relieves us, Kierkegaard notes, for it 'translates' into the general.[7]

The first effect or first destination of language therefore involves depriving me of, or delivering me from, my singularity. By suspending my absolute singularity in speaking, I renounce at the same time my liberty and my responsibility. Once I speak I am never and no longer myself, alone and unique. It is a very strange contract – both paradoxical and terrifying, that binds infinite responsibility to silence and secrecy. It goes against what one usually thinks, even in the most philosophical mode. For common sense, just as for philosophical reasoning, the most widely shared belief is that responsibility is tied to the public and to the non-secret, to the possibility and even the necessity of accounting for one's words and actions in front of others, of justifying and owning up to them. Here on the contrary it appears, just as necessarily, that the absolute responsibility of my actions, to the extent that such a responsibility remains mine, singularly so, something no one else can perform in my place, instead implies secrecy. But what is also implied is that, by not speaking to others, I don't account for my actions, that I answer for nothing [*que je ne réponde de rien*] and to no one, that I make no response to others or before others. It is both a scandal and a paradox. According to Kierkegaard, *ethical* exigency is regulated by generality; and it therefore defines a responsibility that consists of *speaking*, that is, of involving oneself sufficiently in the generality to justify oneself, to give an account of one's decision and to answer for one's actions. One the other hand, what does Abraham teach us, in his approach to sacrifice? That far from ensuring responsibility, the generality of ethics incites to irresponsibility. It impels me to speak, to reply, to account for something, and thus to dissolve my singularity in the medium of the concept.

Such is the aporia of responsibility: one always risks not managing to accede to the concept of responsibility in the process of *forming* it. For responsibility (we would no longer dare speak of 'the universal concept of responsibility') demands on the one hand an accounting, a general answering-for-oneself with respect to the general and before the generality, hence the idea of substitution, and, on the other hand, uniqueness, absolute singularity, hence non-substitution, non-repetition, silence, and secrecy. What I am saying here about responsibility can also be said about decision. The ethical involves me in substitution, as does speaking. Whence the insolence of the paradox: for Abraham, Kierkegaard declares, *the ethical is a temptation.* He must therefore resist it. He keeps quiet in order to avoid the moral temptation which, under the pretext of calling him to responsibility, to self-justification, would make him lose his ultimate responsibility along with his singularity, make him lose his unjustifiable, secret, and absolute responsibility before God. This is ethics as 'irresponsibilization', as an insoluble and paradoxical contradiction between responsibility *in general* and *absolute* responsibility. Absolute responsibility is not a responsibility, at least it is not general responsibility or responsibility in general. It needs to be exceptional or extraordinary, and it needs to be that absolutely and *par excellence*: it is as if absolute responsibility could not be derived from a *concept* of responsibility and therefore, in order for it to be what it must be it must remain inconceivable, indeed unthinkable: it must therefore be irresponsible in order to be absolutely responsible. 'Abraham *cannot* speak, because he cannot say that which would explain everything . . . that it is an ordeal such that, please note, the ethical is the temptation.'[8]

The ethical can therefore end up making us irresponsible. It is a temptation, a tendency, or a facility that would sometimes have to be refused in the name of a responsibility that doesn't keep account or give an account, neither to man, to humans, to society, to one's fellows, or to one's own. Such a responsibility keeps its secret, it cannot and need not present itself. Tyrannically, jealously, it refuses to present itself before the violence that consists of asking for accounts and justifications, summonses to appear before the law of men. It declines the autobiography that is always auto-justification, egodicy [*égodicée*]. Abraham *presents himself*, of course, but before God, the unique, jealous, secret God, the one to whom he says 'Here I am'. But in order to do that, he must renounce his family loyalties, which amounts to violating his oath, and refuse to present himself before men. He no longer speaks to them. That at least is what the sacrifice of Isaac suggests (it would be different for a tragic hero such as Agamemnon).

In the end secrecy is as intolerable for ethics as it is for philosophy or for dialectics in general, from Plato to Hegel:

> The ethical as such is the universal; as the universal it is in turn the disclosed. The single individual, qualified as immediate, sensate, and psychical, is the hidden. Thus his ethical task is to work himself out of his hiddenness and to become disclosed in the universal. Every time he desires to remain in the hidden, he trespasses and is immersed in spiritual trial from which he can emerge only by disclosing himself.
>
> Once again we stand at the same point. If there is no hiddenness rooted in the fact that the single individual as the single individual is higher than the universal, then Abraham's conduct cannot be defended, for he disregarded the intermediary ethical categories. But if there is such a hiddenness, then we face the paradox, which does not allow itself to be mediated, since it is based precisely on this: the single individual as the single individual is higher than the universal. . . . The Hegelian philosophy assumes no justified hiddenness, no justified incommensurability. It is, then, consistent for it to demand disclosure, but it is a little bemuddled when it wants to regard Abraham as the father of faith and to speak about faith.[9]

In the exemplary form of its absolute coherence, Hegel's philosophy represents the irrefutable demand for manifestation, phenomenalization, and unveiling; thus, it is thought, it represents the request for truth that inspires philosophy and ethics in their most powerful forms. There are no final secrets for philosophy, ethics, or politics. The manifest has priority over the hidden or the secret, universal generality is superior to the individual. There is no irreducible secret grounded in right or law; the instance of the law has to be added to those of philosophy and ethics – nothing hidden, no absolutely legitimate secret. But the paradox of faith is that interiority remains 'incommensurable with exteriority'.[10] No manifestation can consist in rendering the interior exterior or show what is hidden. The Knight of Faith can neither communicate to nor be understood by anyone, she can't help the other at all.[11] The absolute duty that obligates her with respect to God cannot have the form of generality that is called duty. If I obey in my duty towards God (which is my absolute duty) *only in terms of duty*, I am not fulfilling my relation to God. In order to fulfil my duty towards God, I must not act *out of duty*, by means of that form of generality that can always be mediated and communicated and that is called duty. The absolute duty that binds me to God himself, in faith, must function beyond and against any duty I have. 'The duty becomes duty by being traced back to God, but in the duty itself I do not enter into relation to God.'[12] Kant explains that to act morally is to act 'out of duty' and not only 'by conforming to duty'.[13] Kierkegaard sees acting 'out of duty', in the universalizable sense of the law, as a dereliction of one's absolute duty. It is in this sense that absolute duty (towards God and in the singularity of faith) implies a sort of gift or sacrifice that functions beyond both debt and duty, beyond duty as a form of debt. This is the dimension that provides for a 'gift of death' which, beyond human responsibility, beyond the universal concept of duty, is a response to absolute duty.

In the order of human generality, a duty of hate is implied. Kierkegaard quotes Luke 14: 26: ' "If any one comes to me and does not hate his own father and mother and wife and children and brothers and sisters, yes, and even his own life, he cannot be my disciple." ' Recognizing that 'this is a hard saying',[14] Kierkegaard nevertheless upholds the necessity for it. He refines its rigour without seeking to make it less shocking or paradoxical. But Abraham's hatred for the ethical and thus for his own (family, friends, neighbours, nation, but at the outside humanity as a whole, his own kind or species) must remain an absolute source of pain. If I put to death or grant death to what I hate it is not a sacrifice. I must sacrifice what I love. I must come to hate what I love, in the same moment, at the instant of granting death. I must hate and betray my own, that is to say offer them the gift of death by means of the sacrifice, not insofar as I hate them, that would be too easy, but insofar as I love them. Hate wouldn't be hate if it only hated the hateful, that would be too easy. I must hate and betray what is most lovable. Hate cannot be hate, it can only be the sacrifice of love to love. It is not a matter of hating, betraying by one's breach of trust, or offering the gift of death to what one doesn't love.

But is this heretical and paradoxical Knight of Faith Jewish, Christian, or Judeo-Christian-Islamic? The sacrifice of Isaac belongs to what one might just dare to call the common treasure, the terrifying secret of the *mysterium tremendum* that is a property of all three so-called religions of the Book, the religions of the nations of Abraham. This rigour, and the exaggerated demands it entails, compel the Knight of Faith to say and do things that will appear (and must even be) atrocious. They will necessarily revolt those who profess allegiance to morality in general, to Judeo-Christian-Islamic morality, or to the religion of love in general. But as Patočka will say,[15] perhaps Christianity has not yet thought through its own essence, any more than it has thought through the irrefutable events through which Judaism, Christianity, and Islam have come to pass. One cannot ignore or erase the sacrifice of Isaac recounted in Genesis, nor that recounted in the Gospel of Luke. It has to be taken into account, which is what Kierkegaard proposes. Abraham comes to hate those closest to him by keeping silent, he comes to hate his only beloved son by consenting to put him to death [*lui donner la mort*]. He hates them not out of hatred, of course, but out of love. He doesn't hate them any less for all that, on the contrary. Abraham must love his son absolutely to come to the point where he will grant him death, to perform what ethics would call hatred and murder.

How does one hate one's own? Kierkegaard rejects the common distinction between love and hate; he finds it egotistical and without interest. He reinterprets it as a paradox. God wouldn't have asked Abraham to put Isaac to death, that is, to make a gift of death as a sacrificial offering to himself, to God, unless Abraham had an absolute, unique, and incommensurable love for his son:

> for it is indeed this love for Isaac that makes his act a sacrifice by its paradoxical contrast to his love for God. But the distress and the anxiety in the paradox is that he, humanly speaking, is thoroughly incapable of making himself understandable. Only *in the instant* [*i det øieblik*] when his act is in absolute contradiction to his feelings, only then does he sacrifice Isaac, but the reality of his act is that by which he belongs to the universal, and there he is and remains a murderer.[16]

I have emphasized the word *instant*: 'the instant [*øieblik*] of decision is *madness* [*Daarskab*]', Kierkegaard says elsewhere.[17] The paradox cannot be grasped in time and through mediation, that is to say in language and through reason. Like the gift and 'the gift of death', it remains irreducible to presence or to presentation, it requires a temporality of the instant without ever constituting a present. It belongs to an atemporal temporality, so to speak, to a duration that cannot be grasped: something one can neither stabilize, establish, *grasp* [*prendre*], *apprehend*, or *comprehend*. Understanding, common sense, and reason cannot seize [*begreifen*], conceive, understand, or mediate it; neither can they negate or deny it, implicate it in the work of negation, make it work: in the act of *giving death*, sacrifice suspends both the work of negation and work itself, perhaps even the work of mourning. The tragic hero enters into mourning. Abraham, on the other hand, is neither a man of mourning nor a tragic hero.

In order to assume his absolute responsibility with respect to absolute duty, to put his faith in God to work, or to the test, he must also in reality remain a hateful murderer, for he consents to put to death. In both general and abstract terms, the absoluteness of duty, of responsibility, and of obligation certainly demands that one transgress ethical duty, although in betraying it one belongs to it and at the same time recognizes it. The contradiction and the paradox must be endured *in the instant itself*. The two duties must contradict one another, one must subordinate (incorporate, repress) the other. Abraham must assume absolute responsibility for sacrificing his son by sacrificing ethics, but in order for there to be a sacrifice, the ethical must retain all its value; the love for his son must remain intact, and the order of human duty must continue to insist on its rights.

The account of Isaac's sacrifice can be read as a narrative development of the paradox constituting the concept of duty and absolute responsibility. This concept puts us into relation (but without relating to it, in a double secret) with the absolute other, with the absolute singularity of the other, whose name here is God. Whether one believes the biblical story or not, whether one gives it credence, doubts it, or transposes it, it could still be said that there is a moral to this story, even if we take it to be a fable (but taking it to be a fable still amounts to losing it to philosophical or poetic generality; it means that it loses the quality of a historic event). The moral of the fable would be morality itself, at the point where morality brings into play the gift of the death that is so given. The absolutes of duty and of responsibility presume that one denounce, refute, and transcend, at the same time, all duty, all responsibility, and every human law. It calls for a betrayal of everything that manifests itself within the order of universal generality, and everything that manifests itself in general, the very order and essence of manifestation; namely, the essence itself, the essence in general to the extent that it is inseparable from presence and from manifestation. Absolute duty demands that one behave in an irresponsible manner (by means of treachery or betrayal), while still recognizing, confirming, and reaffirming the very thing one sacrifices, namely, the order of human ethics and responsibility. In a word, ethics must be sacrificed in the name of duty. It is a duty not to respect, out of duty, ethical duty. One must behave not only in an ethical or responsible manner, but in a non-ethical, non-responsible manner, and one must do that *in the name of* duty, of an infinite duty, *in the name of* absolute duty. And this name which must always be singular is here none other than the name of God as completely other, the nameless name of God, the unpronounceable name of God as other to which I am bound by an absolute, unconditional obligation, by an incomparable, non-negotiable duty. The other as absolute other, namely, God, must remain transcendent, hidden, secret, jealous of the love, requests, and commands that he gives, and that he asks to be kept secret. Secrecy is essential to the exercise of this absolute responsibility as sacrificial responsibility.

In terms of the moral of morality, let us here insist upon what is too often forgotten by the moralizing moralists and good consciences who preach to us with assurance every morning and every week, in newspapers and magazines, on the radio and on television, about the sense of ethical or political responsibility. Philosophers who don't write ethics are failing in their duty, one often hears, and the first duty of the philosopher is to think about ethics, to add a chapter on ethics to each of his or her books and, in order to do that, to come back to Kant as often as possible. What the knights of good conscience don't realize is that 'the sacrifice of Isaac' illustrates – if that is the word in the case of such a nocturnal mystery – the most common and everyday experience of responsibility. The story is no doubt monstrous, outrageous, barely conceivable: a father is ready to put to death his beloved son, his irreplaceable loved one, and that because the Other, the great Other, asks him or orders him without giving the slightest explanation. A father planning infanticide, who hides what he is going to do from his son and from his family without knowing why, what could be more abominable, what mystery could be more frightful (*tremendum*) vis-à-vis love, humanity, the family, or morality?

But isn't this also the most common thing – what the most cursory examination of the concept of responsibility cannot fail to affirm? Duty or responsibility binds me to the other, to the other as other, and ties me in my absolute singularity to the other as other. God is the name of the absolute other as other and as unique (the God of Abraham defined as the one and unique). As soon as I enter into a relation with the absolute other, my absolute singularity enters into relation with his on the level of obligation and duty. I am responsible to the other as other, I answer to him and I answer for what I do before him. But of course, what binds me thus in my singularity to the absolute singularity of the other immediately propels me into the space or risk of absolute sacrifice. There are also others, an infinite number of them, the innumerable generality of others to whom I should be bound by the same responsibility, a general and universal responsibility (what Kierkegaard calls the ethical order). I cannot respond to the call, the request, the obligation, or even the love of another without sacrificing the other, the other others. *Every other (one) is every (bit) other* [*tout autre est tout autre*], every one else is completely or wholly other. The simple concepts of alterity and of singularity constitute the concept of duty as much as that of responsibility. As a result, the concepts of responsibility, of decision, or of duty, are condemned *a priori* to paradox, scandal, and aporia. Paradox, scandal, and aporia are themselves nothing other than sacrifice, the revelation of conceptual thinking at its limit, at its death and finitude. As soon as I enter into a relation with the other, with the gaze, look, request, love, command, or call of the other, I know that I can respond only by sacrificing ethics, that is, by sacrificing whatever obliges me also to respond, in the same way, in the same instant, to all the others. I offer a gift of death, I betray, I don't need to raise my knife over my son on Mount Moriah for that. Day and night, at every instant, on all the Mount Moriahs of this world, I am doing that, raising my knife over what I love and must love, over those to whom I owe absolute fidelity, incommensurably. Abraham is faithful to God only in his absolute treachery, in the betrayal of his own and of the uniqueness of each one of them, exemplified here in his only beloved son. He would not be able to opt for fidelity to his own, or to his son, unless he were to betray the absolute other: God, if you wish.

Let us not look for examples, there would be too many of them, at every step we took. By preferring my work, simply by giving it my time and attention, by preferring my activity as a citizen or as a professorial and professional philosopher, writing and speaking here in a public language, French in my case, I am perhaps fulfilling my duty. But I am sacrificing and betraying at every moment all my other obligations: my obligations to the other others whom I know or don't know, the billions of my fellows (not to mention the animals that are even more other others than my fellows), my fellows who are dying of starvation or sickness. I betray my fidelity or my obligations to other citizens, to those who don't speak my language and to whom I neither speak nor respond, to each of those who listen or read and to whom I neither respond nor address myself in the proper manner, that is, in a singular manner (this for the so-called public space to which I sacrifice my so-called private space), thus also to those I love in private, my own, my family, my sons, each of whom is the only son I sacrifice to the other, every one being sacrificed to every one else in this land of Moriah that is our habitat every second of the day.

This is not just a figure of style or an effect of rhetoric. According to the Second Book of the Chronicles, the place where this occurs, where the sacrifice of Abraham or of Isaac (and it is the sacrifice of both of them, it is the gift of death one makes to the other in putting *oneself* to death, mortifying oneself in order to make a gift of this death as a sacrificial offering to God) takes place, this place where death is given or offered, is the place where Solomon decided to build the House of the Lord in Jerusalem, also the place where God appeared to Solomon's father, David.[18] However, it is also the place where the grand Mosque of Jerusalem stood, the place called the Dome of the Rock near the grand Aksa mosque where Ibrahim's sacrifice is supposed to have taken place and from where Muhammad mounted his horse for paradise after his death. It is just above the destroyed temple of Jerusalem and the Wailing

Wall, not far from the Way of the Cross. It is therefore a holy place but also a place that is in dispute, radically and rabidly, fought over by all the monotheisms, by all the religions of the unique and transcendent God, of the absolute other. These three monotheisms fight over it, it is useless to deny this in terms of some wide-eyed ecumenism; they make war with fire and blood, have always done so and all the more fiercely today, each claiming its particular perspective on this place and claiming an original historical and political interpretation of Messianism and of the sacrifice of Isaac. The reading, interpretation, and tradition of the sacrifice of Isaac are themselves sites of bloody, holocaustic sacrifice. Isaac's sacrifice continues every day. Countless machines of death wage a war that has no front. There is no front between responsibility and irresponsibility but only between different appropriations of the same sacrifice, different orders of responsibility, different other orders: the religious and the ethical, the religious and the ethico-political, the theological and the political, the theologico-political, the theocratic and the ethico-political, and so on; the secret and the public, the profane and the sacred, the specific and the generic, the human and the non-human. Sacrificial war rages not only among the religions of the Book and the nations of Abraham that expressly refer to the sacrifice of Isaac, Abraham, or Ibrahim, but between them and the rest of the starving world, within the immense majority of humankind and even those living (not to mention the others, dead or non-living, dead or not yet born) who don't belong to the people of Abraham or Ibrahim, all those others to whom the names of Abraham and Ibrahim have never meant anything because such names don't conform or correspond to anything.

I can respond only to the one (or to the One), that is, to the other, by sacrificing the other to that one. I am responsible to any one (that is to say to any other) only by failing in my responsibilities to all the others, to the ethical or political generality. And I can never justify this sacrifice, I must always hold my peace about it. Whether I want to or not, I can never justify the fact that I prefer or sacrifice any one (any other) to the other. I will always be secretive, held to secrecy in respect of this, for I have nothing to say about it. What binds me to singularities, to this one or that one, male or female, rather than that one or this one, remains finally unjustifiable (this is Abraham's hyper-ethical sacrifice), as unjustifiable as the infinite sacrifice I make at each moment. These singularities represent others, a wholly other form of alterity: one other or some other persons, but also places, animals, languages. How would you ever justify the fact that you sacrifice all the cats in the world to the cat that you feed at home every morning for years, whereas other cats die of hunger at every instant? Not to mention other people? How would you justify your presence here speaking one particular language, rather than there speaking to others in another language? And yet we also do our duty by behaving thus. There is no language, no reason, no generality or mediation to justify this ultimate responsibility which leads me to absolute sacrifice; absolute sacrifice that is not the sacrifice of irresponsibility on the altar of responsibility, but the sacrifice of the most imperative duty (that which binds me to the other as a singularity in general) in favour of another absolutely imperative duty binding me to the wholly other.

God decides to suspend the sacrificial process, he addresses Abraham who has just said: 'Here I am'. 'Here I am': the first and only possible response to the call by the other, the originary moment of responsibility such as it exposes me to the singular other, the one who appeals to me. 'Here I am' is the only self-presentation presumed by every form of responsibility: I am ready to respond, I reply that I am ready to respond. Whereas Abraham has just said 'Here I am' and taken his knife to slit his son's throat, God says to him: 'Lay not thine hand upon the lad, neither do thou anything unto him: for now I know that thou fearest God, seeing thou hast not withheld thy son, thine only son, from me'.[19] This terrible declaration seems to display God's satisfaction at the terror that has been expressed (I see that 'you fear God [Elohim]', you tremble before me). It causes one to tremble through the fear and trembling it evokes as its only reason (I see that you have trembled before me, all right, we are quits, I free you from your obligation). But it can also be translated or argued as follows: I see that you have understood what absolute duty means, namely, how to respond to the absolute other, to his call, request, or command. These different registers amount to the same thing: by commanding Abraham to sacrifice his son, to put his son to death by offering a gift of death to God, by means of this double gift wherein the gift of death consists in putting to death by raising one's knife over someone and of putting death forward by giving it as an offering, God leaves him free to refuse – and that is the test. The command requests, like a prayer from God, a declaration of love that implores: tell me that you love me, tell me that you turn towards me, towards the unique one, towards the other as unique and, above all, over everything else, unconditionally, and in order to do that, make a gift of death, give death to your only son and give me the death I ask for, that I give to you by asking you for it. In essence God says to Abraham: I can see right away [*à l'instant*] that you have understood what absolute duty towards the unique one means, that it means responding where there is no reason to be asked for or to be given; I see that not only have you understood that as an idea, but that – and here lies responsibility – you have acted on it, you have put it into effect, you were ready to carry it out *at this very instant* (God stops him *at the very instant when there is no more time, where no more time is given*, it is as if Abraham had *already* killed Isaac: the concept of the instant is always indispensable): thus you had *already* put it into effect, you are absolute responsibility, you had the courage to behave like a murderer in the eyes of the world and of your loved ones, in the eyes of morality, politics, and of the generality of the general or of your kind [*le générique*]. And you had even renounced hope.

Abraham is thus at the same time the most moral and the most immoral, the most responsible and the most irresponsible of men, absolutely irresponsible because he is absolutely responsible, absolutely irresponsible in the face of men and his family, and in the face of the ethical, because he responds absolutely to absolute duty, disinterestedly, and without hoping for a reward, without knowing why yet keeping it secret; answering to God and before God. He recognizes neither debt nor duty to his fellows because he is in a relationship to God – a relationship without relation because God is absolutely transcendent, hidden, and secret, not giving any reason he can share in exchange for this doubly given death, not sharing anything in this dissymmetrical alliance. Abraham considers himself to be all square. He acts as if he were discharged of his duty towards his fellows, his son, and humankind; but he continues to love them. He must *love* them and also *owe* them everything in order to be able to sacrifice them. Without being so, then, he nevertheless feels absolved of his duty towards his family, towards the human species [*le genre humain*] and the generality of the ethical, absolved by the absolute of a unique duty that binds him to God the one. Absolute duty absolves him of every debt and releases him from every duty. Absolute ab-solution.

The ideas of secrecy and exclusivity [*non-partage*] are essential here, as is Abraham's silence. He doesn't speak, he doesn't tell his secret to his loved ones. He is, like the Knight of Faith, a witness and not a teacher,[20] and it is true that this witness enters into an absolute relation with the absolute, but he doesn't witness to it in the sense that to witness means to show, teach, illustrate, manifest to others the truth that one can precisely attest to. Abraham is a witness of the absolute faith that cannot and must not witness before men. He must keep his secret. But his silence is not just any silence. Can one witness in silence? By silence?

The tragic hero, on the other hand, can speak, share, weep, complain. He doesn't know 'the dreadful responsibility of loneliness'.[21] Agamemnon can weep and wail with Clytemnestra and Iphigenia. 'Tears and cries are relieving';[22] there is consolation in them. Abraham can neither speak nor commiserate, neither weep nor wail. He is kept in absolute secret. He feels torn, he would like to console the whole world, especially Sarah, Eliezer, and Isaac, he would like to embrace them before taking the final step. But he knows that they will then say to him: 'But why are you doing this? Can't you get an exemption, find another solution, discuss, negotiate with God?' Or else they will accuse him of dissimulation and hypocrisy. So he can't say anything to them. Even if he speaks to them he can't say anything to them. '. . . he speaks no human language. And even if he understood all the languages of the world . . . he still could not speak – he speaks in a divine language, he speaks in tongues'.[23] If he were to speak a common or translatable language, if he were to become intelligible by giving his reasons in a convincing manner, he would be giving in to the temptation of the ethical generality that I have referred to as that which makes one irresponsible. He wouldn't be Abraham any more, the unique Abraham in a singular relation with the unique God. Incapable of making a gift of death, incapable of sacrificing what he loved, hence incapable of loving and of hating, he wouldn't give anything anymore.

Abraham says nothing, but his last words, those that respond to Isaac's question, have been recorded: 'God himself will provide the lamb for the burnt offering [*holocauste*], my son'. If he had said 'There is a lamb, I have one' or 'I don't know, I have no idea where to find the lamb', he would have been lying, speaking in order to speak falsehood. By speaking without lying, he responds without responding. This is a strange responsibility that consists neither of responding nor of not responding. Is one responsible for what one says in an unintelligible language, in the language of the other? But besides that, mustn't responsibility always be expressed in a language that is foreign to what the community can already hear or understand only too well? 'So he does not speak an untruth, but neither does he say anything, for he is speaking in a strange tongue.'[24]

In Melville's 'Bartleby the Scrivener', the narrator, a lawyer, cites Job ('with kings and counsellers').[25] Beyond what is a tempting and obvious comparison, the figure of Bartleby could be compared to Job – not the Job who hoped to join the kings and counsellers after his death, but the Job who dreamed of not being born. Here, instead of the test God makes Job submit to, one could think of that of Abraham. Just as Abraham doesn't speak a human language, just as he speaks in tongues or in a language that is foreign to every other human language, and in order to do that responds without responding, speaks without saying anything either true or false, says nothing determinate that would be equivalent to a statement, a promise or a lie, in the same way Bartleby's 'I would prefer not to' takes on the responsibility of a response without response. It evokes the future without either predicting or promising; it utters nothing fixed, determinable, positive, or negative. The modality of this repeated utterance that says nothing, promises nothing, neither refuses nor accepts anything, the tense of this singularly insignificant statement reminds one of a non-language or a secret language. Is it not as if Bartleby were also speaking 'in tongues'?

But in saying nothing general or determinable, Bartleby doesn't say absolutely nothing. *I would prefer not to* looks like an incomplete sentence. Its indeterminacy creates a tension: it opens on to a sort of reserve of incompleteness; it announces a temporary or provisional reserve, one involving a proviso. Can we not find there the secret of a hypothetical reference to some indecipherable providence or prudence? We don't know what he wants or means to say, or what he doesn't want to do or say, but we are given to understand quite clearly that *he would prefer not to*. The silhouette of a content haunts this response. If Abraham has already consented *to make a gift of death*, and to give to God the death that he is going to put his son to, if he knows that he will do it unless God stops him, can we not say that his disposition is such that he would, precisely, *prefer not to*, without being able to say to the world what is involved? Because he loves his son, he would prefer that God hadn't asked him anything. He would prefer that God didn't let him do it, that he would hold back his hand, that he would provide a lamb for the burnt offering [*holocauste*], that the moment of this mad decision would lean on the side of non-sacrifice, once the sacrifice were to be accepted. He will not decide *not to*, he has decided *to*, but he would prefer not to. He can say nothing more and will do nothing more if God, if the Other, continues to lead him towards death, to the death that is offered as a gift. And Bartleby's 'I would prefer not to' is also a sacrificial passion that will lead him to death, a death given by the law, by a society that doesn't even know why it acts the way it does.

It is difficult not to be struck by the absence of woman in these two monstrous yet banal stories. It is a story of father and son, of masculine figures, of hierarchies among men (God the father, Abraham, Isaac; the woman, Sarah, is she to whom nothing is said; and Bartleby the Scrivener doesn't make a single allusion to anything feminine whatsoever, even less to anything that could be construed as a figure of woman). Would the logic of sacrificial responsibility within the implacable universality of the law, of its law, be altered, inflected, attenuated, or displaced, if a woman were to intervene in some consequential manner? Does the system of this sacrificial responsibility and of the double 'gift of death' imply at its very basis an exclusion or sacrifice of woman? A woman's sacrifice or a sacrifice of woman, according to one sense of the genitive or the other? Let us leave the question in suspense, here between two genitives. In the case of the tragic hero or the tragic sacrifice, however, woman is present, her place is central, just as she is present in other tragic works referred to by Kierkegaard.

The responses without response made by Bartleby are at the same time disconcerting, sinister, and comical; superbly, subtly so. There is concentrated in them a sort of sublime irony. Speaking in order not to say anything or to say something other than what one thinks, speaking in such a way as to intrigue, disconcert, question, or have someone or something else speak (the law, the lawyer), means speaking ironically. Irony, in particular Socratic irony, consists of not saying anything, declaring that one doesn't have any knowledge of something, but doing that in order to interrogate, to have someone or something (the lawyer, the law) speak or think. *Eirōneia* dissimulates, it is the act of questioning by feigning ignorance, by pretending. The *I would prefer not to* is not without irony; it cannot not lead one to suppose that there is some irony in the situation. It isn't unlike the incongruous yet familiar humour, the *Unheimlichkeit* or uncanniness of the story. On the other hand the author of *The Concept of Irony* uncovers irony in the response without response that translates Abraham's responsibility. Precisely in order to distinguish ironic pretence from a lie, he writes:

> But a final word by Abraham has been preserved, and insofar as I can understand the paradox, I can also understand Abraham's total presence in that word. First and foremost, he does not say anything, and in that form he says what he has to say. His response to Isaac is in the form of irony, for it is always irony when I say something and still do not say anything.[26]

Perhaps irony would permit us to find something like a common thread in the questions I have just posed and what Hegel said about woman: that she is 'the eternal irony of the community'.[27]

Abraham doesn't speak in figures, fables, parables, metaphors, ellipses, or enigmas. His irony is meta-rhetorical. If he knew what was going to happen, if for example God had charged him with the mission of leading Isaac on to the mountain so that He could strike him with lightning, then he would have been right to have recourse to enigmatic language. But the problem is precisely that he doesn't know. Not that that makes him hesitate, however. His non-knowledge doesn't in any way suspend his own decision, which remains resolute. The Knight of Faith must not hesitate. He accepts his responsibility by attending to the absolute demand of the other, beyond knowledge. He decides, but his absolute decision is neither guided nor controlled by knowledge. Such, in fact, is the paradoxical condition of every decision: it cannot be deduced from a form of knowledge of which it would simply be the effect, conclusion, or explication. It structurally breaches knowledge and is thus destined to non-manifestation; a decision is, in the end, always secret. It remains secret in the very instant of its performance, and how can the concept of decision be dissociated from this figure of the instant? From the stigma of its punctuality?

Abraham's decision is absolutely responsible because it answers for itself before the absolute other. Paradoxically it is also irresponsible because it is guided neither by reason nor by an ethics justifiable before men or before the law of some universal tribunal. Everything points to the fact that one is unable to be responsible at the same time before the other and before others, before the others of the other. If God is completely other, the figure or name of the wholly other, then every other (one) is every (bit) other. *Tout autre est tout autre*. This formula disturbs Kierkegaard's discourse on one level while at the same time reinforcing its most extreme ramifications. It implies that God, as the wholly other, is to be found everywhere there is something of the wholly other. And since each of us, everyone else, each other is infinitely other in its absolute singularity, inaccessible, solitary, transcendent, non-manifest, originarily non-present to my *ego* (as Husserl would say of the *alter ego* that can never be originarily present to my consciousness and that I can apprehend only through what he calls *appresentation* and analogy[28]), then what can be said about Abraham's relation to God can be said about my relation without relation to *every other (one) as every (bit) other* [*tout autre comme tout autre*], in particular my relation to my neighbour or my loved ones who are as inaccessible to me, as secret and transcendent as Jahweh. Every other (in the sense of each other) is every bit other (absolutely other). From this point of view what *Fear and Trembling* says about the sacrifice of Isaac is the truth. Translated into this extraordinary story, the truth displays the very structure of what occurs every day. Through its paradox it speaks of the responsibility required at every moment for every man and every woman. At the same time, there is no longer any ethical generality that does not fall prey to the paradox of Abraham.[29] At the instant of every decision and through the relation to *every other (one) as every (bit) other*, every one else asks us at every moment to behave like Knights of Faith. Perhaps that displaces a certain emphasis in Kierkegaard's discourse: the absolute uniqueness of Jahweh doesn't tolerate analogy; we are not all Abrahams, Isaacs, or Sarahs either. We are not Jahweh. But what seems thus to universalize or disseminate the exception or the extraordinary by imposing a supplementary complication upon ethical generality, that very thing ensures that Kierkegaard's text gains added force. It speaks to us of the paradoxical truth of our responsibility and of our relation to each instant's *gift of death*. Furthermore, it explains to us its own status, namely its ability to be read by all at the very moment when it is speaking to us of secrets in secret, of illegibility and absolute indecipherability. It stands for Jews, Christians, Muslims, but also for everyone else, for every other in its relation to the wholly other. We no longer know who is called Abraham, and he can no longer even tell us.

Whereas the tragic hero is great, admired, and legendary from generation to generation, Abraham, in remaining faithful to his singular love for the wholly other, is never considered a hero. He doesn't make us shed tears and doesn't inspire admiration: rather stupefied horror, a terror that is also secret. For it is a terror that brings us close to the absolute secret, the secret that we share without sharing it, a secret between someone else, Abraham as the other, and another, God as the other, as wholly other. Abraham himself is in secret, cut off both from man and from God.

But that is perhaps what we share with him. But what does it mean to share a secret? It isn't a matter of knowing what the other knows, for Abraham doesn't know anything. It isn't a matter of sharing his faith, for the latter must remain an initiative of absolute singularity. And moreover, we don't think or speak of Abraham from the point of view of a faith that is sure of itself, any more than did Kierkegaard. Kierkegaard keeps coming back to this, recalling that he doesn't understand Abraham, that he wouldn't be capable of doing what he did. In fact no other attitude seems possible; it is even required by such a prodigious monstrosity, even though it may also be, of all things in the world, the most equally shared.[30] Our faith is not assured, because faith can never be, it must never be a certainty. We share with Abraham what cannot be shared, a secret we know nothing about, neither him nor us. To share a secret is not to know or reveal the secret, it is to share we know not what: nothing that can be determined. What is a secret that is a secret about nothing and a sharing that doesn't share anything?

Such is the secret truth of faith as absolute responsibility and as absolute passion, the 'highest passion' as Kierkegaard will say;[31] it is a passion that, sworn to secrecy, cannot be transmitted from generation to generation. In this sense it has no history. This untransmissibility of the highest passion, the normal condition of a faith which is thus bound to secrecy, nevertheless dictates to us the following: we must always start over. A secret can be transmitted, but in transmitting a secret as a secret that remains secret, has one transmitted at all? Does it amount to history, to a story? Yes and no. The epilogue of *Fear and Trembling* repeats, in sentence after sentence, that this highest passion that is faith must be started over by each generation. Each generation must begin again to involve itself in it without counting on the generation before. It thus describes the non-history of absolute beginnings which are repeated, and the very historicity that presupposes a tradition to be reinvented each step of the way, in this incessant repetition of the absolute beginning.

With *Fear and Trembling*, we hesitate between two generations in the lineage of the so-called religions of the Book: we hesitate at the heart of the Old Testament and of the Jewish religion, but also at the heart of a founding event or a key sacrifice for Islam. As for the sacrifice of the son by his father, the son sacrificed by men and finally saved by a God who seemed to have abandoned him or put him to the test, how can we not recognize there the foreshadowning or the analogy of another passion? As a Christian thinker, Kierkegaard ends by reinscribing the secret of Abraham within a space that seems, in its literality at least, to be evangelical [to refer to the New Testament gospels[32]]. That doesn't necessarily exclude a Judaic or Islamic reading, but it is a certain evangelical or gospel text that seems to orient or dominate Kierkegaard's interpretation. That text isn't cited;[33] rather, like the 'kings and counsellers' of 'Bartleby the Scrivener', it is simply suggested, but this time without the quotation marks, thus being clearly brought to the attention of those who know their texts and have been brought up on the reading of the Gospels:

> But there was no one who could understand Abraham. And yet what did he achieve? He remained true to his love. But anyone who loves God needs no tears, no admiration; he forgets the suffering in the love. Indeed, so completely has he forgotten it that there would not be the slightest trace of his suffering left if God himself did not remember it, *for he sees in secret* and recognizes distress and counts the tears and forgets nothing.
>
> Thus, either there is a paradox, that the single individual as the single individual stands in an absolute relation to the absolute, or Abraham is lost.[34]

NOTES

1 Søren Kierkegaard, *Fear and Trembling, Repetition*, translated by Howard V. Hong and Edna H. Hong (Princeton University Press, Princeton, 1983).

2 [Philippians 2: 12. All biblical quotations are from the Authorized version. – Translator's note.]

3 [Derrida is referring here to Martin Heidegger, *Being and Time*, translated by John Macquarrie and Edward Robinson (Basil Blackwell, Oxford, 1962), ¶47, p. 284.]

4 Philippians 2: 13. I am following the Grosjean and Léturmy translation (Bibliothèque de la Pléiade) here, and will often find it necessary to add Greek or Latin glosses. What they translate by *son bon plaisir* ('his good pleasure') doesn't refer to God's pleasure but to his sovereign will that is not required to consult, just as the king acts as he intends without revealing his secret reasons, without having to account for his actions or explain them. The text doesn't name God's pleasure but his will: *pro bona voluntate* or

hyper tēs eudokias: *Eudokia* means 'good will', not just in the sense of desiring the good, but as the will that judges well, for its pleasure, as in their translation; for that is his will and it suffices. *Eudokeō*: 'I judge well', 'I approve', sometimes 'I am pleased' or 'I take pleasure in', 'I consent'.

5   IV B 78; *Journals and Papers*, translated by Howard V. Hong and Edna H. Hong (7 vols, Indiana University Press, Bloomington and London, 1967–78), 5660, vol. 5, p. 232, see also *Fear and Trembling*, p. 243.

6   Genesis 22: 8. ['Burnt offering' is used here to translate '*holocauste*', which corresponds to '*holocaustum*' in Genesis 22 in the Latin Vulgate Bible where 'burnt offering' is used in the Authorized Version.]

7   *Fear and Trembling*, p. 113. [The English translation gives 'the universal' for *det Almene*, whereas 'the general' is closer to the Danish and is the term Derrida uses. Note also Kierkegaard's distinction between *individuel* ('individual') and *enkelt* ('singular') that anticipates Derrida's here. For this and other clarifications of the English translation I am grateful to Elsebet Jegstrup and Mark Taylor. – Translator's note.]

8   *Fear and Trembling*, p. 115.

9   Ibid., p. 82. [Translation modified – Translator's note.]

10   Ibid., p. 69.

11   Ibid., p. 69.

12   Ibid., p. 68.

13   [Immanuel Kant, *Critique of Practical Reason*, translated by Lewis White Beck, third edition (Macmillan, New York, 1993), p. 84.]

14   *Fear and Trembling*, p. 72.

15   [Derrida is referring here to the Czech philosopher, Jan Patočka, whose work he discusses elsewhere in *The Gift of Death*.]

16   *Fear and Trembling*, p. 74. [Translation modified – Translator's note.]

17   [Søren Kierkegaard, *Philosophical Fragments, Johannes Climacus*, translated by Howard V. Hong and Edna H. Hong (Princeton University Press, Princeton, 1985), p. 52. The Danish word '*Daarskab*' is usually translated as 'foolishness', but the original rendering has been retained here in order to preserve Derrida's contrast with 'reason'.]

18   [II Chronicles 3: 1: 'Then Solomon began to build the house of the LORD at Jerusalem in mount Moriah, where *the LORD* appeared unto David his father, in the place that David had prepared.']

19   Genesis 22: 12.

20   ['The true Knight of Faith is a witness, never the teacher.' *Fear and Trembling*, p. 80.]

21   *Fear and Trembling*, p. 114.

22   Ibid., p. 114.

23   Ibid., p. 114.

24   *Fear and Trembling*, p. 119.

25   [Herman Melville, 'Bartleby', in *Billy Budd, Sailor and Other Stories*, edited by Harold Beaver (Penguin Books, Harmondsworth, 1985). The biblical text is to be found at Job 3: 14.]

26   *Fear and Trembling*, p. 118.

27 In this regard, I refer the reader to my *Glas*, [translated by John P. Leavey], (University of Nebraska Press, Lincoln, 1986), p. 190. [Derrida refers to Hegel's phrase '*die ewige Ironie des Gemeinwesens*', cf. *The Phenomenology of Spirit*, translated by A. V. Miller (Oxford University Press, Oxford, 1977), p. 288.]

28 [See Edmund Husserl, *Cartesian Meditations*, translated by Dorion Cairns (Martinus Nijhoff, The Hague, 1970), ¶50, p. 108.]

29 This is the logic of an objection made by Levinas to Kierkegaard: 'For Kierkegaard, the ethical was essentially general. The individuality of the self would be dissipated, according to him, by any rule that was valid for everyone. Generality would neither contain nor express the secret of the self. But it is not at all clear that Kierkegaard located the ethical accurately. As the consciousness of a responsibility towards others, the ethical does not disperse us into generality [. . .]. On the contrary, it individualizes us, treating everyone as a unique individual, a Self.' Levinas's criticism doesn't prevent him from admiring in Kierkegaard 'something absolutely novel' in 'European philosophy', 'a new modality of the True', the idea of a 'persecuted truth'. [See Emmanuel Levinas, 'Two Comments on Kierkegaard', translated in this volume, pp. 33–6, especially p. 34.]

30 ['*est aussi la chose du monde la mieux partagée. . . .*' Derrida is here alluding to the famous opening sentence of Descartes's *Discourse on Method*: 'Good sense is of all things in the world the most equally distributed.']

31 [*Fear and Trembling*, p. 121.]

32 [The French for gospel is *évangile*.]

33 [Derrida does not cite it either, but he is referring to Matthew 6: 6: 'But thou, when thou prayest, enter into thy closet, and when thou hast shut thy door, pray to thy Father which is in secret; and thy Father which seeeth in secret shall reward thee openly.']

34 *Fear and Trembling*, p. 120. [Derrida's italics.]

Kierkegaard's Publications and their Authors: A Chronology

1813
Born in Copenhagen on 5 May.

1838
From the Papers of One Still Living, published 'against his will' by S. Kierkegaard.

1841
The Concept of Irony, by S. Kierkegaard.

1843
Either/Or, edited by Victor Eremita.
Two Upbuilding Discourses, by S. Kierkegaard.
Fear and Trembling, by Johannes de Silentio.
Repetition, by Constantin Constantius.
Three Upbuilding Discourses, by S. Kierkegaard.
Four Upbuilding Discourses, by S. Kierkegaard.

1844
Two Upbuilding Discourses, by S. Kierkegaard.
Three Upbuilding Discourses, by S. Kierkegaard.
Philosophical Fragments, by Johannes Climacus, edited by S. Kierkegaard.
The Concept of Anxiety, by Vigilius Haufniensis.
Prefaces, by Nicolaus Notabene.

1845
Three Discourses on Imagined Occasions, by S. Kierkegaard.
Stages on Life's Way, edited by Hilarius Bookbinder.
Eighteen Upbuilding Discourses, by S. Kierkegaard.

1846
Concluding Unscientific Postscript, by Johannes Climacus, edited by S. Kierkegaard.
A Literary Review, by S. Kierkegaard.

1847
Upbuilding Discourses in Various Spirits, by S. Kierkegaard.
Works of Love, by S. Kierkegaard.

1848
Christian Discourses, by S. Kierkegaard.
The Crisis and a Crisis in the Life of an Actress, signed 'Inter et Inter'.

1849
The Lilies of the Field and the Birds of the Air, by S. Kierkegaard.
Two Minor Ethico-Religious Treatises, by H. H.
The Sickness Unto Death, by Anti-Climacus, edited by S. Kierkegaard.
Three Discourses at Communion on Fridays, by S. Kierkegaard.

1850
Training in Christianity, by Anti-Climacus.
An Upbuilding Discourse, by S. Kierkegaard.

1851
On my Work as an Author, by S. Kierkegaard.
Two Discourses at Communion on Fridays, by S. Kierkegaard.
For Self-Examination, by S. Kierkegaard.

1855
This Must be Said, So Let It be Said, by S. Kierkegaard.
Christ's Judgement on Official Christianity, by S. Kierkegaard.
The Unchangeableness of God, by S. Kierkegaard.
Died on 11 November.

1859
The Point of View for my Work as an Author, by S. Kierkegaard.

1876
Judge for Yourself, by S. Kierkegaard.

Bibliography

Kierkegaard's Works

In Danish

Samlede Værker, edited by A. B. Drachmann, J. L. Heiberg and H. O. Langes (14 vols, Gyldendal, Copenhagen, 1901–6); second edition (15 vols, Gyldendal, Copenhagen, 1920–36); third edition, with additional editorial material provided by Peter Rohde (20 vols, Gyldendal, Copenhagen, 1962–4).
Søren Kierkegaards Papirer, edited by P. A. Heiberg, V. Kuhr and E. Torsting (11 vols, Gyldendal, Copenhagen, 1909–48); second edition, with supplementary volumes, edited by Niels Thulstrup (13 vols, Gyldendal, Copenhagen, 1968–70).

In English Translation: Journals and Papers

The Journals of Søren Kierkegaard, translated by Alexander Dru (Oxford University Press, London, 1938).
Søren Kierkegaard's Journals and Papers, translated by Howard V. Hong and Edna H. Hong, assisted by Gregor Malantschuk (7 vols, Indiana University Press, Bloomington, 1967–78).
Vol. 1: A–E (1967).
Vol. 2: F–K (1970).
Vol. 3: L–R (1976).
Vol. 4: S–Z (1976).
Vol. 5: Autobiographical. Part 1, 1829–48 (1978).
Vol. 6: Autobiographical. Part 2, 1848–55 (1978).
Vol. 7: Index and composite collation; index prepared by Nathaniel J. Hong and Charles M. Barker (1978).

Papers and Journals: A Selection, translated by Alastair Hannay (Penguin Books, London, 1996).

In English Translation: the Princeton Collected Writings

Vol. 1: *Early Polemical Writings*, translated by Julia Watkin (Princeton University Press, Princeton, 1990); includes *From the Papers of One Still Living*, *Articles from Student Days* and *The Battle Between the Old and the New Soap-Cellars*.

Vol. 2: *The Concept of Irony, Schelling Lecture Notes*, translated by Howard V. Hong and Edna H. Hong (Princeton University Press, Princeton, 1989).

Vol. 3: *Either/Or*, vol. 1, translated by Howard V. Hong and Edna H. Hong (Princeton University Press, Princeton, 1987).

Vol. 4: *Either/Or*, vol. 2, translated by Howard V. Hong and Edna H. Hong (Princeton University Press, Princeton, 1987).

Vol. 5: *Eighteen Upbuilding Discourses*, translated by Howard V. Hong and Edna H. Hong (Princeton University Press, Princeton, 1990).

Vol. 6: *Fear and Trembling, Repetition*, translated by Howard V. Hong and Edna H. Hong (Princeton University Press, Princeton, 1983).

Vol. 7: *Philosophical Fragments, Johannes Climacus*, translated by Howard V. Hong and Edna H. Hong (Princeton University Press, Princeton, 1985).

Vol. 8: *The Concept of Anxiety*, translated by Reidar Thomte and Albert B. Anderson (Princeton University Press, Princeton, 1980).

Vol. 9: *Prefaces* (forthcoming).

Vol. 10: *Three Discourses on Imagined Occasions*, translated by Howard V. Hong and Edna H. Hong (Princeton University Press, Princeton, 1993).

Vol. 11: *Stages on Life's Way*, translated by Howard V. Hong and Edna H. Hong (Princeton University Press, 1988).

Vol. 12: *Concluding Unscientific Postscript*, translated by Howard V. Hong and Edna H. Hong (Princeton University Press, Princeton, 1992).

Vol. 13: *The Corsair Affair and Articles Related to the Writings*, translated by Howard V. Hong and Edna H. Hong (Princeton University Press, Princeton, 1982).

Vol. 14: *Two Ages, A Literary Review*, translated by Howard V. Hong and Edna H. Hong (Princeton University Press, Princeton, 1978).

Vol. 15: *Upbuilding Discourses in Various Spirits*, translated by Howard V. Hong and Edna H. Hong (Princeton University Press, Princeton, 1993).

Vol. 16: *Works of Love*, translated by Howard V. Hong and Edna H. Hong (Princeton University Press, Princeton, 1995).

Vol. 17: *Christian Discourses, The Crisis and a Crisis in the Life of an Actress* (forthcoming).

Vol. 18: *Without Authority: The Lily of the Field and the Bird of the Air, Two Minor Ethical-Religious Essays, Three Discourses at the Communion on Fridays, An Upbuilding Discourse, Two Discourses at the Communion on Fridays* (forthcoming).

Vol. 19: *The Sickness Unto Death*, translated by Howard V. Hong and Edna H. Hong (Princeton University Press, Princeton, 1980).

Vol. 20: *Practice in Christianity*, translated by Howard V. Hong and Edna H. Hong (Princeton University Press, Princeton, 1991).

Vol. 21: *For Self-Examination*; *Judge for Yourself!*, translated by Howard V. Hong and Edna H. Hong (Princeton University Press, Princeton, 1990).

Vol. 22: *The Point of View: The Point of View for my Work as an Author, Armed Neutrality, On My Work as an Author* (forthcoming).

Vol. 23: *The Moment and Late Writings: Articles from Fædrelandet, The Moment, This Must Be Said, So Let It Be Said, Christ's Judgement on Official Christianity, The Changelessness of God* (forthcoming).

Vol. 24: *The Book on Adler* (forthcoming).

Vol. 25: *Kierkegaard: Letters and Documents*, translated by Henrik Rosenmeier (Princeton University Press, Princeton, 1978).

Vol. 26: Cumulative Index.

Philosophical Writings in English Translation: a Historical Selection

Philosophical Fragments; or, A Fragment of Philosophy, translated by David F. Swenson (1936); translation revised by Howard V. Hong (Princeton University Press, Princeton, 1962).

The Point of View for My Work as An Author, translated by Walter Lowrie (1939); (Harper and Row, New York, 1962).

Stages on Life's Way, translated by Walter Lowrie (Princeton University Press, Princeton, 1940).

Repetition, translated by Walter Lowrie (Princeton University Press, Princeton, 1941).

Concluding Unscientific Postscript, translated by David F. Swenson and completed by Walter Lowrie (Princeton University Press, Princeton, 1941).

The Concept of Dread, translated by Walter Lowrie (1944); second edition (Princeton University Press, Princeton, 1957).

Either/Or, vol. 1 translated by David F. Swenson and Lillian Marvin Swenson, vol. 2 translated by Walter Lowrie (1944); translation revised by Howard A. Johnson (2 vols, Princeton University Press, Princeton, 1959).

Fear and Trembling and The Sickness Unto Death, translated by Walter Lowrie (Princeton University Press, Princeton, 1954).

On Authority and Revelation, the Book on Adler, or a Cycle of Ethico-Religious Essays, translated by Walter Lowrie (Princeton University Press, Princeton, 1955; Harper and Row, New York, 1966).

Johannes Climacus, translated by T. H. Croxall (Adam and Charles Black, London, 1958).

Works of Love, translated by Howard V. Hong and Edna H. Hong (Harper and Row, New York, 1962).

The Concept of Irony, with constant reference to Socrates, translated by Lee M. Capel (Collins, London, 1966).

Crisis in the Life of an Actress and Other Essays on Drama, translated by Stephen Crites (Collins, London, 1967).

Fear and Trembling, translated by Alastair Hannay (Penguin Books, Harmondsworth, 1985).

The Sickness Unto Death, translated by Alastair Hannay (Penguin, Harmondsworth, 1989).

Prefaces, translated by William McDonald (Florida State University Press, Tallahassee, 1989).

Either/Or: A Fragment of Life, abridged and translated by Alastair Hannay (Penguin Books, London, 1992).

Fear and Trembling and The Book on Adler, translated by Walter Lowrie (David Campbell, London, 1994).

Further Reading

Theodor W. Adorno, *Kierkegaard: Construction of the Aesthetic*, translated by Robert Hullot-Kentor (University of Minnesota Press, Minneapolis, 1989).

Sylviane Agacinski, *Aparté: Conceptions and Deaths of Søren Kierkegaard*, translated by Kevin Newmark (Florida State University Press, Tallahassee, 1988).

Harold Bloom (ed.), *Søren Kierkegaard: Modern Critical Views* (Chelsea House, New York, 1989).

John D. Caputo, *Radical Hermeneutics* (Indiana University Press, Bloomington, 1987).

John W. Elrod, *Being and Existence in Kierkegaard's Pseudonymous Works* (Princeton University Press, Princeton, 1975).

Peter Fenves, *'Chatter': Language and History in Kierkegaard* (Stanford University Press, Stanford, 1993).

Patrick Gardiner, *Kierkegaard* (Oxford University Press, Oxford, 1988).

Alastair Hannay, *Kierkegaard* (Routledge and Kegan Paul, London, 1982).

Walter Lowrie, *A Short Life of Kierkegaard* (Princeton University Press, Princeton, 1942).

Louis Mackey, *Kierkegaard: A Kind of Poet* (University of Pennsylvania Press, Philadelphia, 1971).

Martin J. Matustik and Merold Westphal (eds), *Kierkegaard in Post/Modernity* (Indiana University Press, Bloomington, 1995).

Christopher Norris, 'Fictions of Authority: narrative and viewpoint in Kierkegaard's writing', in his *The Deconstructive Turn* (Methuen, London, 1983).

Jean-Paul Sartre, 'Kierkegaard: The Singular Universal', in his *Between Existentialism and Marxism*, translated by John Matthews (NLB, London, 1974).

Ronald Schleifer and Robert Markley (eds), *Kierkegaard and Literature* (University of Oklahoma Press, Norman, 1984).

Josiah Thompson (ed.), *Kierkegaard: A Collection of Critical Essays* (Anchor Books, New York, 1972).

David Wood, *Philosophy at the Limit* (Unwin Hyman, London, 1990).

Index